Alternative Approaches
to Assessing Young Children

Alternative Approaches to Assessing Young Children

by

Angela Losardo, Ph.D.
Appalachian State University
Boone, North Carolina

and

Angela Notari-Syverson, Ph.D.
Washington Research Institute
Seattle, Washington

·P A U L·H·
BROOKES
PUBLISHING CO. ®

Baltimore • London • Sydney

Paul H. Brookes Publishing Co.
Post Office Box 10624
Baltimore, Maryland 21285-0624
www.brookespublishing.com

Third printing, May 2007.

Typeset by Barton Matheson Willse & Worthington, Baltimore, Maryland.
Manufactured in the United States of America by
Hamilton Printing Company, Rensselaer, New York.

The vignettes in this book are composite accounts that do not represent the lives or experiences of specific individuals, and no implications should be inferred.

Illustration on cover courtesy of Maya Rose Indrani Losardo.

Library of Congress Cataloging-in-Publication Data

Losardo, Angela.
    Alternative approaches to assessing young children / by Angela Losardo and Angela Notari-Syverson.
        p. cm.
    Includes bibliographical references and index.
    ISBN-13: 978-1-55766-498-3
    ISBN-10: 1-55766-498-6
    1. Psychological tests for children.   2. Child development—Testing.
3. Behavorial assessment of children.   4. Educational tests and measurements.
I. Notari-Syverson, Angela.   II. Title.

BF722.L67·2001
155.4'028'7—dc21   00-052893

British Library Cataloguing in Publication data are available from the British Library.

Contents

About the Authors

Angela Losardo, Ph.D., is Associate Professor in the Department of Language, Reading, and Exceptionalities at Appalachian State University in Boone, North Carolina. Her educational background includes degrees in communication disorders and early childhood special education from the State University of New York at Buffalo and the University of Oregon in Eugene. Dr. Losardo's interdisciplinary training in communication disorders and early childhood special education allows her to synthesize current research in these fields and to communicate effectively with professionals from different disciplines.

Dr. Losardo has considerable experience coordinating and working as a practitioner in inclusive programs for young children in a variety of environments (e.g., home-based programs, center-based preschools, public schools, residential facilities, hospitals, private agencies). Her work has focused primarily on the development of early language and literacy skills in young children. She has coordinated and conducted research projects and has directed interdisciplinary personnel preparation programs at higher education institutions. She has published numerous journal articles, book chapters, and instructional materials for practitioners.

Dr. Losardo's current research interests are alternative and cross-cultural assessment/evaluation procedures, curricular approaches to early language and literacy interventions, and preparing personnel to work in inclusive environments.

Angela Notari-Syverson, Ph.D., is Senior Researcher at the Washington Research Institute in Seattle. Her work focuses on early literacy and language assessment and intervention. She has authored books and journal publications in these areas and is co-author of *Ladders to Literacy: A Preschool Activity Book* (Paul H. Brookes Publishing Co., 1998), an early literacy curriculum developed for use in inclusive education environments.

Dr. Notari-Syverson's educational background includes degrees in psychology and communication disorders from the University of Geneva, Switzerland, and a doctorate in early childhood special education from the University of Oregon in Eugene. Her professional experience involves working with children who have a variety of communication disorders and developmental delays and their families both in the United States of America and in Switzerland. She has directed federal research, demonstration, and training projects in the area of early language and literacy at the Washington Research Institute and the University of Washington, Seattle.

Dr. Notari-Syverson's current research interests are adult–child interactions, assessment, and intervention in multicultural and multilinguistic contexts. She has lived and worked in different countries and is fluent in three languages.

Foreword

Being asked to write a foreword for a book implies that the foreword author is in a position to offer insights that will place the content in a useful perspective, add knowledge that will the aid the readers' understanding, or contribute information that enhances the material presented by the book's authors. Taking any of these reasons seriously poses a significant challenge for creating a beginning piece that contributes in a meaningful way to the material presented in the book. That is the intent of this foreword. To add frosting to this well-baked cake, I will offer observations on this book's authors and their backgrounds, comments about the fundamental importance of the process of assessment, and, finally, a few words about the structure and content of *Alternative Approaches to Assessing Young Children*.

THE AUTHORS

Although it is tempting, I will not return to the early childhoods of Drs. Losardo and Notari-Syverson, but I will venture back to their graduate school days at the University of Oregon's Early Intervention Program. They grew up professionally in a time when early intervention/early childhood special education (EI/ECSE) was solidifying as a legitimate field of study and intervention. Although now accepted as being firmly planted between special education and early childhood education, it (the field) and they (Losardo and Notari-Syverson) had much to learn and to explore during their years as doctoral students. Learn they did, by reading and discussing the many new ideas, concepts, and procedures being introduced to the EI/ECSE field. Their substantive involvement in refining activity-based intervention and the general framework of linking assessment, intervention, and evaluation was equally important. As the many doctoral students who preceded and followed them, their contributions were substantial to the development of an approach that directly links assessment outcomes to the development of goals and objects that, in turn, guide intervention content and, finally, relate directly to evaluation efforts. The impact of this learning is clearly reflected in the content of *Alternative Approaches to Assessing Young Children*.

Let me rush to point out, however, that Drs. Losardo and Notari-Syverson have not reshaped ideas or concepts derived in graduate school but, rather, have significantly expanded the framework surrounding assessment and have presented this framework in a straightforward and digestible manner. What is of particular interest to me is the continuity between what these professionals learned early in their careers and how they have reformed and remolded concepts into more understandable and comprehensive state-of-the art versions. Continuity may be as important a phenomenon for adults as it is for children. The authors reinforce my beliefs in the importance of early education, whether it be in kindergarten or in higher education—indeed, for most of us, university training is the base preparation for the remainder of our professional lives.

THE IMPORTANCE OF ASSESSMENT

I can think of few processes more fundamental to the educational and therapeutic enterprise than assessment. *Alternative Approaches to Assessing Young Children* has in its sights a topic of fundamental importance to personnel in the EI/ECSE and early childhood fields. To emphasize the importance of assessment, I am fond of using an analogy of a map to illustrate the need to know where you are in order to get where you want to go. So, too, comprehensive and accurate assessment outcomes let you know where a child is and where he or she should be going next. In EI/ECSE, assessment outcomes should specify the child's repertoire in important areas of development as well as collect information on the child's social and physical environment. The need to locate a child in developmental space and to specify the surrounding social and environmental conditions that may affect development seems obvious. Yet, this type of comprehensive assessment is done infrequently or in a manner that produces results that do not accurately specify the child's current repertoire, future goals and objectives, and possible intervention content and strategies. Why is this so? I believe there are at least three possible reasons.

First, as Drs. Losardo and Notari-Syverson point out, the purposes of assessment should dictate the type of process and/or tool(s) to be used. For reasons not entirely clear to me, this often is not the case; for example, it is not uncommon to see early childhood or EI/ECSE personnel using standardized tests or screening tools to develop individualized education program (IEP) or individualized family service plan (IFSP) goals and objectives. It is little wonder that the quality of such goals and objectives is poor and their usefulness for developing intervention content highly suspect. Second, adequate time is not spent on the collection of assessment outcomes that can provide the necessary data to determine where the child currently is in developmental space and what goals/objectives should be targeted next. A frequent response to using curriculum-based assessment and evaluation tools is that early childhood or EI/ECSE personnel do not have time for their administration and interpretation. Such responses reflect, at best, a poor or incomplete understanding of the importance of accurate and comprehensive assessment outcomes to the delivery of quality services to young children and their families. A third possible reason that adequate assessments are infrequently conducted may be a lack of appropriate processes and/or tools. Although our understanding of the variables that compose a quality assessment have improved and the number and types of available tools has increased, a significant need remains for alternatives to our existing warehouse of options. This need for alternatives underscores the importance of the current volume of work that is directed to helping personnel understand a variety of assessment frameworks, their strengths and limitations, and practical strategies for their implementation. It is hoped that the advent of such books will improve assessment practices in the early childhood and EI/ECSE fields. Without such assessment, subsequent interventions are likely to be ineffective or even harmful.

ALTERNATIVE ASSESSMENT

The authors correctly define *assessment* in terms of its application to EI/ECSE as a process used to collect a broad range of information that is pertinent to the development of IEPs/IFSPs and intervention content and can be used as the basis for subsequent evaluations. In their excellent overview presented in Chapters 1 and 2, Drs. Losardo and Notari-Syverson develop a strong rationale for the need to understand alternative assessment practices and for practitioners to explore the application of these practices. To further assist the reader, a standard format is used across chapters that enhances comparisons of the varied assessment frameworks and practices.

Although I prefer different nomenclature for some of their frameworks (e.g., I have difficulty thinking of play-based assessment as being focused), the authors do an excellent job of defining the selected frameworks, providing examples of how each approach might be used, offering comparisons across frameworks, and suggesting strategies for application of the various assessment strategies. The descriptions are straightforward and should be understood by most practitioners; however, the material is well referenced, and, thus, abundant resources are provided for readers interested in more detail and depth. Chapter 10, the final chapter, provides a brief recapitulation of the major themes raised throughout the book that many readers will find to be a useful summary.

A number of books on the assessment of young children who are at risk or who have disabilities are available; however, I believe *Alternative Approaches to Assessing Young Children* is the first one directed to early childhood and EI/ECSE personnel that focuses on alternative assessment frameworks. For that reason, I believe this book has the opportunity to draw attention to the important work of exploring and applying alternative strategies. As the authors make clear, many of the children and their families who are eligible for special intervention services require assessment processes that go well beyond the use of traditional standardized tests. Their examples give eloquent testimony to the need to think outside the box.

In the last paragraph of the book's final chapter, Drs. Losardo and Notari-Syverson draw three critical conclusions. First, "assessment is expected to be fair, unbiased, and respectful . . ."—that means we need to move from using traditional approaches to exploring the use of alternative approaches that better accommodate diversity in children's cultures, languages, and learning styles. Second, there is a significant need to study the usefulness and effects of alternative forms of assessment. Currently, we have almost no information on the impact and/or effectiveness of innovative assessment strategies. Clearly, this void must be filled by well-designed and methodologically sound investigations. Finally, we "must not lose sight of the overall goal of assessment, which is to ultimately improve educational outcomes for children"—a fitting conclusion to a substantive new book.

Diane Bricker, Ph.D.
Center on Human Development
University of Oregon

Preface

This book represents the authors' framework for alternative assessment models for young children and families and serves as a practical guide for use with children from birth to 8 years of age. The assessment approaches presented in *Alternative Approaches to Assessing Young Children* have been developed to address the limitations of standardized assessment tools. Practitioners in educational and social services agencies need alternative models of assessment that emanate from new theories of child development and from a new consciousness of the complex factors influencing young children's lives.

Young children develop within a context of social interactions. Thus, a social-interactionist perspective of child development provides the unifying theme that underpins the approaches described in this book. As professionals in human services, our goal is to improve the quality of life for the individuals whom we serve. This book is one way in which we can share our knowledge and what we have learned from others, as well as present our reflections on useful practices and strongly held beliefs. We hope to encourage our readers to examine their own practices and to enjoy the resulting prospect of growth and change. We also believe that it is particularly important for all human services professionals to recognize when their perspectives are different from those of the people they serve, and we address this issue repeatedly in this book.

Throughout each of our careers in the United States of America and in Europe, we have met many children and families who generously shared their experiences, their hopes, and their concerns. Many of these people were from backgrounds and cultures that were different from our own, and it is they who have shown us other ways of viewing and experiencing the world. We learned the importance of setting aside our own opinions and being open to the opinions of others and then being able to adapt our professional services.

Another important theme in *Alternative Approaches to Assessing Young Children* is the interrelationship among theory, research, and practice. Our assumptions and recommendations are influenced by a belief in evolving developmental theories. We draw on those theories for a clearer understanding of the way people act, think, and learn. We also rely on research findings to change and improve our educational practices. Most important, our daily interactions with children have led us to question and test theory and research. Just as theory, research, and practice are interrelated, so are biological and environmental influences on development. Throughout the book, we call for sharing and transdisciplinary collaboration among family members and professionals.

Finally, these are times of exciting technological advances that can influence and change how we live, think, and communicate. Applications of technology to educational practices are opening new paths to overcome the limitations of traditional approaches to assessment. In this book, we attempt to bring together theoretical advances, new research findings, and diverse practical experiences. This information is intended to help professionals build on and improve their services for children and families.

Alternative Approaches to Assessing Young Children begins with an overview of historical perspectives on child development. The evolution of traditional and contemporary approaches to assessment is traced, and the limitations of traditional approaches are discussed in terms of their educational relevance and appropriateness for use with children from various cultural and linguistic backgrounds. We present a framework for implementing alternative assessment models. All chapters provide a detailed description of the approach, a theoretical orientation and rationale for its use, advantages and limitations, and specific guidelines for implementation with a primary focus on early language and literacy development. Suggestions for practitioners working in inclusive environments are also provided. In addition, we provide a transdisciplinary framework for comprehensive, multidimensional approaches to assessment. Finally, a glossary of terms that are in bold print in the text and an appendix of data collection forms for each type of assessment appear at the end of the book.

Practitioners in the human services are continuously engaged in the delicate task of balancing professional knowledge and technique with intuition and personal emotion. With each child and family encountered, new and unique relationships are formed through the sharing of expertise, experiences, beliefs, and feelings. It is our sincere hope that this book will assist students and professionals everywhere to adopt current best practices for serving young children and families from diverse cultural and linguistic backgrounds in the context of mutually respectful relationships.

For the Course Companion Web Site User

Alternative Approaches to Assessing Young Children has a course companion web site designed to enhance the learning experience of instructors and students using the book in a college course. For instructors, there is a sample course syllabus that outlines each chapter, provides learning objectives, lists key terms and concepts, and suggests supplementary readings. PowerPoint slides, discussion strategies, and focus topics are provided to support in-class lectures. For students, there are self-study questions with answer keys, downloadable versions of the assessment forms printed in the book, and links to web sites and on-line discussion groups.

The course companion web site is free for all readers. Readers can access the web site at http://textbooks.brookespublishing.com/losardo.

Acknowledgments

We acknowledge our gratitude to all of the families and children with whom we have worked throughout the years in the United States of America and in Europe. We extend a heartfelt thank you to our own families, friends, and mentors, to whom we are deeply indebted for all of their support and encouragement. Finally, we appreciate the assistance of our manuscript reviewers: Alice Naylor, who is a close and highly valued academic colleague and mentor; Terry Losardo, a critical thinker and an impeccable editor; and Anne Stafford, who began as a graduate assistant on the project and ultimately contributed a high degree of professional assistance.

Select material for this book was developed, in part, through funding from the U.S. Department of Education, Office of Special Education and Rehabilitative Services, Early Education Program for Children with Disabilities: Grant No. H024B20031, Supporting Literacy Development in Young Children with Disabilities: A Comprehensive Interactive Emergent Literacy Curriculum for Preschoolers; Grant No. H024D600008, Mediated Learning Outreach Training: Promoting Developmentally Appropriate Practices in Inclusive Settings; and Grant No. H024B50020, Supporting Neurobehavioral Organizational Development in Infants with Disabilities: The Neurobehavioral Curriculum for Early Intervention.

To Maya and Don

And to our parents,
John and Teresa Losardo
and
Mafalda and Arnaldo Notari

And to Adalgisa Gatti

Historical Perspectives on Alternative Assessment

After reading this chapter, you will be able to:

- Highlight the importance of theoretical frameworks and how they guide views on the study of child development

- Summarize the major influences behind changes in the study of child development

- Describe the evolution of traditional and contemporary theoretical perspectives on child development

- Explain the relationship between theories on child development and assessment and intervention practices

*T*he world is undergoing astounding change in the new millennium. Economic and political forces, along with rapid technological advances, are making distance and national borders less relevant. The increasing globalization of economies has resulted in the movement and exchange of people, goods, and ideas. Communication systems such as cable and the Internet have made information more easily and rapidly available than ever before. Many benefits have resulted from these changes even as new challenges have emerged. Exposure to other cultures and ways of life enriches and broadens conventional ways of thinking. Early 21st-century models and views of the world appear too narrow and are unable to account for the variation in beliefs and customs of diverse cultures and the complexity of continuous adaptation to changing conditions.

These changes have had an enormous impact on the field of human services. Educational and clinical practitioners in today's work force interact with children and families who live in environments of increasing diversity and change. Remarkable progress has occurred since the early 1980s, including changes in professional development standards and educational services provided to young children and their families. Yet, legislative changes in the 1990s (e.g., welfare reform) reduced resources, bringing a new set of challenges to professional services. In addition to these cutbacks, societal trends such as increased poverty and environmental health hazards continue to place increasing numbers of children at risk for educational failure (Hodgkinson, 1992; U.S. General Accounting Office, 1994).

The influence of environmental factors on child development and learning has been well documented (e.g., Sameroff & Chandler, 1975). Demographic trends in the 1990s regarding ethnic diversity and household composition reflected greater variability (Hodgkinson, 1992). There is a growing awareness of the complexity of the interactions between environmental and biological factors that influence child development. For example, research findings have shown the detrimental effects of the lack of a nurturing environment on a child's brain development (Shore, 1997).

Over the years, a variety of clinical and educational assessment and intervention tools have been created based on new theories of and assumptions about child development (Berkeley & Ludlow, 1992). Practitioners at the beginning of the 21st century need models that 1) accurately reflect the complex factors influencing young children and their family's lives and 2) provide a comprehensive understanding of children's development in the context of their families, larger communities, and cultures (Meisels, 1996). To make informed decisions regarding assessment and intervention, practitioners need to be aware that procedures, materials, instruments, and interactions are embedded in particular world views, expectations, values, and behavioral preferences (Barrera, 1996). This chapter shows educators and clinicians how to recognize and identify their own practices and approaches and to realize that these are based on specific theoretical views and assumptions about how children develop and learn.

IMPORTANCE OF THEORETICAL FRAMEWORKS

A **theory** is extremely useful when viewed as a framework to organize and give meaning to facts, to guide decisions, and to give direction for further action: "There is nothing so practical as a good theory" (Lewin, 1943, cited in Bronfenbrenner, 1993, p. 5). Educators and practitioners must be aware that they too operate according to their own theories about development and learning and that these theories evolved from training and experience over the years. How an individual answers the following questions reflects his or her theoretical perspectives:

- What do children need in order to develop and learn?

- What are the *most important* things children need to learn?

- What is the role of adults, of caregivers, of teachers?

- What are the goals of education?

Answers to these and other questions reflect the underlying assumptions and beliefs that guide and influence a practitioner's interactions with children, families, and colleagues.

Generally speaking, research and developments in theoretical models have had a positive influence on educational and clinical practice by stimulating the creation of new tools and technologies. Sometimes how technologies have influenced theory or experience has led to the refinement and verification of theories (Warren & Reichle, 1992). For example, the developmental outcomes of early intervention studies (e.g., Lazar, Darlington, Murray, Royce, & Snipper, 1982) have played a role in questioning the stability of the types of abilities that are measured by IQ tests. Similarly, advances in computer technology have helped broaden notions of intelligence, as assistive aids have provided a means of communication for people with severe motor impairments. In some instances, technological innovations may come before conceptual understanding and empirical verification (Gregory, 1984). For instance, one does not need to understand the underlying structures and rules of language in order to use language. This broader idea is illustrated by an example from earlier times, when cooking and food preservation were undertaken with no conceptual knowledge of the causes of decomposition and the role of cooking in the reduction of disease.

As new conceptual and technological advances made possible the study of behaviors in complex, real-life settings, the assumption that practice is a direct application of findings from theory and research was questioned. Piaget himself recognized that "all hypotheses derived from psychology must be verified, through actual classroom practices and educational results rather than merely based on simple deductions" (1973, p. ix). Theory, research, and practice should be viewed as complementary, interrelated activities that continuously influence each other in a reciprocal manner.

HISTORICAL PERSPECTIVE

Over the years, assessment and educational practices have been modified to reflect the predominant theory of child development. Theory and research in child development have provided a comprehensive knowledge base regarding the sequence of developmental accomplishments of young children and the environmental conditions needed to support development (Kohlberg & Mayer, 1972; Scott & Bowman, 1997). This has had a major impact on applied disciplines such as education and speech-language pathology. The theoretical bases for assessment and instructional procedures are not always evident to the user. It is important that practitioners be aware of how the assessment tools and curricula they use reflect new and broader assumptions about how children develop and learn. Such awareness leads to the questioning of whether the methods in use are consistent with the practitioner's espoused beliefs and values.

Traditional Models of Child Development: Nature versus Nurture

Two polarized views about the nature of human development have dominated scientific thinking throughout modern history: the nativist model and the behavioral model. Each offered a different perspective on the impetus to human development. These models were viewed as incompatible, and researchers and practitioners tended to adhere to either one or the other, with little communication between the two camps (Warren, 1993). Many assessment and instructional procedures that reflect one or the other of these two theoretical models are still widely used in educational and clinical practice.

Nativist Model

The **nativist perspective** emphasizes the intrinsic potential for optimal development to occur, given a healthy environment. Development is viewed as genetically determined and occurring primarily through maturation. The nativist model focuses on abilities believed to be independent of and separate from everyday experience, such as cognitive abilities being biologically determined and constant.

Chomsky's (1957) model of generative language was based on a nativist view that language originated from an internal and innate set of competencies and was not derived from the environment. Studies of child development, such as those by Gesell (1940), were motivated by the concern to describe internal maturational processes. These studies resulted in the description of major developmental milestones that serve as the basis for the standardized infant assessment and curricula still used at the beginning of the 21st century. During the time that these studies occurred, educational and clinical applications focused on test construction, establishing developmental norms, and the assessment of biological readiness. Few educational or therapeutic programs were available for people with disabilities because environmental modifications were assumed to have a limited effect on intelligence and behavior.

Behavioral Model

The **behavioral perspective** (Skinner, 1957) is based on an empiricist or cultural transmission model. Learning is believed to occur as a result of external reinforcement of associations between environmental stimuli and behavior responses. Development is viewed as an additive accumulation of independent skills that are culturally, rather than biologically, determined.

For example, in this model language was considered similar to other behaviors and subject to principles of operant conditioning. It was believed that children learn language by imitating adult verbal models and that adults selectively reinforce these imitations. From a behavioral perspective, the aims of education were to socialize children into mainstream school culture through the use of a standard, uniform curriculum. A major emphasis was placed on the direct teaching of skills using behavioral principles that entailed manipulating environmental stimuli and rewarding children for culturally desired behaviors. The behavioral model had a major influence on special education programs for people with moderate and severe disabilities (e.g., autism). Highly prescribed intervention programs were devised using teaching sequences and specific correction procedures. Quantitative assessment measures (e.g., frequency counts) of task-related behaviors measured performance against arbitrarily set criteria.

Beginning of Integration

Findings from empirical research and observations of real-life behaviors revealed the limitations of models that reduced human development simply to either biological or environmental factors. The nativist model proved inconsistent with findings of variations in children's development as a result of contextual factors. The behavioral model failed to account for the emergence of novel behavior that appeared independent of any adult models, such as children's error patterns (e.g., saying "goed" for *went*) in early language acquisition. These limitations stimulated interest in the interactionist position, which viewed development as the result of interactions between an organism and its environment. **Information processing models** of development were also emerging. The three perspectives that address integration are discussed next.

Interactionist Perspective

An early proponent of the **interactionist perspective** was Dewey (1916). The interactionist model, however, became widely popular in the 1970s, when Piaget's theory began to have a strong influence on educational research and practice. Piaget's theory considers development as a series of sequential stages of development with earlier stages providing necessary bases for later learning. The generation of novel and idiosyncratic behaviors results from children's interactions with objects and people in their environment and their active participation in the construction and transformation of knowledge according to their own intellectual resources.

Bloom (1970) used this model to explain the origin of language development as the dynamic interplay between children's growing cognitive abilities and their encounters with the social world. From this perspective, the goal of education was to stimulate intellectual and moral development through the provision of environments that allowed children to actively manipulate and experiment with objects and materials (Kohlberg & Mayer, 1972). Piagetian content and developmental sequences were used as a basis for a number of curricula and intervention programs (e.g., Bricker & Bricker, 1974; Hohmann, Banet, & Weikart, 1979; Kamii & DeVries, 1978). Assessment focused on identifying prerequisite behaviors (e.g., sensorimotor prerequisites to oral language). Qualitative methods were used to analyze children's use of learning strategies rather than quantitative measurements of skill mastery.

Information Processing Theories

A metaphor for the information processing model is the computer. Humans encode and transform information to solve cognitive tasks. Development is viewed in terms of changes in memory-storage capacities and the use of different types of cognitive strategies rather than an accumulation of knowledge. The interest in cognitive strategies stimulated the development of metacognitive approaches. These metacognitive approaches focused on teaching students how to think and make explicit those processes necessary to the understanding and completion of a task.

Connectionist Models

Connectionist models are computer models that are loosely based on the principles of neural information processing (Elman et al., 1996). The connectionist model attempts to explain complex cognitive processes using concepts from both behavioral science and neuroscience. Drawing on an analogy to the central nervous system in which neurons activate and inhibit each other in complex networks, information processing is viewed as involving large numbers of units stimulating or inhibiting each other through networks of connections. This model has been used in research on the early cognitive abilities of infants (Mareschal, French, & Quinn, 2000) and in psycholinguistic research to identify the processes necessary for learning grammar (Bates, Thal, & Marchman, 1991).

Toward a More Comprehensive Approach: Social-Constructivist Model

Piagetian and information processing models recognize the importance of social experience but give comparatively little attention to interaction with others in the generation of new knowledge. The increasing recognition that development cannot be separated from social and cultural contexts brought renewed interest in work conducted by Vygotsky in the 1930s (Vygotsky, 1978). Later accounts of and elaborations on Vygotsky's theory (e.g., Bruner, 1975; Cole & Scribner, 1974; Wertsch, 1985) strongly emphasized the social origin of knowledge. They attributed children's progression from simple to more complex behaviors primarily to the introduction of new knowledge by a more advanced individual (Meadows, 1993). Assuming a social-constructivist perspective, development in this model is viewed as the internalization and transformation of routines, skills, and ideas that children learn through participation in shared activities with an adult or a more capable peer. Children develop more sophisticated competence because the adult or peer guides them through the learning process. The social-constructivist model had profound implications for educational and clinical practice. Two concepts that had a major impact on educational practices, the zone of proximal development (ZPD) and mediation, are explored in the following paragraphs.

Zone of Proximal Development

Vygotsky used the term **zone of proximal development** to refer to "the distance between the actual developmental level as determined by independent problem-solving and the level of potential development as determined through problem-solving under adult guidance or in collaboration with more capable peers" (1978, p. 86). This notion that adult assistance can improve a child's performance on tasks was applied to the development of assessment procedures. These procedures could be used to evaluate children's potential in terms of their responsiveness to instruction. The strong emphasis on the role of the adult as a mediator in helping children learn transformed classroom practices. Curricular programs (e.g., Gutierrez-Clellen & Quinn, 1993; Norris & Hoffman, 1990; Osborn, Sherwood, & Cole, 1991; Tharp & Gallimore, 1988) were devised that delineated specific teaching or scaffolding strategies for teachers to assist children in learning cognitive, language, and literacy skills.

Mediation

The Vygotskian perspective stresses the role played by **mediation** or the social transmission of psychological and cultural tools to the developing child. Adults teach children important cultural and cognitive tools that are socially constructed and transmitted through generations (e.g., language, literacy, mathematical systems, maps, computers). Children appropriate or make these cultural tools their own through a process of guided participation. In the context of sociocultural activities, the adult provides the necessary structure or scaffolding for the child to transform and "reinvent" his or her understanding and knowledge (Rogoff, 1993). Psychological growth is viewed as a movement from "other-regulation" to "self-regulation." Adults take on less and less responsibility as children learn to provide their own scaffolding through the mediation of psychological and cultural tools.

Studies of social institutions that play a fundamental role in the transmission of cultural-cognitive tools, such as schools, highlight the existence of a unique school-based culture referred to as a *"hidden" curriculum*. The hidden curriculum consists of unspoken expectations for children in terms of knowledge and familiarity with mainstream culture, rules for communication and behavior in school, and rules for peer acceptance and interaction (Nelson, 1994). Research findings have revealed that the match or mismatch between the home and school cultures exerts a strong influence on children's academic success (Cazden, 1988; Heath, 1983; Labov, 1972). For example, the school culture of the Anglo American middle class typically emphasizes individual achievement and competition, which is not compatible with the values of children from traditional Hawaiian cultures, where cooperation and mutual help are stressed (Tharp, 1989). Similarly, African American oral traditions of verbal challenge games may be viewed as rude and impertinent by those with different ethnic backgrounds and may clash with a classroom's communication style (Heath, 1989). Assessments and curricula have been developed to identify problems due to cultural differences and unfamiliarity with the hidden curriculum, and at the explicit teaching of language, intellectual activities, and social rules typical to schools (Barrera, 1993; Nelson, 1994).

Models of child development have evolved over time from simplistic explanations that focus on single factors or causes of behaviors (etiology or environment) to models that account for reciprocal influences among multiple factors, including culture. These newer models, aided by conceptual, methodological, and technical advances, provide increasingly sophisticated views that better reflect the complexity of human behavior.

AN INTEGRATED UNIFIED MODEL: SYSTEMS PERSPECTIVE

At the end of the 20th century, trends in the search for a comprehensive framework for the study of human development moved toward a synthesis and integration of diverse perspectives (Mallory, 1992; Warren, 1993). Holistic models have replaced **reductionist models** that break complex wholes into separate units. Holistic models offer broader conceptual frameworks, emphasizing the unification of concepts and methods and rejecting dualistic thinking based on separation and contrasts. Traditional distinctions—such as those between objective and subjective, mind and body, innate and acquired—have been questioned (Overton, 1994).

Knowledge and meaning do not exist independent of an individual's thoughts and understanding, thereby nullifying a distinction between the objective and the subjective. Though rejecting the notion of absolute truth, the systems perspective recognizes that knowledge is not totally private, arbitrary, or independent of rational thought. Emphasis here is placed on the interrelationships between the cognitive-rational and the affective-emotional aspects of human thought. Along with traditional quantitative approaches, researchers and practitioners are beginning to employ qualitative methodologies that allow for subjective views on how children learn (e.g., different ways of knowing). Qualitative approaches to assessment and intervention are particularly useful in cross-cultural environments, in which the acknowledgment of one's own subjectivity and cultural values is essential in order to recognize and respect the way a family's subjective world affects a child's behavior and development (Barrera, 1996).

The mind and the brain do not work separately but, rather, constitute a unified whole. Research in the neurological and cognitive fields suggests that the human mind is constrained and structured by the human body. For example, extreme environmental deprivation and stress can cause changes to the physiological structure of the brain and neurochemical response patterns. At the same time, cultural experiences such as language and early social interactions can have a positive impact on the early development of the brain (Shore, 1997).

The distinction between which behaviors are innate (i.e., genetically transmitted) and which are acquired through experience and environmental influence is artificial. The theory of evolution demonstrates that experience and adaptation to the environment have influenced the development and selection of genetic material. Even genetically prewired systems need particular environmental conditions in order to unfold.

Systems theory is designed to study unified whole and self-organizing systems. It provides a comprehensive account for the entire realm of human experience including the cognitive, imaginative, emotional, social, and practical aspects of everyday existence (Thelen & Smith, 1994). As no priority is accorded to individual components, the systems perspective makes possible an integration of objective and subjective, individual and cultural, and biological and environmental elements (Overton, 1994). Early 21st-century methodologies based on a systems perspective account for the complexity of human behaviors in real-life settings. The basic tenets of a systems theory are that 1) complex interdependencies exist among all components of a system, 2) the interaction among these components differs under different conditions, and 3) these interdependencies result in the emergence of different global patterns of behavior without the specification or control of the individual components (Evans, 1996). Dynamic systems theory, for example, recognizes aspects of human behavior such as change, variability, flexibility, interrelations, and bidirectional influences among components, as well as the production of novel forms of behavior that have been problematic for reductionist models (Bronfenbrenner, 1979; Sameroff & Chandler, 1975; Thelen & Smith, 1994). Table 1.1 summarizes the history of the major theoretical perspectives on child development.

Broad Ecological Approach

Many researchers in the field of child development, as well as in applied clinical and educational disciplines, have adopted the systems approach to guide research and practice efforts. Bronfenbrenner (1979) formulated the

Table 1.1.   Theoretical perspectives on child development

Nativist	Development is genetically determined and occurs through maturation.
Behavioral	Development is viewed as resulting from the external reinforcement of associations between environmental stimuli and behavioral responses.
Interactionist	Development is viewed as resulting from interactions between an organism and its environment.
Information processing	Development is viewed in terms of changes in memory storage capacities and use of different types of cognitive strategies.
Connectionist	Development or the acquisition of knowledge is similar to the central nervous system, in which neurons activate and inhibit each other in complex networks.
Social-constructivist	Development is viewed as the internalization and transformation of routines, skills, and ideas that children learn through participation in shared activities with adults or more capable peers.
Systems theory	Development occurs as a result of complex interactions among interdependent subcomponents of a system. New global patterns of behaviors that are different from the sum of their individual components emerge.

ecological model, which has had a strong influence on educational programs. The ecological model allows for a holistic approach. The unit of analysis is not the child but the child and the environment, as first expressed by Lewin in the 1940s. Bronfenbrenner proposed a conceptual framework for analyzing the environment as a system of nested, interdependent, dynamic structures that include 1) the child and the immediate environment (e.g., the family, child care, school), 2) more distal environments in which the child does not participate directly but in which events occur that can indirectly influence the child (e.g., a parent's workplace), and 3) the broader social context (e.g., cultural beliefs, social structures). This recognition that the child cannot be studied in isolation from the family, the community, and the values and institutions of the society has broadened the scope of research and practice.

The search for methodologies that can provide a valid portrayal of how children function in real-life situations has resulted in the development of several new and innovative assessment procedures. Contemporary instructional procedures address not only the child's needs but also those of the family and the community. The involvement of families in the assessment and instructional process is essential to the implementation of ecologically valid practices. Professionals who are aware of cultural influences on development are concerned about the sensitivity of assessments and curriculum materials. They feel the need to establish relationships of mutual respect and understanding with families from diverse cultural backgrounds (Harry, Rueda, & Kalyanpur, 1999).

CONCLUSION

At the beginning of the 21st century, a huge gap exists between research, theory, and practice. A holistic-ecological approach to human development reflects more accurately how children actually live and develop in a world filled with people, things, and events that are in continuous interaction (Thelen & Smith, 1994). Many professionals are modifying program models and procedures to better meet the needs and priorities of the children and families they serve. For example, early interventionists have expanded the scope of individualized education programs (IEPs) and individualized family service plans (IFSPs) to include family participation and input.

Implementation of new program models is not without problems. New procedures and tools often lack sufficient validation and systematic application. Instruments designed for research purposes are too time-consuming and impractical for daily, real-life application (Bricker, 1992). Although well-researched assessment instruments and curricula are available, they are based on a body of knowledge derived from research in laboratory-type settings, insightfully characterized by Bronfenbrenner as "the strange behavior of children, in strange situations with strange adults for the briefest possible periods of time" (1979, p. 19). Many standardized and criterion-referenced tests, for example, are divided into specific domains or areas of development (e.g., cognition, communication, fine motor, gross motor, social, self-help). This is useful for practical purposes. Many behaviors, however, may fit in multiple domains. For example, is the category "initiates social interaction" a communication or a social skill? Is "puts together two puzzle pieces" a cognitive or fine motor skill? Other behaviors are complex and involve skills from multiple areas of development. Reading, for instance, involves social, cognitive, linguistic, and sensory abilities.

The study of human behaviors as they occur in real-life situations has increased the value of contributions from research in applied environments (e.g., empirical investigations of the effects of intervention programs) to inform theory and basic research. Stronger collaborative endeavors between researchers and practitioners are needed in which practitioners are actively involved in clinically and classroom-based research (e.g., Bricker, 1993c; Mallory, 1992; Peck, 1993). Although theory and research in child development can serve to guide and enhance practices, real-life observations and research by practitioners can contribute to a better understanding of the development of children and families.

Review Questions

What are the major theoretical perspectives on child development?

Identify the major tenets of the social-constructivist perspective.

How have ecological models influenced assessment and educational practices?

What is your own view on what children need to develop and learn?

How are theory, research, and practice related? Identify an instance in your professional life that illustrates the relationship among them.

Traditional and Contemporary Assessment Models

2

After reading this chapter, you will be able to:

- Define the types and purposes of assessment

- Describe the evolution of traditional and contemporary approaches to assessment

- Summarize the limitations of traditional models of assessment

- Discuss a framework for alternative assessment models

*A*long with new conceptualizations of child development and learning, approaches to assessment have changed dramatically over the years. Practitioners and researchers have come to realize that traditional methods provide only a limited view of children's functioning in real-life settings, so they have sought models and practices that represent deeper understanding of the developmental process. This chapter provides basic definitions of assessment and discusses traditional approaches. Two major types of assessment and their purposes are reviewed. The evolution of traditional and contemporary approaches to assessment is traced, and the limitations of traditional approaches in terms of their educational relevance and their approriateness for use with culturally and linguistically diverse children are discussed.

DEFINITIONS AND TERMINOLOGY

Assessment can be broadly defined as the process of observing, gathering, and/or recording information (Cohen & Spenciner, 1994). Practitioners conduct assessments mainly to obtain information for the purpose of making evaluative decisions. With a multitude of decisions to make, professionals rely on procedures and instruments that are specific to the principles and needs of their practices (Bergen, 1994a). For example, a common assessment practice in the medical field is conducting routine screening of large numbers of children in order to identify those who may need more specific assessment. Once a problem is suspected, such as a language delay, the child may be referred to a communication specialist who will conduct an in-depth assessment to determine whether a specific language disorder exists. Educators are primarily concerned with collecting information on children's progress over time that will assist them in making decisions about educational planning. Social workers need information about the broader social and community context to make decisions about which kinds of social, financial, or legal assistance a family might need. A variety of assessment approaches and methods are available, and the choice of a given tool depends on the type of decision the professional needs to make (Greenspan & Meisels, 1996).

ASSESSMENT APPROACHES AND TOOLS

An assessment procedure is usually derived from one of two broad assessment approaches: quantitative or qualitative (Schwartz & Olswang, 1996). From a **quantitative perspective,** assessment is viewed primarily as an objective measurement process that results in a numerical representation of children's behaviors and abilities. The process begins with the identification of well-defined target behaviors, which are usually tested in pre-specified and standardized conditions. From a **qualitative perspective,** assessment is viewed as the documentation of more complex and holistic behaviors as they occur in natural environments. Methods such as observations, interviews, and questionnaires provide information on qualitative aspects of behaviors rather than mastery of skills.

Formal Assessments

Traditional types of assessment are based on a quantitative perspective. They rely on predefined, highly structured tasks and focus on isolated aspects of development that are easy to observe and to measure. These assessments may be categorized as **formal assessments** as opposed to nonformal. Formal assessments are tests that yield information on a preset content and have specified guidelines for administration. Information is usually collected on a one-time basis and compared with normative data. Standardized tests belong in this category.

Nonformal Assessments

Nonformal assessments consist of structured and systematic observations of behaviors within meaningful, context-bound activities (e.g., children's block constructions, drawing and writing, dramatic play, conversations about books, participation in class discussions). Information is collected on an ongoing basis at different times and across multiple environments, using a broad variety of quantitative and qualitative methods. Silliman and Wilkinson (1991) classified nonformal assessment tools into three main categories: categorical, narrative, and descriptive.

Categorical Tools

Categorical tools have predetermined categories into which all events and behaviors are coded during the observation. This type of observation can be quantified and summarized by a numerical representation. Typical examples of categorical tools are rating scales and checklists. They are relatively easy and inexpensive to use, but they are not suitable when detailed information on qualitative aspects of behaviors is needed. For example, a checklist will provide information on whether a child can say more than 50 single words but does not necessarily describe specific types of words; similarly, if a child uses invented spelling, a checklist will not provide samples of particular spelling patterns that the child may use.

Narrative Tools

Narrative tools include journals, running records, anecdotal notes of observations of critical incidents, and ethnographic notes recorded during observations. These tools are systematic and detailed written descriptions of behaviors. They are easy to record and to share with others; however, the accuracy and the selection of the information may be subject to interpretative biases.

Descriptive Tools

Descriptive tools are verbatim accounts of actual language use and provide a detailed record of behaviors (e.g., language transcripts) and a description of the various contexts in which the behaviors are exhibited. Their use requires trained staff and typically involves technological tools such as audiotaping and videotaping. Analysis of a descriptive record is time-consuming.

These nonformal tools are not exclusive but are meant to complement each other to provide an integration of multiple perspectives. Both quantitative and qualitative measures are used to assess young children. For instance, a psychologist may present information based on a child's performance on a standardized test; a teacher may contribute information on the child's progress toward specific educational goals using data from curriculum-based checklists. Caregivers can describe significant incidents involving the child observed at home and in the community.

TYPES OF ASSESSMENT

Until the early 1990s, educational and clinical practitioners relied primarily on two major types of assessment: norm-referenced and criterion-referenced. **Norm-referenced assessments** are used primarily for diagnostic purposes; **criterion-referenced assessments** are used to measure a child's mastery of specific skills. **Curriculum-based assessment (CBA)** is a special type of criterion-referenced assessment in which test items represent functional skills that can serve as educational goals and objectives.

Norm-Referenced Assessment

Norm-referenced tests provide information on how a child is developing in relation to a larger group of children of the same chronological age. These tests undergo an extensive development and standardization process. Items are chosen based on not their educational relevance but primarily on statistical criteria such as the percentage of children who master a particular skill at a certain age or whether the item correlates well with the total test.

The value of a standardized test is judged by statistical measures of its psychometric properties, mainly its reliability and validity. **Reliability** refers to the consistency or stability of test performance over time and across observers. If a child is tested twice, for example, within a short time period, the test should yield similar scores. Also, two testers independently testing the same child should obtain similar test results. **Validity** is the extent to which the test measures what it says it measures. If a test is said to assess pragmatic language, for instance, it is important that items represent an adequately comprehensive range of skills that are specifically pragmatic, such as turn taking or topic initiation.

Criterion-Referenced Assessment

Rather than comparing a child's performance to a normative group or a standardized sample, criterion-referenced tests measure mastery of specific objectives defined by predetermined standards of criteria. Items are usually sequentially arranged within developmental domains or subject areas, and numerical scores represent the proportion of the specific domain or subject area the child has mastered. Because these instruments are not standardized, adaptations are allowed and encouraged to elicit a representative sample of children's behavior in optimal conditions.

Curriculum-Based Assessment

CBA is a direct application of criterion-referenced assessment strategies to educational content (Notari, Slentz, & Bricker, 1991). It is a form of criterion-referenced measurement in which curricular objectives serve as the criteria for the identification of educational targets (Bagnato & Neisworth, 1991). Because of the direct congruence among testing, teaching, and progress evaluation, CBA is a direct means for identifying a child's entry point within an educational program and for refining and readjusting instruction. Assessment and curricular content are coordinated to address the same skills and abilities, and repeated testing occurs over time to measure the child's progress on these skills.

Bagnato and Neisworth (1991) distinguished two types of CBA: curriculum-referenced scales and curriculum-embedded scales. Curriculum-referenced scales include skills that are common to most educational programs but are not particular to any specific curriculum. Two examples of curriculum-referenced scales are the Brigance Diagnostic Inventory of Early Development–Revised (Brigance, 1991) and the Callier-Azusa Scale: Assessment of Deaf-Blind Children (Stillman, 1974). In curriculum-embedded scales, assessment items are identical to skills included in a specific curriculum. Examples include the Assessment, Evaluation, and Programming System (AEPS) for Infants and Young Children (Bricker, 1993a), the Hawaii Early Learning Profile (HELP; Parks et al., 1994), and the Creative Curriculum for Early Childhood (Dodge & Colker, 1992). Curriculum-embedded assessments provide specific guidelines for administering assessment items, developing instructional goals and objectives, and conducting activities to facilitate the acquisition of functional skills.

CBAs focus on skills that are part of the daily curriculum, making it easier for teachers to collect information on an ongoing basis and to monitor children's learning so they can adjust the curriculum and teaching strategies to an individual child. Table 2.1 summarizes the characteristics of norm-referenced assessment, criterion-referenced assessment, and CBA.

PURPOSES OF ASSESSMENT

Practitioners should understand why they are measuring a child's performance before choosing an assessment instrument. A discrepancy often exists between the purpose of an assessment tool and how it is used (Sheehan, 1982). Standardized tests, for example, were developed to compare a child's performance to that of a normative sample and should not be used for evaluating the quality of educational programs (Popham, 1999).

✳A comprehensive assessment should involve four processes, each with its own unique purpose: 1) **screening,** 2) **diagnostic assessment,** 3) **program assessment,** and 4) **evaluation.** Screening is conducted to identify children who may be at risk for health or developmental problems and should occur prior to the other measurement processes. Because it entails the testing of large groups of children, screening procedures should be brief and relatively easy to administer. The purpose of using screening tools is to

Table 2.1.   Characteristics of norm-referenced, criterion-referenced, and curriculum-based assessment

Norm-referenced assessment

Provides information on how a child is developing in relation to a larger group of children of the same chronological age

Items are chosen based on statistical criteria, such as percentage of children who master a particular skill at a certain age or whether the item correlates well with the total test

Criterion-referenced assessment

Measures the mastery of specific objectives defined by predetermined standards of criteria

Items are usually sequentially arranged within developmental domains or subject areas

Numerical scores represent proportion of specific domain or subject area that a child has mastered

Curriculum-based assessment

Curricular activities are provided for each assessment item

Used as direct means for identifying a child's entry point within an educational program and for refining and readjusting instruction

Assessment and curricular content are coordinated to address same skills and abilities

Repeated testing occurs over time to measure child's progress on these skills

determine whether a child's performance is sufficiently different from other children's of the same chronological age to warrant more testing.

Following an initial suspicion of a delay, a diagnostic assessment is conducted to provide in-depth information regarding the specific nature and extent of the problem. These assessments are highly specialized and need to be administered by trained professionals. Diagnostic tools are used to qualify children for special services and to make referral and placement decisions. Screening and diagnostic instruments are generally norm-referenced.

Program assessment specifically addresses the need to obtain educationally relevant information and provide guidance in the development of educational programs. Program assessment serves at least three functions (Bricker & Littman, 1982). First, this type of assessment provides information for identifying appropriate intervention content. Second, caregivers may use results from these assessments to compare their goals for children with those of service providers. Third, program assessments may be used to document children's progress and learning of new skills over time.

When used as an evaluation tool, results of children's performance on a program assessment are compared before and after intervention. Program assessments can draw upon a variety of methods. Most programs use criterion-referenced tests, which are more sensitive to progress than norm-referenced tests. Other methods suitable for evaluating progress can include anecdotal records and diverse types of documentation of children's work, such as drawings, writing samples, or photographs. Table 2.2 summarizes the four purposes of assessment.

LIMITATIONS OF TRADITIONAL APPROACHES

Norm-referenced instruments are best used for screening and diagnostic purposes, when it is important to compare a child's performance to that of

Table 2.2.   Purposes of assessment

Screening

To determine whether the child is in need of further assessment in one or more areas of development

Diagnostic assessment

To determine whether a problem exists, identify the nature of the problem, and conclude whether the child is eligible for services

Program assessment

To determine a child's current skill level or baseline skills before intervention

Evaluation

To determine how children progress over time by comparing a child's skills before and after intervention

same-age peers. However, assessments administered with standardized procedures during a single session often lead to an underestimation of the capabilities of children with disabilities (Bagnato & Neisworth, 1991). Because standardized tests use criteria that discriminate between groups of children of different ages, the behaviors tested may not necessarily be educationally relevant. Examples include asking a child to remove a large round peg from a board or to point to a pellet in a bottle. Standardized tests do not yield direct information for making program decisions or choosing curricular content, nor have they proved sensitive to intervention efforts (Darby, 1979; Garwood, 1982).

Norm-referenced and criterion-referenced assessments are based on different assumptions about child development and learning. They differ primarily in two ways: 1) the criteria or standards for judging progress and 2) the relevance of information for educational planning and intervention. In a norm-referenced approach, progress is considered a function of the degree to which a child "catches up" with his or her peers. Little information is gathered on environmental factors and instructional strategies that may promote or hinder the child's progress. A criterion-referenced approach is more specifically focused on determining whether the instruction is benefiting the child, and progress is based on criteria determined for a particular child and context. A curriculum-based approach aims to evaluate the actual instruction provided. Information is collected on an ongoing basis so that teaching adjustments can be made continuously to best support the child's individual needs.

Traditional assessment approaches have proved inadequate to address important questions raised by new theoretical formulations and research findings, as well as the daily experiences of professionals. Two interrelated issues have led to significant modifications in assessment practices: 1) the complexity and holistic nature of development and 2) the role of context and culture in learning.

Complexity and Holistic Nature of Development

Assessment approaches tend to reflect the predominant theory of child development. Contemporary models consider development a complex and dynamic process determined by multiple biological and environmental factors that interact with each other in a continuous and reciprocal manner. Within this perspective, assessment provides information on all factors that may influence a child's behavior, which allows one to obtain a comprehensive, holistic understanding of how the factors are interconnected and related to each other (Meltzer, 1994). For example, before assuming a language delay in a toddler who is not yet using language to communicate in child care, many areas need to be assessed: hearing, oral-motor skills, cognitive abilities, and emotional development. It is also important to look at how the child interacts across contexts and with different people. Some children may be proficient in the language used at home but have not yet had sufficient exposure to English.

Traditional approaches to assessment do not necessarily take into account contextual variations in performance. Norm-referenced tests are based on nativistic assumptions that abilities are relatively stable over time and independent of environmental influences (e.g., the cognitive abilities measured in IQ tests). A one-time assessment that is considered representative of the child's overall functioning is conducted to make decisions about treatment based on a diagnostic label or category.

Based on the behavioral perspective, criterion-referenced assessment approaches focus on the analysis of environments and tasks, as well as on the measurement of observable behaviors that can be manipulated and taught using prescriptive and highly structured instructional approaches. Organized by separate domains or areas of development rather than by an integrated and holistic approach, these tests often result in a fragmented and, at times, distorted view. Assessment tends to be limited to behaviors for which tests and scales already exist and ignore aspects that are difficult to measure, such as emotional development, social and family contexts, or self-regulatory processes (Greenspan & Meisels, 1996).

Although criterion-referenced instruments are more sensitive to intervention than norm-referenced approaches, they too have serious shortcomings. Many were developed by selecting isolated items from various norm-referenced instruments, a procedure that invalidates age equivalency scores for individual items and limits their educational relevance (Johnson, 1982). Items drawn from standardized tests, such as "shows fear of strangers" or "places 10 pellets in a small bottle," do not necessarily represent functional behaviors that can be used to develop educational goals. Also, many criterion-referenced assessments are based on a fragmented skill, test-teach-test approach that does not reflect current models of the way children develop and learn. Many tests, for instance, limit the assessment of math skills to asking children to count. Learning to count, however, involves the understanding and mastery of other skills that need to be assessed, such as one-to-one correspondence, conservation of numbers, and the cardinal principle (the notion that the last word in the counting sequence represents the total number of objects counted). Also, development is not just progressive mastery of skills; it proceeds by a trial-and-error process in which children create and test their own hypotheses. In learning language, children go through a phase of overextending grammatical rules, adding, for example, an *s* to *foot* to form the plural *foots*. This may be considered an error on a traditional test even though it is, in reality, an important step in a child's language development.

Ecological conceptualizations of development have resulted in a broader approach to assessment that incorporates descriptive and qualitative methods. These newer methods enable the assessment of broader holistic behaviors of children and observation of behaviors across contexts.

Focus on the Whole Child

Specialized assessment tools are not always the most appropriate methods for assessing all types of behaviors. For example, emotional and social behaviors are best assessed through naturalistic observations of interactions between the child and primary caregivers during play or daily activities and routines. Important processes—such as strategies that children may use to inhibit inappropriate behaviors, self-regulate in situations of stress, or focus attention on specific stimuli—are best documented through observation rather than direct testing. The attention to interrelationships among domains has led to the recognition of reciprocal influences between domains of development and behaviors that were formerly viewed as unrelated. To illustrate this point, the early-1990s emphasis on the interrelated nature of early language and literacy led to the examination of multiple aspects of behavior, including 1) pragmatic, semantic, syntactic, and graphophonemic language abilities; 2) early phonemic awareness skills; 3) metacognitive and metalinguistic abilities; and 4) text schema and text structure knowledge (Ball, 1993; Marvin, 1989; Westby & Costlow, 1991). This view supports recommendations for teaching reading using a balanced approach (Snow, Burns, & Griffin, 1998). Reading is not just associating letters and sounds (i.e., phonics) and the mechanical decoding of words. Being a good reader also involves mastering vocabulary and grammar, understanding that words are made of individual sounds, having knowledge and ideas to communicate, being motivated to read, using strategies to self-monitor comprehension and repair errors, and knowing how to organize and sequence different aspects of a story or narrative. Furthermore, children who experience problems in oral language development are likely to develop later literacy learning difficulties—evidence that has important implications for the early identification of reading disabilities (Aram & Nation, 1980; Catts & Kamhi, 1987).

Assessment Across Multiple Contexts

The realization that the match or mismatch between the home and school cultures exerts a strong influence on children's academic success has promoted the development of assessments aimed at identifying testing problems related to cultural differences (Barrera, 1993; Nelson, 1994). A comprehensive and integrated view of the child can be obtained only if caregivers and practitioners across disciplines collaborate and share information. The use of qualitative tools such as interviews and oral reports broadens the sources and scope of the assessment to include information not only from professionals about children's performance in specific situations but also from people who know the children best (e.g., family members) and observe their behaviors across multiple daily contexts and routines.

Role of Context and Culture on Learning

The ecological model no longer views behaviors as separated from the context of everyday experiences. New assessment models incorporate alternative methods and procedures that can address two critical areas that traditional approaches failed to take into consideration: 1) the influences of family and sociocultural contexts on child behavior and 2) the child's functioning within natural environments (Bricker, 1992; Brown, Collins, & Duguid, 1989).

Influences of Family and Sociocultural Contexts

An accurate understanding of a child's functioning needs to include information about the child's behaviors, not only in the traditional classroom or clinical assessment environments but also in the context of the family and the community (Bricker, 1992; Neisworth & Bagnato, 1988). Because children display competence differently across school and other social environments, information from family members is critical in making decisions about the need for intervention services (Thomas, 1993). This is especially important when a child's family background is different from the mainstream culture and traditional assessments may underestimate the child's abilities (Lapp, Flood, Tinajero, Lundgren, & Nagel, 1996; Thorp, 1997).

Children from different cultural backgrounds may score poorly on norm-referenced tests, not because they have delays but because of the external biases of tests constructed to reflect the mainstream culture and beliefs (Cummins, 1984; Gutierrez-Clellen, 1996). Academic achievement tests, for example, focus on written language and ignore many oral language skills for which African American children may demonstrate greater competence (Hale, 1992). These tests do not differentiate developmental problems from difficulties that arise from a sociocultural mismatch between experiences in the home and the social conventions and rules used in the school (Cazden, 1988; Heath, 1982; Labov, 1972; Snow, 1983). Responses to the stress caused by acculturation factors can be easily confused with learning disabilities (Adler, 1981; Barrera, 1993; Gavillàn-Torres, 1984; Westby, 1985). Children with limited proficiency in the language used for instruction need to pay attention to both the instructional content and the language used to convey that content. Language use in the context of the school curriculum is the most significant factor in placing certain groups at a disadvantage (Miller, 1984).

For children who are bilingual, assessment must also provide information about the child's knowledge of languages other than English so that the assessment of language development can be differentiated from the use of language as a medium for instruction (Westby, 1985). Barrera (1993) recommended examining several aspects of language: 1) the presence of receptive and expressive skills in non-English language, 2) the use of diverse rules and styles of language usage, 3) second-language learning, and 4) concept and skill learning through a nonnative language.

Practitioners need to become familiar with a child's cultural background—in terms of acculturation and schooling experiences—before assuming that a difficulty is due to a learning disability or developmental delay (Lopez-Reyna & Bay, 1997; Thorp, 1997). Assessment should be viewed as a process of formulating hypotheses, by addressing questions about the how (e.g., how cultural differences influence performance, how the environment promotes knowledge of rules of the learning environment) and why of behaviors (Gregory, 1997; Schwartz & Olswang, 1996). Preschools generally espouse a child-centered approach to learning, in which children are expected to engage in independent learning and exploration. A child who does not speak up and actively participate in activities may come across as shy and lacking in self-confidence. In the child's home, however, children may engage mostly in functional daily family activities—rather than drawing, painting, and playing with Legos—and adults may be more directive, so children are expected to listen and observe and are not asked for their opinions. Another child may be extremely fluent in the language and literacy skills of his or her home and community, in which oral traditions, visual media (e.g., television, films), and popular print (e.g., advertisements, magazines) are stressed. Yet, these experiences may differ from the more formal types of language and literacy used in school to the extent that the child is seen as having a learning disability.

Socioculturally competent assessment requires the ability to perceive and assess skills in a multifaceted fashion. This allows information and meaning to be exchanged in a truly communicative manner among different observers, including caregivers and culture-language mediators such as interpreters (Barrera, 1996; Thomas, 1993). Assessment practices can include an "ethnography" of the child's behaviors by using qualitative, informal observation and interview tools and various forms of documentation of performance (e.g., videotapes, audio recordings) (Ballard, 1991; Gavillàn-Torres, 1984).

Assessment within Natural Contexts

One of the most important purposes of assessment is to yield information about the contexts in which children learn best and how they respond to instruction (Nelson, 1994). Research findings show that children perform better when the context and tasks are familiar and make sense to them. African American children perform better on language tasks when they are presented with culturally appropriate pictures (Cazden, 1970). Differences in performance on Piagetian tasks between Western and non-Western populations disappear when tests use tasks and materials that are familiar and culturally appropriate (Fischer & Silvern, 1985). Young children show evidence of more sophisticated abilities when materials and tasks are developmentally appropriate and meaningful to them (Donaldson, 1978).

FRAMEWORK FOR ALTERNATIVE ASSESSMENT MODELS

A major challenge exists for the development and the adoption of assessment instruments and procedures that reflect early 21st-century theories of learning. Assessment practices must expand to include the contextual and cultural influences that either facilitate or hinder learning. The following chapters describe state-of-the-art, alternative assessment approaches that can easily be integrated into and across everyday activities, draw from observations and interactions with children and families involved in actual tasks and activities, and measure children's learning potential by measuring changes in performance following mediation by an adult.

These alternative assessment models can be classified into three major categories: 1) embedded models, 2) authentic models, and 3) mediated models. In addition, transdisciplinary models draw on various approaches. A framework for alternative assessment models is depicted in Figure 2.1.

Embedded approaches include assessment approaches in which opportunities to observe children's behavior are embedded in natural contexts. This approach focuses on providing children with multiple opportunities to perform skills across domains of development with different people, using different materials, in multiple environments. Specific applications of embedded approaches are naturalistic assessment (see Chapter 3) and focused assessment (see Chapter 4).

Authentic assessments include approaches in which a profile of the abilities of children are documented through completion of real-life tasks. Authentic models are based on the assumption that behavior must be observed in real-life contexts. The focus of authentic assessment is to document how and why instructional procedures work—or do not work—to achieve "authentic" changes in learning and development. Specific applications of authentic approaches include performance assessment (see Chapter 5) and portfolio assessment (see Chapter 6).

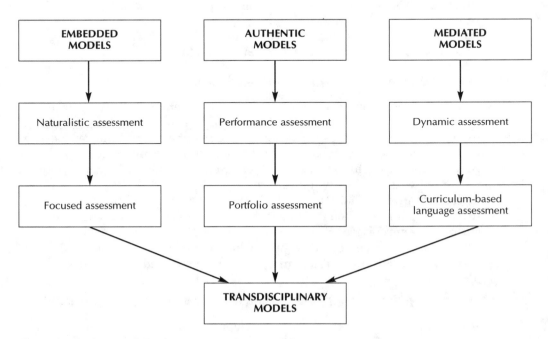

Figure 2.1.   A framework for alternative assessment models.

Mediated assessment approaches are assessments in which guided teaching is used to provide information on children's responsivity to instruction and their mastery of the language of instruction. Assessment through teaching is the collection of information by participating directly in student–teacher interactions, observing student–student interactions, and observing children's language use when working with ideas and materials. This type of assessment relies on the assumption that children's responsivity to instruction can be used as a powerful predictor of future outcomes. The focus on process and learning potential over mastery makes this approach extremely appropriate for testing in cross-cultural environments. Specific applications of mediated approaches are dynamic assessment (see Chapter 7) and curriculum-based language assessment (see Chapter 8).

A transdiciplinary model uses multiple methods and sources to make a comprehensive and multidimensional assessment of children's abilities across contexts (see Chapter 9). Combinations of procedures are used, ranging from formal, standardized tests to nonformal, naturalistic observations. These models utilize a transdisciplinary framework and require collaboration among caregivers and professionals from a variety of disciplines. Assessment procedures are individualized to match unique characteristics of children and families and take into account the different ways in which the children may respond to assessment procedures.

CONCLUSION

This chapter presents an overview of traditional models of assessment and illustrates their shortcomings in view of early 21st-century theory and research. The traditional practice of collecting information on a child's performance in standardized situations and restricted settings (e.g., resource rooms) does not adequately account for variations in performance across social and physical environments and is insensitive to intervention efforts. Although CBAs provide teachers with information on instructional content, they rarely provide information on how to change instruction and adjust teaching strategies to a child's individual needs (Mehrens & Clarizio, 1993). Little, if any, information is provided on the child's ability to learn. In many classrooms, the curriculum is actually driven by the assessment, as teachers focus on preparing their students for successful performance on standardized tests (Darling-Hammond, 1989). Still worse, some practitioners continue to consider assessment and instruction two distinct and separate procedures. Following an assessment, children typically qualify for specific treatments or educational placements, but instructional planning and monitoring are conducted with no relationship to the initial assessment (Notari, Slentz, & Bricker, 1991).

Review Questions

■ What is the difference between a quantitative approach and a qualitative approach to assessment?

■ Give a brief description and one example of each of the following nonformal assessment tools: categorical, narrative, and descriptive.

■ Describe the following types of assessment: norm-referenced, criterion-referenced, and curriculum-based. Identify one limitation of each.

■ Describe the measurement processes and their purposes.

■ When conducting assessments of children from different cultural and linguistic backgrounds, what is one factor that a professional should take into consideration? Why?

Naturalistic
Assessment

3

After reading this chapter, you will be able to:

■ Define naturalistic assessment, and discuss the rationale for its use

■ Give examples of models and methods that fit into a naturalistic assessment framework

■ Identify considerations and guidelines for implementing naturalistic assessment

*M*s. Martinez, a preschool teacher, stands in the doorway of her empty classroom and surveys the room in preparation for a new school year. Around the room are three small tables with four chairs each, a teacher's desk and work table, an aquarium that illuminates the darkened room, and a supply closet. In 2 weeks, she will be greeted by 12 new young students. As always, in preparation for the start of a new year, Ms. Martinez visits each child's home.

On these initial home visits, Ms. Martinez has several objectives. She finds it beneficial to meet each family at home to learn more about the family members' background and traditions and ask about their child's likes, dislikes, and typical routines. She explains that the overall goals of her program are to 1) encourage family involvement and 2) enhance the developmental status of children, encourage their independence, and promote social interaction among the children in her program. She invites all families to participate as fully as they wish in accomplishing these objectives.

On her first home visit this year, Ms. Martinez visited the Ghose family. Their 4-year-old daughter, Indrani, was diagnosed at 2 years of age with cerebral palsy and a profound hearing loss. Although she has hearing aids for both ears, she does not wear them consistently because of frequent ear drainage. During the meeting, Ms. Martinez asked questions about Indrani's developmental history. Ms. Ghose reported that Indrani's motor milestones were delayed and that she began to crawl and pull up to stand at 30 months of age. Both Mr. and Ms. Ghose expressed concern about the delays in their daughter's development, particularly in the motor and social-communication areas.

Ms. Martinez explained that one of her first tasks each year is to determine the current developmental status of the children in her program. She showed them a copy of the curriculum-based assessment that she uses to do this. This particular assessment has an associated form that is designed for family members to fill out while observing their children during typical activities in the home. Ms. Martinez explained that during the first 3–4 weeks of the program, she and other team members (an audiologist, a speech-language pathologist, and a physical therapist) would be getting to know Indrani and recording their observations of her behaviors across developmental domains. She invited Mr. and Ms. Ghose to participate in the assessment process, and they readily agreed to fill out the family-completed assessment form.

While reviewing the protocol given to him by Ms. Martinez, Mr. Ghose commented that most items would be easy to rate based on their present knowledge of what Indrani could and could not do at home. Ms. Ghose said that she could not respond to a few of the items, and Ms. Martinez suggested that some skills might require direct testing. Ms. Martinez stated that she would contact Mr. and Ms. Ghose, as well as the other team members, in approximately 1 month to schedule a meeting. The purpose of the meeting would be to share the assessment findings of all team members and to develop an IEP for Indrani. Finally, she explained that the same assessment would be readministered midway through the year and again at the end of the year to monitor Indrani's progress.

Naturalistic, or milieu, teaching procedures for young children have been described as a group of strategies for teaching language in its functional context (Kaiser, Yoder, & Keetz, 1990). The term **naturalistic instruction** evolved to refer to adult–child interactions that share three attributes (Rule, Losardo, Dinnebeil, Kaiser, & Rowland, 1998). First, naturalistic instruction typically refers to an instructional context in which intervention occurs during routine events and everyday activities in a variety of environments, including homes and preschools. Second, the interaction between the adult and the child typically follows the child's lead or capitalizes on a child's interest; that is, the child may initiate the interaction or the adult may focus on the object of the child's attention and then initiate the interaction. The consequences of the child's behavior are usually those that are inherent to the interaction. Third, naturalistic interventions address functional skills. Instruction occurs in the contexts in which children apply skills—such as asking for more snacks, obtaining materials that they wish to use, or taking turns with a peer—so the skills to be learned have immediate application.

Naturalistic assessment is based on this instructional approach and, thus, has similar characteristics. Naturalistic assessment also refers to an instructional context. Multiple opportunities for the child to perform skills across domains of development occur or can be embedded in the context of child-initiated, routine, and planned activities. Caregivers and others who interact with the child on a regular basis are responsible for observing the child and recording assessment information. Generally, an adult observes the child during play and may even join in the activity, being careful to follow the child's attentional lead. Some behaviors are difficult to observe, however, so it may be necessary to directly test a child or obtain information through reports. Naturalistic assessment addresses functional skills that will enhance the child's independence and social interactions across environments.

THEORETICAL FRAMEWORK

Naturalistic assessment occurs in the context of typical routines. Functional, developmental skills are observed by familiar adults using a combination of categorical, narrative, and descriptive tools. The ecological approach provides the basis for where the assessment will occur, developmental theory defines which behaviors will be observed, and applied behavior analysis provides guidance for how to observe and elicit these behaviors.

The **ecological approach** (Brofenbrenner, 1979) provides the basis and context for assessment within a child's typical environment and emphasizes the nested, interdependent systems (i.e., home, school, community) of which the family is a part. Assessments are implemented in naturalistic contexts and involve individuals who have the greatest opportunity to interact with the child on a regular basis (e.g., caregivers, teachers). The information collected in the child's natural environment is likely to provide an accurate view of the child's true functioning needs. This is especially important for a child whose family background is different from the mainstream culture or that of the assessor.

Naturalistic assessment addresses developmental, functional skills that facilitate a child's independence and control of his or her environment. Normative developmental studies provide the basis for most early childhood education and early childhood special education assessment tools and curricula in use at the beginning of the 21st century. Most criterion-referenced tools are based on age-related sequences of developmental milestones in infants and young children and are designed to assist practitioners to determine functional target behaviors and intervention activities to teach those behaviors.

Naturalistic assessment procedures draw from applied behavioral analysis to describe the environmental conditions necessary for eliciting desired behavior. Some curriculum-based assessment tools commonly used to conduct naturalistic assessment make suggestions for ways to arrange the environment and the types of activities and materials to use. Discrete skills are operationally defined so they can be observed, measured, and quantified. A typical method used in this framework is event sampling. **Event sampling** involves measuring specific behaviors by counting the number of times they occur or recording how long each lasts (Bailey & Wolery, 1992). Another method involves determining specific quantitative criteria for mastery, such as measuring whether the child can respond to simple questions in three out of five trials.

MODELS AND APPLICATIONS

Naturalistic approaches are designed to measure discrete, functional skills across naturalistic contexts. A combination of categorical, narrative, and descriptive tools can be utilized to record information. Naturalistic approaches are implemented by familiar adults using a moderate to high degree of structure. For example, children are typically observed in the context of child-initiated and routine activities, but the behaviors to be observed are identified in advance by the assessment team and outlined on the assessment protocol. Although the adult generally follows the attentional lead of the child to record observations, sometimes direct testing and report measures are required. Data are reported both quantitatively and qualitatively.

Several naturalistic assessment models and procedures are described in the literature. Bailey (1989) described an approach to assessment that is based on Brofenbrenner's (1979) ecological model. He provided the following suggestions for practitioners:

- Invite caregivers and others who are most familiar with the child to participate as partners in all assessment activities using tools and instruments that encourage collaboration.

- Become knowledgeable about the cultural, linguistic, and ethnic characteristics of children and families.

- Conduct assessment activities in realistic contexts and naturalistic environments to increase the ecological validity of observational data.

- Use the assessment data to plan for the child's immediate placement and his or her transition to future environments.

Barnett, Macmann, and Carey (1992) described a model for naturalistic assessment in which information on the behavioral repertoire of a child is collected through **ecobehavioral interviews,** observation, and curriculum-based assessment. Ecobehavioral interviews are based on the premise that a caregiver and others who interact with the child on a regular basis can provide the most detailed information about that child's abilities, possible areas of concern, and areas in which the child may be experiencing difficulties. Observations of children in natural environments—such as home, child care, and preschool programs—can be used to supplement the information acquired through interview. Curriculum-based assessment is used to ensure that the links among assessment, intervention, and evaluation are straightforward. Information garnered during the initial assessment is used to develop intervention goals and content. Intervention efforts are evaluated on an ongoing basis using the same method.

Another approach, activity-based intervention (Bricker, 1998), provides specific guidelines for naturalistic assessment activities. Activity-based intervention is part of a larger framework that links assessment, intervention, and evaluation activities. A series of seven assessment activity plans have been developed to use in coordination with the AEPS Measurement for Birth to Three Years (Bricker, 1993b) and six activity plans for use with the AEPS Measurement for Three to Six Years (Bricker & Pretti-Frontczak, 1996). Opportunities to observe children's behaviors are integrated into child-initiated, routine, and planned activities. These assessment plans provide multiple opportunities for children to perform skills when interacting with different people, using familiar materials across different environments. Each plan contains assessment items from several developmental domains that are likely to be observed during a specific activity, as well as a materials list and directions for preparing the environment for assessment. An example of an AEPS snack activity plan for children birth to 3 years of age is contained in Figure 3.1.

During a snack activity, the following behaviors of children are likely to be observed: the ability to get into and out of a child-size chair (gross motor domain), rotate the wrist on a horizontal plane while opening a jar (fine motor domain), use alternative strategies to solve problems (cognitive domain), and transfer liquids (adaptive domain). In addition to these behaviors that are most likely to be observed, other behaviors may be noted, such as the ability to use two-word utterances (social-communication domain) and the ability to take turns (social domain). Practitioners can use anecdotal notes to record these and any other observed behaviors. In this way, comprehensive and detailed information about children's behavioral repertoires is obtained. Figure 3.2 is an example of a data recording form for the snack activity plan.

Watson, Layton, Pierce, and Abraham (1994) described a similar approach to the assessment of early literacy skills in which skills are embedded within specific classroom activities. They identified six components of emergent literacy:

1.   Print awareness

2.   Concepts of book print

Activity: Snack

Domain(s):   Adaptive, Fine Motor, Gross Motor, Cognitive

Materials: Child-size cups, small bowls, napkins, spoons
Juice in lightweight pitchers
Raisins in small transparent jar with twist-off lid
Yogurt or applesauce
Foods in pieces large enough to require the children to bite (e.g., quartered apples or saltine crackers)
Waterproof tarp to protect floor
Bibs or child-size aprons

Directions: 1. Arrange a child-size table on a tarp *without* chairs around it in a semi-enclosed area, and request that each child retrieve a chair and bring it to the table to get ready for snack. Observe each child's ability to navigate a large object around the barrier, move barrier or go around barrier to obtain objects, and move around barrier to change location (Cognitive, Strand E: 3.0, 3.1, and 3.2).

2. Group 2–4 children at the table. Observe each child's ability to get into and out of a child-size chair (Gross Motor, Strand B: 2.0).

3. Offer raisins in a small, transparent jar to children. The lid on the jar should require the child to unscrew it, but it should not be secured too tightly. Observe each child's ability to rotate wrist on a horizontal plane while opening the jar (Fine Motor, Strand B: 1.0). Allow each child to put the lid back on the jar before passing it on to the next child. Observe each child's ability to assemble the jar and lid (Fine Motor, Strand B: 2.0). If the child cannot open or close the jar successfully, observe the child's use of alternative strategies to solve problems (Cognitive, Strand E: 4.0).

4. Observe each child's grasp when obtaining raisins and other small pieces of food and when grasping a spoon (Fine Motor, Strand A: 4.0 and 3.0).

5. Allow children opportunities to pour juice into their own cups. Observe each child's ability to transfer liquids (Adaptive, Strand A: 5.1).

6. Allow children to distribute the remaining eating utensils. (If a child did not successfully assign one item to two or more people, allow the child additional opportunities.) Observe each child's ability to assign one object to two or more people (Cognitive, Strand F: 3.0).

7. Allow children opportunities to spoon yogurt or applesauce into their own bowls. Observe each child's ability to transfer food with a spoon (Adaptive, Strand A: 5.2).

8. Observe each child's ability to eat a variety of foods, to eat independently with a spoon or fork, and to drink from a cup (Adaptive, Strand A: 1.0, 2.0, 3.0, 4.0, and 5.0).

Figure 3.1. Snack assessment activity plan. (From Bricker, D. [1993b]. *Assessment, Evaluation, and Programming System for Infants and Children: Vol. 1. AEPS measurement for birth to three years* [p. 254]. Baltimore: Paul H. Brookes Publishing Co.; reprinted by permission.)

Naturalistic Assessment Collection Form

Gross motor	Strand	Objective	Child 1	Child 2	Child 3	Child 4	Child 5
Cognitive	E 3.0	Navigates large object around barriers					
	E 3.1	Moves barrier or goes around barrier to obtain object					
	E 3.2	Moves around barrier to change location					
Cognitive	E 4.0	Uses alternative strategies to solve problems					
Cognitive	F 3.0	Assigns one object to two or more people					
Fine motor	B 1.0	Rotates wrist on horizontal plane while opening jar					
	B 2.0	Assembles jar and lid					
Fine motor	A 3.0	Grasps spoon					
	A 4.0	Grasps small pieces of food					
Gross motor	B 2.0	Gets into and out of child-sized chair					
Adaptive	A 5.1	Transfers liquids					
Adaptive	A 5.2	Transfers food with a spoon					
Adaptive	A 1.0–2.0	Eats a variety of foods					
	A 3.0	Drinks from a cup and/or glass					
	A 4.0–5.0	Eats independently with a spoon or fork					

Anecdotal Notes: Record any other behaviors observed.

Figure 3.2. Naturalistic assessment data collection form. (From Bricker, D. [1993b]. *Assessment, Evaluation, and Programming System for Infants and Children: Vol. 1. AEPS measurement for birth to three years* [p. 254]. Baltimore: Paul H. Brookes Publishing Co.; adapted by permission.)

3.   Story sense

4.   Phonological awareness

5.   Matching speech to print

6.   Control of reading and writing

These components are used to structure routine classroom activities. For example, concepts of books and print can be assessed during storybook reading at opening circle time, story structure during dramatic play, and phonological awareness during writing and library time. Although it is preferable to obtain information through observation, direct testing and report often become necessary. Notari-Syverson, O'Connor, and Vadasy (1998) created a sample data collection form for naturalistic assessment of early literacy skills, shown in Figure 3.3.

Grisham-Brown (2000) described a naturalistic model designed to assess children with multiple disabilities. The person initiating the assessment gathers from the child's family information about the child's medical, developmental, and educational history. This information is then used by the initial contact person and the family to select relevant team members. One of three different elicitation formats is used to collect assessment information: 1) the arena or episodic format, in which all assessment information is collected at one time by all team members; 2) the collaborative-ongoing format, in which data are collected throughout the day by one or two team members; and 3) the activity-based format described previously, in which preplanned assessment activities (e.g., AEPS assessment activities) are used and data are collected by one or more team members. Similar to the activity-based application, the Grisham-Brown model uses activities as the context for the assessment but assesses only one child at a time. The team generates an individualized assessment form on which specific skills to be measured are recorded, along with a list of the materials necessary to elicit the desired behaviors. Although other children can participate in an assessment activity, the team's focus is on the child with multiple disabilities. During the assessment, caregivers assume a variety of roles, such as offering their perceptions of the representativeness of the child's performance, suggesting modifications to the activity, or actually administering assessment items. After the assessment, the caregivers and practitioners meet to develop an education plan that contains learning objectives (e.g., using five manual signs), suggested activities in which the objective can be taught (e.g., snack time), the support services or personnel needed (e.g., a speech-language pathologist), and any necessary adaptations (e.g., hand-over-hand assistance to produce the manual signs).

ADVANTAGES AND LIMITATIONS

Naturalistic assessment is used to measure children's performance across instructional contexts. Children are observed in the context of typical classroom activities as well as planned situations to elicit behaviors that are not readily observed in the classroom (e.g., dressing and undressing). Informa-

Emergent Literacy Data Collection Form

Observer: Anne Stapleton

Date: May 6, 2000

Activity	Emergent Literacy	Component	Behavior Observed	Child 1	Child 2	Child 3	Child 4	Child 5
Opening circle	Print/book awareness: Symbolic representation	Play	Uses symbols in play					
		Pictures	Identifies objects, people, and actions represented in pictures					
		Graphics	Scribbles					
	Print/book awareness: Print	Book conventions	Knows where book begins and ends					
		Awareness of graphic symbols	Identifies a printed word					
		Letter identification	Recites part of alphabet					
		Writing	Copies letters					
	Print/book awareness: Letter–sound correspondence	Single sounds and letters	Says most common sound for each letter					
		Words	Uses letter sounds to write words					
	Metalinguistic awareness: Perception and memory for sounds	Environmental sounds	Uses sounds to represent objects and animals					
		Words	Repeats short words					
		Phrases	Repeats phrases					

(continued)

Figure 3.3. Emergent Literacy Data Collection Form. (From Notari-Syverson, A., O'Connor, R.E., & Vadasy, P.F. [1998]. *Ladders to literacy: A preschool activity book* [pp. 321–326]. Baltimore: Paul H. Brookes Publishing Co.; adapted by permission.)

35

Figure 3.3. (continued)

Activity	Emergent Literacy	Component	Behavior Observed	Child 1	Child 2	Child 3	Child 4	Child 5
	Metalinguistic awareness: Word awareness	Phonemes	Repeats single phonemes after a short delay (1–2 seconds)					
		Words	Identifies a word from a spoken sentence					
	Metalinguistic awareness: Phonological skills	Rhyming	Says common rhymes along with teacher or peers					
		Alliteration	Recognizes words that start with the same sound					
		Blending	Blends syllables into words					
		Segmentation	Segments words into syllables					
	Oral language: Vocabulary	Words and sentences	Uses one-word utterances to label a variety of objects, people, and events					
	Oral language: Narrative skills	Narrations of real events	Relates events with beginning, middle, and end					
		Book	Attends to and labels pictures in book					
		Narrations of fictional story	Adds simple comments and asks questions					
	Oral language: Literate discourse	Conversations	Maintains social interaction over two or more turns					
		Categorical organization	Uses superordinate labels to indicate general categories					
		Decontextualization	Generalizes experiences to other settings					
		Interpretive/ analytic discourse	Uses internal state words to express feelings and motivations					

36

tion that is collected by familiar adults while the child is in a natural environment potentially provides a more accurate assessment of the child's true functioning needs. This is especially important for a child whose family background is different from the mainstream culture or that of the assessor.

Advantages

Among the advantages of naturalistic assessment are the naturalistic context itself, the use of familiar and culturally appropriate materials, and the use of activities that may sustain a child's interest. These elements are discussed in more detail next.

Naturalistic Context

Research shows that an accurate assessment that is representative of children's abilities—particularly in the areas of language and literacy—is best obtained from low-structured, child-centered, familiar activities. For example, young children use more complex language during low-structured situations than in elicited production tests (Lahey, Launer, & Shiff-Myers, 1983; Longhurst & Grubb, 1974; Prutting, Gallagher, & Mulac, 1975) and when they talk about a self-initiated topic (Strandberg & Griffith, 1968, cited in Cazden, 1977). Similarly, young children with disabilities talk more when questions are embedded within a conversational context and are more likely to address questions about child-initiated topics than questions about a new topic (Yoder, Davies, & Bishop, 1992). Children's language is also more complex during routine versus nonroutine interactions (Yoder & Davies, 1990).

Familiar and Culturally Appropriate Materials

Standardized tests do not take into account the contextual influences on a child's behavior. Bergen and Mosley-Howard (1994) suggested that children who are not familiar with certain materials (e.g., toy blocks) may perform poorly on developmental tests. Naturalistic assessment occurs in contexts such as the home, with familiar toys and culturally appropriate materials.

Interest Level of Children

During standardized testing situations, children are asked to respond to a series of questions or tasks that bear little resemblance to real-life activities. Children are often taken to an unfamiliar environment on a one-time basis and tested by adults whom they may not know. It can be difficult to maintain children's attention and/or cooperation in these test situations. Naturalistic assessments utilize typical activities that are inherently interesting to children, so little external support or reward is necessary to maintain their interest and participation.

Limitations

Limitations inherent in naturalistic assessment include the required planning time, reduced efficiency, and the high level of expertise required to conduct such assessment. Each of these areas is explored in the following paragraphs.

Required Planning Time

When using naturalistic assessment procedures, observation of children's behavior occurs throughout the day. If using checklists or rating scales, the daily activity schedule and the behaviors that are likely to be observed during each activity must be planned in advance of the observational period. Although some commercially available assessment tools, such as AEPS, provide assessment activities that specify in which context certain behaviors are likely to occur, most curriculum-based assessment tools do not. Specific behaviors must be observed in a variety of natural contexts.

Reduced Efficiency

Observational assessment of children's behaviors in natural contexts may not always be time efficient. In general, when using standardized testing procedures, a child is seen on a one-time basis for a few hours or perhaps for an entire morning or afternoon. When observing a child in the home, rapport must be established with the child and the family before a sample of the child's behavior can be considered representative. It may take several hours or even several visits to the child's home to obtain an accurate picture of the child's abilities. Observing and collecting information on several children in child care facilities or preschool classrooms can take as long as 2–4 weeks. In addition, relevant behaviors, such as dressing and undressing, may not easily be observed in classroom-based programs. Therefore, interviews with caregivers and examinations by report will likely be necessary.

High Level of Expertise Required

It requires both skill and practice to conduct naturalistic assessment. If a child walks over to the snack table and grasps a cup that another child offers, the practitioner could record that behavior in several ways. The child has demonstrated the fine motor action of reaching and grasping, the gross motor ability of walking independently, the adaptive ability of drinking from a cup, the social-communication act of using a gesture to request an object, and the social skill of initiating a transaction. The practitioner must be skilled in observing and recording behaviors across all domains of development.

GUIDELINES FOR IMPLEMENTATION

In naturalistic instruction, child-initiated, routine, and planned activities are used as the context for teaching. Bricker (1998) differentiated the three types of activities in the following way. **Child-initiated activities** are those that a child selects; **routine activities** are events that occur on a predictable or regular basis, such as mealtime, diapering, and dressing. **Planned activities** refer to designed events that ordinarily do not happen without adult intervention, such as the play activity of washing a baby doll. When planned activities are used, they should be enjoyable, motivating, and developmentally appropriate.

As with naturalistic instruction, activities are the framework in which naturalistic assessment occurs, thus making the development and implementation of activities critical to the assessment process. The first step in naturalistic assessment is to determine where the assessment will take place. If the practitioner is assessing an infant or a toddler, the most likely assessment context is the home. The practitioner must spend time getting to know the child and his or her family and the family's typical activities and routines.

Another decision to be made before assessment begins concerns where and when to observe the child. Assessment schedules, which identify the child's typical activities and routines across environments, can assist the assessment team in this process. If the assessment will be conducted at home, caregivers can provide an overview of the child's activities. Likewise, if the assessment will occur in a center-based program, practitioners can use the daily classroom schedule to structure the assessment activities. Figure 3.4 is an example of an assessment schedule for a child across different environments (e.g., home, preschool program). This schedule specifies which areas will be assessed, who will be responsible for assessing which areas, where the assessment activities will occur, and how data will be recorded. Figure 3.5 is an assessment schedule containing similar information that can be used in a center-based program.

The team members also need to discuss with the family the behaviors to be assessed. The child may be assessed across domains of development or in select areas. For example, Mr. and Ms. Ghose expressed concerns that Indrani was not yet speaking and about her delayed motor development. In this case, the team could well decide to assess the social-communication and motor domains.

In addition, interviews are necessary to obtain relevant background information on the child and his or her family. The practitioner selects appropriate tools to use and then explains to the family the pros and cons of available options. A unified, systematic approach that links assessment with intervention and evaluation is preferred for conducting developmental assessment (Bagnato, Neisworth, & Munson, 1997; Bricker, 1998). The application of a unified systems approach is based on the use of appropriate assessment tools. CBA, a type of criterion-referenced measure, is the most frequently used tool for linked assessment, intervention, and evaluation (Bagnato, Neisworth, & Munson, 1989; Bagnato et al., 1997). Brief descriptions of some commonly used CBAs are provided in Table 3.1.

Now the team members are ready to discuss their respective roles and responsibilities. Caregivers are full participants in the assessment process and are provided with options as to the role(s) they can choose (Bailey, 1989). Bricker (1998) suggested that the caregiver's involvement may vary depending on his or her values, availability, comfort level, experience, education, and background. Practitioners would do well to be aware of their

Naturalistic Assessment: Assessment Schedule for an Individual Child

Child's name: _Indrani_

Child's routine	Area of assessment	Assessor	Where	How
Changing diapers and dressing	Adaptive	Caregiver	Home	Anecdotal notes
Breakfast	Adaptive	Caregiver	Home	Anecdotal notes
Play time	Social-communication	Speech-language pathologist	Morning preschool program	Curriculum-based assessment Language sample
Snack time	Social	Speech-language pathologist	Morning preschool program	Curriculum-based assessment
Planned activity	Cognitive Fine motor	Preschool teacher	Morning preschool program	Curriculum-based assessment
Outdoor time	Gross motor	Physical therapist	Morning preschool program	Curriculum-based assessment
Storytime	Social-communication Early literacy	Speech-language pathologist	Morning preschool program	Curriculum-based assessment
Lunch time	Adaptive	Caregiver Occupational therapist	Home	Anecdotal notes

Figure 3.4. Activity schedule for assessing a child across environments.

Naturalistic Assessment: Assessment Schedule for a Center-Based Program

Classroom routine	Area of assessment	Who	How
Arrival time	Social	Preschool teacher	Anecdotal notes
Free play	Adaptive	Physical therapist Speech-language pathologist	Curriculum-based assessment Language sample
Opening circle time	Social-communication	Speech-language pathologist	Anecdotal notes
Planned activity	Cognitive Fine motor	Preschool teacher Occupational therapist	Curriculum-based assessment
Snack time	Adaptive	Preschool teacher	Curriculum-based assessment
Outdoor time	Gross motor	Physical therapist	Curriculum-based assessment
Clean up/bathroom time	Adaptive	Preschool teacher	Curriculum-based assessment
Lunch time	Adaptive	Occupational therapist	Curriculum-based assessment
Storytime	Social-communication Early literacy	Speech-language pathologist Preschool teacher	Curriculum-based assessment Checklists

Figure 3.5. Activity schedule for assessing several children across classroom environments.

Table 3.1.   Examples of commonly used curriculum-based assessment tools

---

Assessment, Evaluation, and Programming System for Infants and Children: Vol 1. AEPS measurement for birth to three years (Bricker, 1993b)

Assessment, Evaluation, and Programming System for Infants and Children: Vol 2. AEPS curriculum for birth to three years (Cripe, Slentz, & Bricker, 1993)

Assessment, Evaluation, and Programming System for Infants and Children: Vol 3. AEPS measurement for three to six years (Bricker & Pretti-Frontczak, 1996)

Assessment, Evaluation, and Programming System for Infants and Children: Vol 4. AEPS curriculum for three to six years (Bricker & Waddell, 1996)

Description: AEPS is designed to be used with children from birth to six years developmentally. Assessment items are functional and generic and are arranged in a hierarchical and sequential order. Adaptations are specified, and a range of scoring options are provided.

The Carolina Curriculum for Infants and Toddlers with Special Needs (2nd ed.) (Johnson-Martin, Jens, Attermeier, & Hacker, 1991)

The Carolina Curriculum for Preschoolers with Special Needs (Johnson-Martin, Attermeier, & Hacker, 1990)

Description: The Carolina Curriculum is designed to be used with children who have mild delays and severe disabilities from birth to 24 months developmentally. The preschool version is an extension of the curriculum to accommodate the needs of children beyond the 24-month level. Specific adaptations are provided, and a range of scoring options is available.

Hawaii Early Learning Profile (HELP): Birth to 3 (6th ed.) (Parks et al., 1994)

Hawaii Early Learning Profile (HELP) for Preschoolers (VORT Corporation, 1995)

Description: HELP is designed to be used with children from birth to six years developmentally. It can be used by both professionals and parents. General guidelines for adaptations are provided as well as a range of scoring options.

Developmental Programming for Infants and Young Children–Early Intervention Developmental Programming and Profile (Rev. ed.) (Schaefer & Moersch, 1981)

Description: Developmental Programming for Infants and Young Children–Early Intervention Developmental Programming and Profile is designed to be used with children from birth to 36 months developmentally. This curriculum-based assessment provides general guidelines for adaptations and contains a range of scoring options.

---

own preconceived attitudes toward caregivers who are different from themselves. The increased availability of assessment tools and procedures that provide a formal mechanism for including families has allowed more participation options (Bricker, 1998; Crais, 1995).

Crais (1995) presented several options for facilitating caregiver participation throughout the assessment process. First, she suggested that caregivers can be invited to participate in an arena-type assessment of their child. Using this approach, caregivers and practitioners observe and assess the child together. Second, caregivers can be invited to complete both formal and nonformal observations of their child's developmental behaviors at home. In addition, caregivers may be asked to select the most appropriate activities for observing their child, interpret their child's behavior, and validate the representativeness of the assessment results.

When determining the level of caregiver participation, keep in mind that tools such as CBA give practitioners the opportunity to work with caregivers and other professionals to obtain relevant behavioral information. For example, if the assessment is conducted in an arena-type format, the caregiver typically interacts with the child while other team members observe and record data. The occupational therapist assesses the child's fine motor abilities; the physical therapist assesses the gross motor domain; the speech-language pathologist assesses the child's speech, language, and communication abilities; and the preschool teacher assesses the child's social skills. The caregiver provides information about the child's adaptive behaviors (e.g., using a cup to drink) through report or demonstration, such as providing the child with a snack during the observation period.

Once these preliminary decisions have been made, the team is ready to begin the actual assessment process. Most behaviors can be observed as the child engages in typical activities and routines. Although observational methods are preferred, it may be necessary to directly test some items or obtain some information from reports. Reports are often related to adaptive skills such as dressing and undressing or preacademic skills such as copying simple shapes. The practitioner may interview the caregiver or elicit behaviors directly from the child. Table 3.2 is a summary of guidelines for implementing naturalistic assessment.

SUGGESTIONS FOR PRACTITIONERS IN INCLUSIVE ENVIRONMENTS

The relationship among assessment, intervention, and evaluation should be straightforward. Ideally, the information collected during the initial assessment period is used to develop intervention goals for the child. In turn, in-

Table 3.2.   Guidelines for implementing naturalistic assessment

Determine when and where the assessment will take place.
 If assessing an infant or toddler, the most likely assessment context will be the home.
 If assessing the child at home, the caregiver can provide an overview of the activities that may be used.
 Spend time getting to know the child and his or her family and the family's typical activities and routines.
 If assessing a child in a center-based program, practitioners can use the daily classroom schedule to structure the assessment activities.

Meet with team members to discuss the behaviors to be assessed.
 The child may be assessed across domains of development or in select areas.

Select appropriate assessment tools.
 Use interviews to obtain relevant background information on the child and his or her family.
 Evaluate the pros and cons of all available options.
 Choose tools that link assessment and intervention with evaluation.

Discuss the respective roles and responsibilities of the team.
 Caregivers are full participants in the assessment process and are provided with options as to the role(s) they can choose.

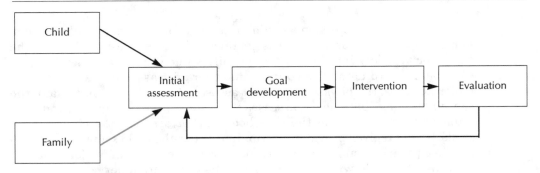

Figure 3.6.   A model directly linking program components.

tervention efforts should address the goals determined by the assessment. Finally, evaluation measures should focus on determining the effectiveness of intervention efforts. Figure 3.6 is a schematic illustration of a **linked systems approach** that directly connects assessment, intervention, and evaluation. Several variations of this simple model have been described elsewhere (Bagnato et al., 1997; Bricker, 1989, 1998; Bricker & Losardo, 2000; Hutinger, 1988).

A linked system can be divided into four phases: 1) initial assessment, 2) goal development, 3) intervention, and 4) evaluation. Each phase is linked to the next, and all four components are reciprocally related. These phases are described in detail next.

Initial Assessment

During the first phase, initial assessment, the practitioner uses an assessment tool that facilitates the direct relationship among testing, teaching, and evaluation. The major objective of an initial assessment is the formulation of realistic and appropriate goals and objectives. The importance of including caregivers in this process, particularly when assessing young children, cannot be overemphasized. During the initial assessment phase, practitioners direct their efforts toward using tools that measure functional skills of children in real-life social interactions with adults. For instance, a functional skill may involve naming essential objects or events in the environment, such as a desired toy, or communicating a physical need, such as thirst. Therefore, a repertoire of functional and generic activities that demonstrate independent functioning in young children form the basis of effective assessment tools.

Goal Development

To develop goals, caregivers and practitioners first share assessment results. They then collaboratively select relevant goals and objectives for the child. Once the annual goals and their associated short-term objectives are selected, the next step is to prioritize them and develop an education or intervention plan. Priorities are chosen based on their functional relevance across a variety of natural environments, such as home, church, and school.

Intervention

The team members develop an IFSP for infants and toddlers or an IEP for preschool-age or primary-grade children. Intervention plans can vary in format, but all contain the following elements:

- Identifying information for the child and his or her family
- Dates for expected initiation and completion of program
- Target goals and corresponding objectives
- A description of the places where the intervention may occur
- Teaching and intervention procedures and activities
- Specification of procedures to evaluate a child's progress

Evaluation

Without systematic documentation of change, practitioners and caregivers cannot determine the effects of educational or intervention efforts. As shown previously in Figure 3.6, the final phase of a linked system involves collecting evaluation data. These data provide systematic feedback on the success of intervention plans and determine progress on priority child goals and family outcomes. A variety of formal and nonformal strategies can be used for daily or weekly monitoring of child progress. Collecting evaluation data should be viewed as an essential part of the program, rather than as something that is only necessary for federal and state accountability purposes. Evaluation data can be used effectively to make modifications in program plans or to make adjustments in teaching strategies. Table 3.3 summarizes suggestions for practitioners using naturalistic assessment in inclusive environments.

CONCLUSION

Naturalistic assessment is a viable alternative to standardized measures when 1) the purpose of assessment is to determine the developmental level of functioning of young children and 2) that information is used to develop functional educational outcomes. Measurement of developmental skills may be accomplished through formal and nonformal methods. Categorical tools, such as CBAs, are well suited to the naturalistic approach. They contain functionally relevant behavioral items that are designed to enhance the child's independence and social interactions across environments. Informa-

Table 3.3.   Suggestions for practitioners using naturalistic assessment in inclusive environments

Initial assessment

The child is assessed using an assessment tool that facilitates the direct congruence among testing, teaching, and evaluation.

The major objective of an initial assessment is the formulation of realistic and appropriate goals and objectives.

Practitioners should direct their efforts toward using tools that measure functional skills of children in real-life social interactions with adults.

Practitioners should use assessment tools that contain functional and generic items that build repertoires that demonstrate independent functioning in young children.

Goal development

Caregivers and practitioners share assessment results and collaboratively select relevant goals and objectives for the child.

Prioritize goals and objectives and develop an education or intervention plan.

Intervention

Develop an individualized family service plan (IFSP) or an individualized education program (IEP). Intervention plans should contain:

Identifying information

Dates for expected initiation and completion of program

Target goals and corresponding objectives

A description of the places where the intervention may occur

Teaching and intervention procedures and activities

Specification of procedures to evaluate a child's progress

Evaluation

A variety of formal and nonformal strategies can be used for daily or weekly monitoring of child progress.

Evaluation data can be used effectively to make modifications to program plans or make adjustments in teaching strategies.

---

tion gathered from the assessment is used to design education and intervention programs, allowing teaching activities to be created for each developmental goal and objective. Children's progress is evaluated using the same assessment tool. Nonformal measures, such as narrative and descriptive tools, are also used to collect information and monitor children's progress.

Review Questions

■ What is the rationale for using naturalistic assessment?

■ What are the three salient characteristics of naturalistic assessment?

■ How do underlying theoretical perspectives and assumptions influence naturalistic assessment tools and procedures?

■ Identify the formal and nonformal tools that practitioners might use to conduct naturalistic assessment in an early childhood or early childhood special education program.

Focused Assessment

After reading this chapter, you will be able to:

■ Define focused assessment, and discuss the rationale for its use

■ Give examples of models and methods that fit into a focused assessment framework

■ Identify considerations and guidelines for implementing focused assessment

*M*s. Hirschy initially thought that developing an IEP for Sergio was going to be quite a challenge. The 5-year-old had autism and was nonverbal, and he had been labeled "untestable" by multidisciplinary team members because he did not perform any of their test items. The psychologist had tried to observe Sergio in the classroom during his first week at school, but he just sat in a corner and refused to interact with any adult or child. Sergio's mother said that he liked puzzles and stacking blocks, but when Ms. Hirschy offered some blocks and Legos to him, Sergio grunted in protest and pushed them away. Children with autism often deal poorly with change, so the psychologist thought that Sergio's reaction was because the school materials were not exactly the same as the ones he had at home.

The team decided to observe Sergio using Transdisciplinary Play-Based Assessment (TPBA; Linder, 1993). Sergio's mother was willing to return to the clinic and bring Sergio's favorite toys with him. While she played and interacted with Sergio, the psychologist, the speech-language pathologist, the physical therapist, and Ms. Hirschy were surprised to see that Sergio was indeed very good at puzzles and engaged in this activity for quite some time. Sergio also used objects functionally, such as bringing a cup to his lips and a comb to his hair. He took his mother's hand on multiple occasions. Once he placed it on a box lid to get a block that had been placed in the box and was now invisible; another time he pushed her hand to a wind-up toy, as if asking her to turn the key and make the toy move. The physical therapist noticed that Sergio squatted for most of the time in a frog-like, or W-sit, position and that, in general, his muscle tone was high and his movements jerky.

During the IEP meeting, Sergio's parents accepted the team's suggestion to work on tool use and the understanding of causality, two important sensorimotor precursors to the development of oral language. They were most concerned about Sergio's lack of response to their displays of affection. When they attempted to hug or kiss him, he often protested, stiffening his body and pushing them away. Sergio really seemed to enjoy rough-and-tumble games, however, such as when his mother played "horsey" with him (by jogging him up and down on her knees) or his father played "airplane" with him (by whirling Sergio around). His parents were also very concerned about Sergio's getting upset when things changed suddenly. One day he even starting banging his head when his mother removed her blue sweater to reveal a red shirt underneath. Another time, he refused to enter the neighborhood grocery store after it had been remodeled.

The team agreed that these were priorities and discussed how to translate them into IEP long-term goals and short-term objectives. The team members needed to know which kinds of physical interactions and situations Sergio responded to best. It was also necessary to recognize how Sergio showed pleasure and affection, what degree of change he could tolerate, and which strategies worked best to help him cope with change. Qualitative descriptive data would be the best way to obtain this type of information. The team decided that the best times to observe Sergio and collect data would be during free play time (when the teaching staff could easily initiate various types of physical contact) and transitions (when changes were most likely to occur).

The team discussed the most efficient way for the staff to collect data consistently on a weekly basis. Although it would be easy to observe Sergio during free play and transition times, the team members could not be certain that Sergio would spontaneously engage in the behaviors they wanted to assess. Everyone agreed that it would be more practical and efficient to structure specific situations that provide opportunities for the relevant behaviors to occur. Introducing a certain degree of control gave the team the additional advantage of being able to observe Sergio's behaviors in the same situation over a period of time, making comparisons and evaluation of changes more accurate (Cazden, 1981).

This chapter uses the term **focused assessment** to refer to observations that use adult-structured interactions to elicit specific behaviors for assessment purposes. In focused assessments, the assessor concentrates multiple behaviors across different areas into a single situation and uses specific strategies to elicit targeted skills (Rice & Wilcox, 1995). Assessment scenarios can be created by the child's teacher and usually occur within the context of familiar activities and situations, although they may not necessarily be a part of daily classroom routines (Genishi & Brainard, 1995). Nonformal methods, such as anecdotal notes and checklists, are used and allow for the documentation of holistic, complex behaviors and skills.

CONTEXTS FOR ASSESSMENT

Assessment situations vary greatly, depending on the focus of the assessment and the child's interests and age. They tend to be adult directed, however, as the adult structures interactions and manipulates materials to elicit specific skills in a short period of time. When assessing younger children, play and snack time offer many opportunities for children to demonstrate a broad variety of social, cognitive, and motor skills. With older children, the assessment may focus more specifically on academic skills, so more appropriate contexts may be looking at a book or conducting a science project. In all cases, the situations are somewhat contrived in that the adult selects materials and guides interactions to directly elicit targeted skills rather than wait for the child to spontaneously manifest behaviors.

Ms. Voiland sets up the dramatic play area as a restaurant three times per year to observe children's progress in language, cognitive, and early literacy skills. She also creates an obstacle course to evaluate motor skills. Ms. Voiland and other members of the assessment team developed recording sheets based on a tool that assesses skills across multiple developmental domains in the context of play interactions. (Figure 4.1 is an example of an observation sheet.)

For weekly monitoring of children's IEP goals and objectives, Ms. Voiland uses daily picture book reading time to assess early literacy and language skills. While the children look at books individually or with a peer, Ms. Voiland interacts with one or two selected children to elicit targeted language or early literacy

Observation Sheet

Child's name: _Leila_   Date of birth: _3/30/97_   Age: _3:6_

Observer: _Ms. Voiland_   Role: _Teacher_   Date of assessment: _10/2/00_

Domain/discipline: _Cognitive development_

Area   _Representation/use of symbols_

    Subarea   _Imaginary play_

    Focus   _What roles and actions, themes/storylines does Leila engage in during imaginary play?_
        What kinds of imaginary props does she use?

    Observations   _Leila pretended to be a customer. Ordered "macaroni and cheese." Pretended to eat using plastic fork. Also fed teddy bear. Said "He hungry too and wants to drink juice."_

Area   _Attention_

    Subarea   _Engagement in activity_

    Focus   _What is the average length of time Leila remains focused on an activity?_
        In which kinds of activities does she remain focused:
           The longest? How long?
           The shortest? How short?
           Is she easily distracted? By what?

    Observations   _Engaged in pretend feeding for about 5 minutes. Then it was her turn to be the waiter. Asked Rui "Want to eat?" Heard Malcolm playing in the water area and left Rui to join Malcolm._

Figure 4.1. Focused play assessment observation sheet. (*Source:* Linder, 1993.)

Early Literacy Observation Form

Child's name: *Malcolm*

Print/Book Awareness: Things about my play, drawing, and writing, and what I know about print and books.

Date	What I did or said	Where/with whom
2/15/00	*Wrote name*	*On drawing (small group with Natalia and Denzel)*

Metalinguistic Awareness: What I know about sounds, words, and sentences; nursery rhymes; and word play (breaking down words into syllables and phonemes, putting sounds together, finding the first sound and words that sound the same).

Date	What I did or said	Where/with whom
2/15/00	*Changed "alphabet" to "alphazet"* *Recited: Humpty Dumpty*	*Circletime: Songs*

Oral Language: Words I know; things I say about what I do, what I feel, and what I think; and stories I can tell.

Date	What I did or said	Where/with whom
2/16/00	*I think this is right, but I'm not sure*	*Drawing a bicycle (small group with Ms. Norman)*

Figure 4.2. An example of an early literacy observation form. (From Notari-Syverson, A., O'Connor, R.E., & Vadasy, P. [1998]. *Ladders to literacy: A preschool activity book* [p. 22]. Baltimore: Paul H. Brookes Publishing Co.; adapted by permission.)

skills. She then records each child's data on separate Early Literacy Observation Forms (see example in Figure 4.2) and an Early Literacy Weekly Notes (see example in Figure 4.3).

The daily art activity presents an excellent opportunity to elicit fine motor and social-interaction behaviors, as well as some self-help skills during cleanup time. In the previous year, Ms. Voiland set up five different situations to test skills in each of these areas of development. That was time consuming, and she was not always able to collect data for all of the children every week. Now, by concentrating skills into specific situations, she had to do a bit more initial planning, but the actual data collection process proceeded in a more efficient manner. During art activities, for example, she made sure that Rui got to practice his IEP ob-

Early Literacy Weekly Notes

Week of: <u>March 30, 2000</u>

What we did and said this week.

Child's name	Date	What I did or said
Leila	3/30	Making blueberry muffins: In the stove . . . hot. We put food in the stove.
Natasha	3/30	Block construction: used picture as model for construction. Drew picture of block tower.
Malcolm	4/1	Storybook reading: The Very Quiet Cricket. Crickets like food. He's always bigger. He looks like a monster.
Rui	4/2	Clapping syllables 2 claps for Rui 3 claps for banana 2 claps for dinosaur
Leila	4/2	Wrote name: LLA
Aimee	4/2	Recited: Twinkle, twinkle and ABC song
Natasha	4/3	Wrote on drawing: the cat and the bat

Figure 4.3.   Weekly anecdotal notes for early literacy. (From Notari-Syverson, A., O'Connor, R.E., & Vadasy, P. [1998]. *Ladders to literacy: A preschool activity book* [p. 23]. Baltimore: Paul H. Brookes Publishing Co.; adapted by permission.)

jective of picking up small objects (e.g., dried peas) to paste on his pictures and that Natasha had opportunities to initiate social interactions in order to get other children to pass her art supplies. Ms. Voiland also elicited language by encouraging children to tell each other about their projects. She asked them to write, or pretend to write, their names on their pictures, especially Leila and Malcolm, whose IEP objectives included learning to print their names.

At the end of the project, she had the children wash their hands and observed Aimee's progress in independently carrying out all of the steps. Ms. Voiland was especially interested in keeping track of which children Natasha interacted with the most, because she wanted to pair Natasha with a special friend during free play time. Ms. Voiland also noted Aimee's reactions to changes during the cleanup and hand-washing routines, situations in which Aimee tended to get upset easily. At the physical therapist's request, Ms. Voiland also observed the quality of Rui's movements and muscle tone. To be sure that all of this information would be recorded in a systematic manner, Ms. Voiland prepared in advance a Focused Assessment Data Collection Form (see Figure 4.4) for herself and her staff to note descriptive observations of each child's relevant behaviors.

COLLECTING DATA

Focused assessment differs from the naturalistic assessment approach described in Chapter 3 in that it follows more flexible testing procedures and uses nondirective questions and more open-ended methods of observation, such as checklists and anecdotal records. These methods enable the assessment of more complex and holistic behaviors, as well as the qualitative and process aspects of performance. Naturalistic assessment approaches draw from applied behavioral technology. They use child-responsive interaction styles and environmental arrangement to provide a social and physical context for assessing observable skills. These skills are operationally defined in order to be measured and quantified. Because of these requirements, skills are typically discrete and focus on a single task. Task analysis is used to break down complex behaviors into smaller components.

Some aspects of children's behaviors, however, are difficult to quantify or to break down into smaller components and are better documented in a holistic manner. This is shown in the following example involving Sergio, the child introduced at the beginning of this chapter:

Sergio communicated in highly idiosyncratic ways. Thus, it was difficult to choose one communication method and develop a specific definition and objective criteria that would represent an appropriate affective response. It seemed important to focus on the qualitative aspects of an interaction, relying on a certain amount of subjective clinical judgment. For example, Sergio often averted his gaze and would not look at his parents directly even if he initiated an interaction with them. Most often, his way of interacting and expressing affection was to sit with his back against the adult's body and bang his head lightly against the adult's chest—a behavior that was initially interpreted as aggressive rather than affectionate. Yet, a slight smile on Sergio's face gave a clue to the true intention of this behavior. When Sergio was anxious or upset, however, his head banging became stronger and qualitatively different. The team developed an individualized focused observation form specifically for Sergio (see Figure 4.5). They used a simple open-ended checklist with columns and blank spaces to record relevant aspects of Sergio's behavior (e.g., context, adult behavior, child's reaction, facial expression,

Focused Assessment: Data Collection Form

Activity: Art   Date: 01/05/00   Observer(s): Ms. Voiland

Child: Rui	Child: Natasha	Child: Leila	Child: Malcolm	Child: Aimee
Objective: Picks up small objects	**Objective:** Initiates social interaction	**Objective:** Prints name	**Objective:** Prints name	**Objective:** Washes hands independently
Note: Observe quality of movement and muscle tone	**Note:** With whom?	**Note:**	**Note:**	**Note:** Reactions to change
Picked up three peas and two corn kernels Used thumb/index finger for first—all fingers for last two Effort and multiple attempts (two or three) Noticed that opposite arm was stiff and hand tightly fisted	Asked Leila for red paint (pointed and said, "Me, please") Asked Ms. Bates to roll up apron sleeves (held up arms) Went over to Lina and looked at Lina's painting	Wrote "Lela"	Wrote "Malm" Asked me to write his first name, then copied model correctly	Followed Toni to sink and washed hands—wiped hands dry on apron Toni told Aimee to use paper towel—Aimee placed hands on ear and moved away to library corner Refused to come to circle time—stayed quietly in library corner and seemed to listen to circle-time songs

Figure 4.4. Focused assessment data collection form for monitoring the progress of several children.

Focused Assessment: Individualized Observation Form

Child's name: _Sergio_   Activity: _Free play_   Date: _04/15/00_ Observer(s): _Ms. Binek (PT)_

Objectives/focus	Child behavior	Where	With whom	Qualitative aspects
Initiates social interaction	Took my hand and placed it on toy truck	Block construction area	With me, one-on-one—Rui and Leila were nearby but not interacting directly with Sergio	Clear intent was for me to make truck move Laughed when I made the truck roll down a slope
Gaze	Gazed directly at me once while he laughed at the truck rolling down the slope			
Stereotyped behaviors (head banging)	Banged head lightly against my arm when truck stopped rolling			

Figure 4.5. Focused assessment observation form for monitoring a child's progress.

57

communicative intent, affective quality) and to note his affective responses during free play time. The physical therapist also thought that free play would be an appropriate time to observe his tone and quality of movement, so extra columns were added to Sergio's checklist.

Play-Based Assessments

Play is an ideal situation for conducting focused assessments in early childhood and early childhood special education environments. It is an activity in which young children engage for a significant amount of time (Rubin, Fein, & Vandenberg, 1983). Because of its pleasurable and flexible nature, play has long been acknowledged by a broad variety of disciplines as an ideal context for observing the cognitive, social, emotional, linguistic, and motor development of young children (Bruner, 1972; Garvey, 1977; Segal & Webber, 1996; Vygotsky, 1967; Winnicott, 1971) and recommended as a context for early assessment and intervention with children with disabilities (Bufkin & Bryde, 1996; Fewell & Kaminski, 1988; Lifter, Sulzer-Azaroff, Anderson, & Cowdery, 1993; Odom & Strain, 1984; Rogers, 1988).

Segal and Webber (1996) distinguished two major types of play observations: structured and nonstructured. **Structured play observations** are specifically designed to assess play behaviors. They usually consist of checklists or rating scales and involve predefined procedural directions that specify the environment, toys, and strategies to use for eliciting behaviors. Some may also utilize normed scales or developmental levels to rate a child's behaviors. Examples are the Play Assessment Scale (PAS; Fewell, 1986), which yields numerical scores and developmental ages for children from 2 to 36 months, and the Dunst version of the Uzgiris and Hunt Scales of Infant Psychological Development (Dunst, 1980), which identifies age placement and developmental stages for children from birth to 24 months of age.

In **nonstructured play observations,** play is most often used as a context for assessing behaviors across multiple domains of development. The child is observed in spontaneous play with a caregiver or another adult without restrictions in the environment, toys, or timing. Nonstructured play observations are designed to identify all behaviors that occur during play that may be relevant to a referral question or help guide intervention (Segal & Webber, 1996). Behaviors are reported in narrative forms (e.g., notes, videotaping, audiotaping) and are assessed according to broad guidelines from literature and open-ended scales.

The context of play provides a comprehensive, integrated view of a child's interactions with people and objects within a meaningful context. The unstructured nature of the situation allows for an expansion of the assessment beyond traditional developmental skills to include an observation of the child's ability to organize emotions, sensations, and self-regulatory behaviors (Wieder, 1996). Nonstructured play observations provide an opportunity to observe a child in a naturalistic situation and to identify capabilities that may not be recognized in a formal test, such as engagement, persistence, attention span, and exploration diversity (Segal & Webber,

1996). They are especially useful in assessing functional behavior of a young child who either cannot or will not perform in a formal testing situation (e.g., children younger than 3 years of age, children with autism, children with severe motor impairments, children who do not speak English).

THEORETICAL FRAMEWORK

Focused assessments provide a middle ground between traditional standardized testing and naturalistic observation of spontaneous behaviors. The tester uses probing questions to elicit responses from children rather than waiting for behaviors to occur spontaneously. Testing procedures follow the child's lead and are adapted to the characteristics of the individual child.

Clinical Approach

The purpose of using a focused approach to assessment is not to record the absence or presence of behaviors or correct or incorrect responses but to describe and identify patterns of behaviors, strategies, and processes. This type of approach is commonly used by clinicians to log observations and clinical impressions for assessment and therapeutic intervention purposes. Clinical methods emphasize qualitative aspects of behaviors and flexibility in procedures and interpretation of behaviors (Rey, 1958). The method consists of having a general framework for testing rather than a set of specified procedures. The tester observes and listens to the child and adapts the pace and level of questioning to the individual child. The basic aim is to reveal the underlying reasons for the child's behaviors (Ginsberg & Opper, 1979). The principles of clinical assessment methods have useful applications to the classroom. Prizant and Rydell (1993), for example, discussed the assessment of unconventional verbal behavior (e.g., echolalia) that is characteristic of many children with autism. Echolalia is often considered a meaningless and inappropriate repetition of words or phrases; Prizant and Rydell, however, described echolalia as an intentional communicative strategy that should be viewed as compensatory within a developmental perspective. In younger children, an increase in functional use of echolalia may be desirable, and teachers may want to document types, communicative functions, and contexts in which echolalia occurs. A clinical approach may also be helpful when monitoring children who are learning to use augmentative and alternative communication systems, wheelchairs, or other assistive technology for which behavior observations are used to make changes and adjustments to the technology.

Because objective standards and criteria are often lacking, it is critical that the practitioner be aware of the impact of potential biases due to personal beliefs and assumptions. The practitioner must learn to rigorously develop and consider multiple explanations for behaviors and continually self-monitor the assessment process (Leung, 1996). If a 4-year-old child with a language delay has frequent temper tantrums, one clinician may interpret this behavior as the result of frustration about not being able to communicate; another may see it as undesirable attention-seeking behavior that needs to be extinguished. If a mother pays little attention when her 2-year-old daughter falls and slightly scrapes her knee, one person may believe that the mother is encouraging her daughter's independence; another may think that the mother lacks affection.

More systematic and structured approaches have been proposed. Neisworth and Bagnato (1988), for example, described a judgment-based assessment model that provides a systematic method for structuring impressions of professionals and caregivers. **Judgment-based assessment** is a subjective rating of behaviors based on overall impressions. This method focuses on assessing broad dimensions of behavior, including tolerance for frustration, task persistence, attention, engagement, and motivation. It bases ratings on professional judgment and expertise rather than on explicit criteria (Bailey & Wolery, 1992). Ratings can be quantified with numerical ratings representing ascending or descending levels of intensity or quantity for each behavior. Each numerical level is accompanied by a qualitative description of exemplar behaviors.

Developmental Theory

A wealth of research has highlighted the interrelationships among various domains of development—in particular, play and aspects of development such as cognition (Piaget, 1962; Watson & Fischer, 1980), language (Bates, Camaioni, & Volterra, 1975; Vygotsky, 1967), and literacy (Cazden, 1984; Galda & Pellegrini, 1985; Isenberg & Jacob, 1983; Morrow, 1989; Pellegrini, 1983). Studies have found strong relationships between play and diverse aspects of language development both in children who are developing typically (e.g., Bates, Benigni, Bretherton, Camaioni, & Volterra, 1979; McCune-Nicolich & Bruskin, 1982; Ogura, 1991; Shore, 1986) and in those with disabilities (e.g., Cunningham, Glenn, Wilkinson, & Sloper, 1985; Fewell, Ogura, Notari-Syverson, & Wheeden, 1997; Kennedy, Sheridan, Radlinski, & Beeghly, 1991; Ogura, Notari, & Fewell, 1991). In addition to providing children with opportunities to directly explore the various uses and functions of print and practice different literacy skills, play appears to facilitate the representational abilities that serve as a foundation for literacy development. The language used during play is similar to the more formal, literate language required of children in school and has been found to facilitate the development of metalinguistic awareness, an ability thought to be strongly related to literacy outcomes.

Transdisciplinary Approach

Transdisciplinary assessment is also referred to as **arena assessment** because of the physical arrangement of observers around the child in the middle (Child Development Resources Training Center, 1992). One person interacts with the child while other team members observe, record observations, and score on identical or different tests. This model is particularly useful for young children and preschoolers with severe disabilities. In Wolery and Dyk's study (1984), parents and professionals believed the arena model provided a more accurate picture of the child's strengths and needs and was less time consuming than individual assessments. Diagnostic teams often use arena assessments in conjunction with or instead of standardized measures when assessing infants and preschool-age children (Bagnato & Neisworth, 1994).

MODELS AND APPLICATIONS

Focused assessments draw on situations and activities that are part of regular daily routines. These situations are structured and directed by an adult in order to elicit from the child the specific skills and behaviors that are the focus of the assessment. Depending on practitioners' preferences, observations may be guided by specific checklists and scoring systems or they may be devised on an individual basis by the team.

Creating their own systems of assessment can be time consuming for teachers. A number of models and methods that fit into a focused-assessment framework are available. For instance, Cazden (1977) proposed assessment through **concentrated encounters.** These situations are representative of real-life events and familiar interaction experiences, but they are condensed and focused by teacher direction to yield more information in less time. Instead of conducting separate tests, for example, the teacher may condense the assessment of early language and literacy skills into a single observation of a child's behaviors during storybook reading. If the book is carefully selected, the teacher will be able to elicit a variety of skills, from book handling behaviors and picture labeling to knowledge of story structure and nursery rhymes, as well as word and letter recognition and letter sounds.

Lahey (1988) referred to **nonstandardized elicitations,** in which the adult takes an active role within naturalistic situations by suggesting certain tasks to elicit particular responses. To assess sentence construction, for example, the adult may manipulate puppets and ask the child to describe the puppet's specific actions. Similarly, the adult may prepare specific materials for an art project to elicit the labeling of colors, shapes, and sizes.

Notari-Syverson et al. (1998) described a clinical approach to elicit and assess specific early language and literacy skills during structured play with miniature toys, storybook reading, and drawing and writing activities. Using this method, observed behaviors can be recorded on an itemized checklist along with samples of children's dictations and drawings.

The Communication and Symbolic Behavior Scales (CSBS; Wetherby & Prizant, 1993) is another example of an informal flexible format for gathering data on young children's communicative behaviors (e.g., reciprocity, social-affective signaling). The CSBS is based on direct assessment of children using a continuum of structured to unstructured contexts that require rating on a quantifiable scale (Wetherby & Prizant, 1992).

Bartoli and Botel (1988) proposed a framework for observation of children's oral and written language during routine events in the classroom. The teacher structures observations of children's learning around selected critical experiences such as transactions with text, independent reading and writing, and oral and written composition. Within these experiences, observations are made of children's oral and written language skills (e.g., narrative structure, syntactic complexity) that can serve as a basis for developing an IEP. Subsequent intervention also takes place around the same critical learning events.

Play-Based Assessments

There are two broad categories of play assessments. One type specifically assesses play behaviors and developmental levels that are, for the most part, based on Piagetian approaches. Play is seen as a window for assessing children's knowledge and development of cognitive, language, and communication skills—areas strongly related to play in infants and preschool-age children (Lifter & Bloom, 1989; Nicolich, 1977). Other tools use play as a natural context for assessing a broad variety of skills across developmental domains. Play is an activity in which young children commonly and readily engage, although specific materials and interactions may differ across cultures.

Various structured assessments are available to observe and evaluate play behaviors. One is PAS, an observational assessment of play development for children between the ages of 2 and 36 months. The scale consists of 45 developmentally sequenced items that are observed as the child plays. The scale yields numerical scores that can be converted to developmental play ages. Data are available on its use with children with disabilities (Fewell et al., 1997).

An example of an open-ended scale for specifically assessing play behaviors is Nicolich's (1977) Symbolic Play Scale. It identifies five different levels of play, beginning with presymbolic schemes that involve the simple functional use of objects to elaborate planned sequences of pretend play. A manual describing specific procedures and scoring criteria is also available (McCune-Nicolich, 1980). Other examples include the Symbolic Play Scale Checklist (Westby, 1980), the Symbolic Play Test (Lowe & Costello, 1976), and procedures described in Largo and Howard (1979); Gitlin-Weiner, Sandgrund, and Schaefer (2000); and Sheridan, Foley, and Radlinski (1995). A number of play observations have been used with children with disabilities (Lifter et al., 1993; Newson & Newson, 1979; Ogura et al., 1991; Wieder, 1996).

A well-known and useful model that uses play as a context for the assessment of skills across developmental domains is TPBA. TPBA is a type of arena assessment in which all members use a common set of assessment forms and procedures. It provides a wealth of guidelines, information, and forms for assessing the cognitive, socioemotional, communication, language, and sensorimotor domains of children between the developmental ages of birth and 6 years. TPBA is implemented by a team (consisting of parents and representatives of diverse disciplines) that observes a child for 1–1½ hours during play activities with a play facilitator. The TPBA approach is based on theories and practices related to play in numerous disciplines of study (Calhoun & Newson, 1984; Fewell, 1986; McCune-Nicolich, 1980; Nicolich, 1977; Parten, 1932; Rogers, 1988; Westby, 1980). Myers, McBride, and Peterson (1996) compared a traditional multidisciplinary standardized assessment to the TPBA. Overall, the transdisciplinary approach is favored by practitioners and parents in terms of efficiency, the functional utility of assessment reports, and the high congruence in developmental ratings by observers.

ADVANTAGES AND LIMITATIONS

Focused assessment approaches are useful and time-efficient tools for practitioners seeking to assess children's skills and behaviors across multiple domains or curriculum areas. The assessment takes place within a context or situation that is meaningful and familiar to the child; however, the adult may modify materials and activities and direct interactions to elicit specific targeted behaviors from the child. Skills may be individualized to the child or consist of predetermined standardized checklist items. Different observers may use different tests or scoring systems. Yet, remember that it is important to consider the familiarity and cultural relevance of the assessment activities, materials, and social interactions when assessing children from diverse cultural backgrounds. People from all cultures engage in caregiving and play activities with young children, but forms of interaction, meanings, and customs may vary across cultures (Lifter & Bloom, 1998).

Advantages

The use of a transdisciplinary approach and meaningful context, as well as flexibility and efficiency, are focused assessment's advantages. Each of these characteristics is examined in the following discussion.

Transdisciplinary Approach

Multiple aspects of development can be assessed simultaneously using a transdisciplinary assessment approach. Practitioners from different disciplines can observe a child together and easily involve caregivers (Crais, 1995). A transdisciplinary approach facilitates communication and caregiver–professional partnerships.

Meaningful Context

Similar to naturalistic assessment, focused assessment occurs within the context of meaningful activities. The child is actively engaged in routine tasks and activities, which facilitates the building of rapport between the practitioner and the child. Focused assessment promotes generalization of learned behaviors because the child can practice a skill using a variety of materials in a variety of environments.

Flexibility

Focused assessment allows for the qualitative analysis of complex behaviors and learning strategies. Procedures can be adapted and accommodated to suit each child's characteristics. For example, culturally relevant materials can be used when appropriate.

Efficiency

When conducting focused assessments, caregivers and practitioners can structure their interactions with the child in order to elicit targeted behaviors. Data may be collected by multiple sources using checklists and anecdotal notes in a concentrated period of time.

Limitations

Among the limitations of focused assessment are the required planning time, the lack of standardized procedures, and the high level of expertise required to conduct the assessment. These characteristics are explored in further detail next.

Required Planning Time

Practitioners must work with other team members to develop activities, criteria, and standards for evaluating a child's performance. If using transdisciplinary observation procedures, coordinating team members' schedules can be difficult. In addition, multiple observations may be necessary to obtain a representative sample of the child's behaviors.

Lack of Standardized Procedures

Practitioners must develop individualized activities and data collection procedures for each child. Professionals have also observational criteria specific to their disciplines, so these need to be shared, discussed, and agreed upon prior to the assessment.

High Level of Expertise Required

The qualitative nature of a focused assessment requires in-depth knowledge of child development and clinical expertise. Practitioners must be adept at discerning relevant child behaviors within the context of daily routines. They must be able to simultaneously observe and record behaviors across multiple domains of development.

GUIDELINES FOR IMPLEMENTATION

To begin planning for a focused assessment, it is important to specify the purpose of the assessment and observation. Will the observation focus on one child or a group of children? Will multiple areas and skills be observed? Will the assessment involve caregivers and professionals from diverse disciplines?

Next, the team must agree on criteria for skill mastery based on a review of developmental normative data and available assessment instruments. Then, the participants in the assessment must determine specific roles and responsibilities. Who will observe which skills? Who will interact with the child or children?

Now the team is ready to select the most appropriate context, activity, and materials for eliciting the skills targeted for observation. Familiarity and meaningfulness are key elements because the goal is to optimize children's participation in selected activities (Cazden, 1977). Play and story-book reading are ideal activities for conducting a focused assessment with young children. In addition, cultural relevance of activities, materials, and interactions are important aspects to consider. The team may contact the child's family or colleagues who are familiar with the child's culture to obtain information on the cultural sensitivity of the assessment plan.

Careful planning is important. The team member who interacts with the children must structure the situation to elicit the targeted skills within the time frame designated for the assessment. The examiner can use a variety of strategies to direct and focus interactions ranging from intentional arrangement of the environment and materials to asking questions, modeling, or using direct instruction techniques. The examiner's behavior should not be scripted. The examiner should, however, structure and direct the interactions by following children's focus of interest.

Finally, decisions must be made on how to best record data (e.g., videotape, audiotape, notes, memory). After the assessment data are shared among team members, a summary or evaluative report can be written. Each team member should be given the opportunity to review the assessment report for accuracy and possible revisions. Table 4.1 is a summary of guidelines for implementing focused assessment.

SUGGESTIONS FOR PRACTITIONERS IN INCLUSIVE ENVIRONMENTS

The flexible and open-ended nature of focused assessments make them ideal for inclusive early childhood environments. Early childhood staff can use

Table 4.1.　Guidelines for implementing focused assessment

Specify the purpose of the assessment.
　Will the observation focus on one child or a group of children?
　Will multiple areas and skills be observed?
　Will the assessment involve parents and professionals from diverse disciplines?

Agree on criteria for skill mastery, and determine procedures and responsibilities.
　Who will observe which skills?
　Who will interact with the child or children?

Select the most appropriate context, activity, and materials for eliciting the skills targeted for observation.
　Familiarity and meaningfulness are key elements.
　Use culturally relevant materials and activities.
　Play and storybook reading are ideal activities for assessing young children.

Plan carefully.
　Determine how to structure the situation to elicit targeted skills within the designated time frame.
　Determine strategies to direct and focus interactions.

Decide how to record data.
　Methods may include videotape, audiotape, notes, or memory.

them to make observations of typically developing children and children who may be at risk for developmental delays. They can also be used by teachers and members of the IEP team to monitor the progress of children with disabilities on specific IEP objectives.

Initial Assessment

First, it is important to gather background information on the child by interviewing family members and others who know the child best. Either a CBA or a transdisciplinary approach can be used to identify the child's strengths and areas of concern. When using a transdisciplinary approach, the practitioner must specify the purpose of the assessment and which areas to observe (e.g., parent–child interactions, language, cognitive development, motor skills). The environment for the observation also must be determined (e.g., home, clinic, child care center, school), as well as who will interact with child (e.g., team member, parent) and who will observe. Each team member should share information on developmental guidelines and decide how to record data (e.g., videotape, audiotape, notes, memory). Team members may elect to use different methods.

Goal Development

Goals and objectives are identified based on the results of the CBA or the transdisciplinary focused assessment, as well as caregiver input. The context in which these objectives will be implemented and monitored for progress should be considered (Bufkin & Bryde, 1996). Selected goals and objectives should represent generic, broad-based skills that can be practiced in naturalistic daily routines (Notari-Syverson & Shuster, 1995). The general objective *the child will use an object as a tool to solve a problem* (e.g., use a broom to push a ball from under a bed; step on a stool to reach a toy on a shelf) takes into account the many ways a behavior can manifest itself, compared with the more specific *the child will use a string to obtain a pull-toy*.

Intervention

Familiar routines that offer the best opportunities for observing areas of concern are used for both assessment and intervention activities. A variety of appropriate materials should be used, such as sensory toys (e.g., squeeze animals, playdough, musical instruments), cause-and-effect toys (e.g., pop-up toys, telephones, wind-up toys, cash registers), and miniature toys for symbolic play (e.g., toy cars, pretend dining set, doctor kit, dolls, stuffed animals).

Evaluation

A focused or play-based approach can be used for ongoing monitoring of a child's progress in the classroom or other environments. First, develop a data collection plan for gathering information on IEP objectives. Then, determine the frequency of data collection and the most appropriate method (e.g., checklists, anecdotal notes, videotape) for recording the behaviors

Table 4.2.   Suggestions for practitioners using focused assessment in inclusive environments

Initial assessment

First gather background information by interviewing family members and others who know the child well.

Either a curriculum-based assessment (CBA) or a transdisciplinary approach can be used initially to identify the child's strengths and areas of concern.

Specify the purpose of assessment and which areas to observe.

Determine the environment for observation, who will interact with the child, and who will observe.

Have each team member share information on developmental guidelines, and decide how to record data.

Goal development

Identify goals and objectives based upon the results of the CBA or transdisciplinary focused assessment and caregiver input.

Consider the context in which these objectives will be implemented and monitored for progress.

Goals and objectives should represent generic, broad-based skills that can be practiced in naturalistic daily routines.

Intervention

Plan familiar activities that offer the best opportunities for observing areas of concern.

When assessing young children, choose a variety of appropriate materials/toys:

Sensory toys

Cause-and-effect toys

Miniature toys for symbolic play

Evaluation

Develop data collection plan for gathering information on IEP objectives.

Determine the frequency of data collection and the most appropriate method for recording the behaviors under observation.

When recording written observations, describe actual behaviors and events; avoid subjective interpretations.

Criteria for skill mastery should be meaningful within the context of the assessment situation.

Staff should meet on a regular basis to monitor the child's progress and to revise instruction as needed.

At the end of the year, readminister the same curriculum-based or transdisciplinary assessment originally used to evaluate the child's progress.

under observation. When recording written observations, describe actual behaviors and events; avoid subjective interpretations. For example, instead of the term *enjoys,* use a term such as *smiles*; instead of *angry,* use *hits* or *cries.*

Criteria for skill mastery should be meaningful within the context of the assessment situation. Staff should meet on a regular basis to monitor the child's progress and to revise instruction as needed. The following questions can be used to guide the meetings:

- Is the skill acquired? If not, can the child do it with help?

- Which kinds of support, materials, and situations work best in helping the child perform the skill?

- Does the child partially perform the skill?

- Is the skill generalized?

- Is the skill socially validated in other environments?

At the end of the year, readminister the CBA or transdisciplinary assessment originally used to evaluate the child's progress. Table 4.2 summarizes suggestions for practitioners using focused assessment in inclusive environments.

CONCLUSION

Focused assessment is a useful and time-efficient approach that is particularly well suited for transdisciplinary team assessments and ongoing monitoring of a child's progress on general classroom curriculum goals or IEP/IFSP goals and objectives. In a focused assessment approach, the adult assumes a directive role by eliciting targeted behaviors to obtain a maximum amount of information within the specified assessment time frame.

Data can be gathered using various methods. While observing the child during snack time, for example, each professional may focus on behaviors that are relevant to his or her particular discipline and use different methods for recording observations. The speech-language pathologist may transcribe utterances verbatim in order to calculate the child's mean length of utterance; the physical therapist may check off a list of observed items.

Focused assessments take place in a context or an activity that is meaningful and familiar to the child. For young children, play is an ideal context because children readily engage in play activities across cultures. Other caregiving routines, such as mealtime, are also common across cultures. Particular materials and adult–child interactions, however, may vary. Cultures assign different meanings and customs to meals in terms of food, utensils, social interactions, and expectations for independence. It is important for the practitioner to use culturally sensitive assessment materials, activities, and adult–child interactions as appropriate.

Review Questions

■ What are four salient characteristics of focused assessment?

■ What is one way in which focused assessment differs from naturalistic assessment as described in Chapter 3?

■ What are two advantages to using nonstructured play observations in focused assessment?

■ Describe arena assessment. What is the rationale for conducting arena assessments?

5

Performance Assessment

After reading this chapter, you will be able to:

- Define performance assessment, and discuss the rationale for its use

- Give examples of models and methods that fit into a performance assessment framework

- Identify considerations and guidelines for implementing performance assessment

*M*s. Byrd proudly pinned 4-year-old Anna's drawing on the wall near the library corner. She would show it to Anna's mother tomorrow morning. Anna had been talking about Cinderella ever since her friend Jenny had read the story to her 2 weeks ago. She had made three drawings of Cinderella this week. The most recent one showed two figures side by side on bright yellow paper. Both had hair, eyes, a nose, and a mouth, as well as arms and hands, legs, and feet. Under the figures, Ms. Byrd had written exactly what Anna had said while drawing:

> Cinderella got yellow hair . . . And footprints. I got Cinderella . . . red dress [Anna had colored the body of one of the figures red]. Cinderella dress. I just make Cinderella a beautiful dress. Red long dress. I got to draw Cinderella getting married. Pants and a hands, a hair, blue. A prince. Cinderella married to Prince Charming. This is the Prince and Cinderella.

Anna, who had significant language, cognitive, and motor development delays, had been included in Ms. Byrd's Head Start program since September. At first Ms. Byrd was worried that a child with such delays would not be able to learn in her bustling classroom environment. Would she be able to give the child the necessary attention and help? Fortunately, Ms. Gonzales, the itinerant special education teacher, had been very responsive and helpful. Now Ms. Byrd believed that Anna was doing very well. Ms. Byrd compared Anna's new drawing to an earlier one from Anna's file. This drawing had a tall stick figure in the foreground with Anna's dictation: "It got feet. It got a head. The mouth. My mommy's face." Above the head were some simple shapes and the words: "And her kitchen." Next to the tall stick figure were three other smaller, similar figures: "And this is me . . . and my brother. My Daddy in there." Surrounding the figures were more scribbles and shapes: "And the windows there and the door there . . . and lots of toys." Thus, it was evident that Anna had made a lot of progress in her language and drawing skills.

Teachers often display samples of children's work in the classroom. Children engage in many activities, ranging from gross motor play to quiet storybook reading. Some of the classroom activities are routine functional events (e.g., eating a snack, toileting); others involve fantasy play and artistic expression. Children's artwork on the walls or science projects on display in the classroom evidence children's participation in these activities. Displaying children's work makes the environment warm and friendly and gives children a strong sense of ownership.

Yet, these samples can serve another important role. They can be used as a meaningful way of assessing a child's abilities and evaluating progress. Systematically using children's behaviors and projects to make judgments for assessment purposes is referred to as **performance assessment.** Traditional approaches to data collection relied on eliciting specific behaviors from children on demand and in contrived testing situations. Many times, children's performance in these situations did not match what teachers and parents had witnessed their children doing during home and classroom routines or when engaged in meaningful real-life tasks. The following classroom vignette shows how children's behaviors and performance may vary as a function of task and context:

Kilhyum, a 4-year-old Korean boy, spoke in monosyllables during traditional testing. When given a picture book, however, he lit up and started talking in sentences about the pictures: "Penguin hold on to gorae's kori [whale's tail]!" For the science project, Jon had made a beautiful drawing of a sunflower. Nonetheless, when Ms. Nguyen, his teacher, asked Jon to draw a picture of a person for her weekly IEP objective probe, she got scribbles. Ms. Nguyen was also having a hard time observing Diana's independent eating skills because Diana refused to eat the school snack. Yet, Diana's mother said that her daughter was a voracious eater of the spicy foods cooked at home. Shona refused to play with puzzles in class, but at home she and her sister beaded a beautiful necklace. Ms. Nguyen also recalled how surprised she was when Ms. Lew, her assistant, showed her the story that the children had dictated to her:

A Pirate, Elephant, Crocodile, Peter Pan, and Big Bad Wolf Story
by Kilhyum, Jon, Diana, and Shona

Once there were two pirates and an elephant. It was fun sailing in the pirate ship because there were so many pirates. It was so much fun. Then they all got into a fight. The crocodile was swimming in the water. The elephant was catching food. Peter Pan swoops down. The alligator snapped at him and missed. The Big Bad Wolf frightened the crocodile and the crocodile swam off.

Ms. Nguyen printed extra copies of the story, which she laminated and made into books. She placed one copy in the library corner and also sent copies home.

Performance assessment is a broad term that refers to methods in which children are given the opportunity to demonstrate and apply knowledge. Telling a story, building a model of a playground area, climbing a ladder, drawing a picture of a pet, and creating a shopping list before a grocery store visit are examples of performance tasks in which children show a variety of language, literacy, cognitive, social, and motor skills. The tasks can be developed specifically for the assessment, or they can occur as part of daily routines. When tasks are completed in a real-life context (e.g., writing a letter to a friend, reading a list of products to buy at the store, swimming at the local pool), it is referred to as **authentic assessment** (Cohen & Spenciner, 1994). Performance assessment, uses a broad variety of methods and products, including traditional observation techniques and anecdotal records, videotaping, audiotaping, photographs, transcriptions of children's comments and discussions, and actual work samples in various media (e.g., a drawing, writing, a block construction).

Documentation is a particular type of performance assessment. The use of documentation to understand and make decisions about children's thoughts, ideas, and work was first emphasized and used systematically in Reggio Emilia schools (Helm, Beneke, & Steinheimer, 1998). **Documentation** is any activity that provides a sufficiently detailed performance record to help others understand the behavior recorded (Forman & Fyfe, 1998). Documentation goes beyond merely displaying or assessing performance; it also provides an explanation of the child's learning processes. For example, in addition to displaying a selection of children's drawings, documentation would also include commentaries from teachers, family members, and the children themselves explaining the reasons, processes, and meanings for the different drawings. It is typically used to assess the development of a group of children working together on a project and focuses on the social dynamics of learning.

Performance assessment is rapidly becoming one of the most widely used approaches to assessment of preschool- and school-age children, and it is being used as part of statewide and districtwide evaluations (Darling-Hammond, Ancess, & Falk, 1993; Khattri, Kane, & Reeve, 1995). Traditional data collection methods, such as frequency counts, do not always fit well into the real-world demands of day-to-day life in a preschool classroom (Schwartz & Olswang, 1996; Wolery, 1996) and do not represent the actual behavior in the most meaningful way for parents, paraprofessionals, and child care staff. For instance, learning to read and construct maps and diagrams (Maxim, 1997), using technology such as computers, understanding environmental issues (Puckett & Black, 1994), having visual and musical artistic abilities (Bond & Dean, 1997), demonstrating cognitive processes such as problem solving, and experimenting (Meisels, 1996; Micklo, 1997) are all important abilities and real-life skills that are rarely represented in traditional tests or CBA checklists of developmental milestones or academic skills.

Real-life skills are often complex and holistic and cannot be broken down into individual components. Performance samples allow practitioners to record highly complex behaviors—visual, musical, or kinesthetic—using a variety of methods and tasks that approximate the conditions and resources the child normally encounters in the classroom or other real-life settings (Genishi & Brainard, 1995; Teale, 1988). Reading and writing, for example, are complex tasks that require the integration of many processes and are best documented by children's actual work samples.

A performance assessment also provides information about children's strategies and processes and, therefore, captures qualitative metacognitive and motivational processes such as higher-order thinking skills, initiative, creativity, emotional and relational factors, motivation, attitudes, interest, general comfort, and well-being (Meisels, 1996; Schwartz & Olswang, 1996). Two children may have the same score on a test, but performance assessment will show qualitative differences in the ways each child may demonstrate the skills (Meisels, 1996). One child may, for instance, reflect and think before giving a response; another may act impulsively and proceed by trial and error and self-corrections. Yet, both complete the test with the same number of correct responses. Similarly, writing samples may show that one child wrote all of the words correctly the first time and that another child erased and corrected mistakes. Thus, the teacher should not look only at correct responses but also at strategies and errors.

Performance-based assessment measures offer the necessary flexibility to ask questions such as, "In what ways does each child incorporate print into play?" "For what purposes does the child use gestures?" "What types of books does the child read?" "With which children does he interact the most?" It also allows for accommodations and adaptations, such as assistive technology or augmentative and alternative communication (AAC) systems for children with significant sensory impairments (Miller & Robinson, 1996). This is shown in the following vignette:

Jamie, a 6-year-old child with severe cerebral palsy, had just received a new wheelchair. His parents said it was important that Jamie learn to move around in it during community outings and wanted that to be one of Jamie's IEP goals. How could the team and the parents collect data on progress? The traditional checklists used in the classroom were not of much use because they did not address wheelchair use. Ms. Nagasawa, Jamie's teacher, decided to use anecdotal notes to record how Jamie performed getting on and off the bus and going to the playground. Because the observations would take place outside the classroom, she decided to use a small notebook that would fit into her pocket and a larger notebook affixed to a clipboard for more extensive observations. She also prepared a folder for collecting the notes. Jamie's family was willing to be involved. His parents had a camcorder and could videotape Jamie during visits to the grocery store and to his grandmother's house on Sundays. Jamie's parents also wanted him to learn to write his name using his home computer, and Eric, Jamie's older brother, offered to work with Jamie on the weekends. Jamie's grandmother was interested in learning about computers, so she was going to sit in. They would print out Jamie's attempts and send a copy to school on Mondays for the teachers to file in Jamie's folder.

A performance assessment approach is conducive to involving families. Rather than conducting trials of target behaviors and counting frequencies, nonprofessionals can easily document what children do in real-life settings such as home and the community by taking a few notes, making a telephone call to the teacher, or sending a sample of the child's work to school. Performance assessment also allows documentation of behaviors with culturally relevant and meaningful materials and contexts. Because many behaviors—especially language—reflect the influences of cultural contexts (e.g., home, school), it is important to observe children in culturally relevant environments. Situations defined by formal academic or school-related culture are not sufficient for assessing language development in children who do not speak English at home; they need to be observed in environments where children communicate the most competently and receive the mediation and support to which they are accustomed (Gutierrez-Clellen, 1996). Because of the various cultures and languages encountered in early childhood programs, performance assessment can provide valuable cross-validation of test results, as tests are usually culture specific and may not be appropriate for the child being tested (Leung, 1996). If a child does not do well on a test but does well in the classroom or at home, then one cannot infer the problem is inherent to the child.

Following are some examples of how Ms. Nguyen, the teacher from the first vignette, used performance assessments to involve families. By broadening her approach to include home and classroom observations and examples of children's work and behaviors in addition to checklists, frequency counts, and IEP progress charts, she was able to develop a comprehensive assessment of her students' abilities:

Feedback from Kilhyum's mother reassured Ms. Nguyen that he was learning new skills in school and generalizing them to the home. His mother wrote the teacher notes such as "K. loves the 'Teddy Bear, Teddy Bear' song, and it helps him get ready for bed. We will make this his bedtime activity."

Ms. Nguyen was also getting information from other children's parents. Jon's mother showed her a picture that Jon had drawn of himself on a swing at the park. Diana's father sent a videotape of Diana eating lunch at home with her brothers and sisters. Shona's mother had sent Ms. Nguyen the following note: "Shona loves helping put away the dishes from the dishwasher. She also puts away her clothes—socks, pajamas, T-shirts, shirts, and pants."

Ms. Nguyen decided to expand her assessment approach. She would look at picture books with Kilhyum and take notes at least once per week on his language. Instead of having Jon draw a person, she was going to have the children keep their own journals or albums, in which they would draw pictures and insert photographs and write or dictate about family members and friends throughout the year. This would allow her to look at Jon's progress in drawing a person and also keep track of other children's fine motor, language, and early literacy development. She would use checklists from a CBA for language and fine motor skills and the drawing criteria from a normed assessment for the drawings. As for Diana, her mother agreed to complete a checklist that she and Ms. Nguyen designed together to observe Diana's progress in independent eating at home, shown in Figure 5.1.

To monitor Shona's fine motor skills, Ms. Nguyen and Ms. Lew decided to introduce a crafts area where children could display selected pieces of fine arts created in school: jewelry constructed with beads, pastings on pictures, and masks. Other children had fine motor IEP goals, too, so they could all contribute to the exhibit. Labels needed to be made, objects organized into categories, and exhibits discussed and visited so the teachers would be able to observe and document children's use and progress on a variety of early literacy, language, social, and cognitive skills. This would require a bit of planning, but it would be fun. When the teachers proposed this idea to the class, the children seemed quite excited. Ms. Nguyen needed to make a plan to make sure that she collected data on each child on a regular basis. She devised three performance assessment forms for collecting IEP data. She would use two different forms to monitor progress on children who had IEP objectives: One was for observing a child individually, and the other was for observing multiple children in a small group. Examples of both versions of the performance assessment IEP/IFSP data collection forms are contained in Figures 5.2 and 5.3.

She would use the third form for recording observations on behaviors, products, or new skills learned by the other children who did not have IEPs. An example of this form is shown in Figure 5.4. Ms. Nguyen also thought it would be interesting to keep a log of how the crafts area project progressed. She could also

Performance Assessment: Things My Child Can Do at Home

Child's name: _Diana_   Observer(s): _Mother_

Observation period/dates: _1/15/00–1/30/00_

Did Diana eat regularly? _Yes_

Which foods did she enjoy the most? _Tamales, ice cream_

Were there any foods she did not like? _No_

Did Diana use her spoon or fork? _Yes_

    By herself? (Please describe) _No_

        I sliced the tamales, and Diana ate them with her fingers

    With help? (Please describe)

        Used spoon to eat ice cream—had to help her scoop, but she was able to bring the spoon to her mouth by herself.

Did Diana drink out of her cup? _Yes_

    By herself? (Please describe) _No_

    With help? (Please describe)

        Had to help her hold her cup

Were there other important things Diana did or learned?

        Said "more," "ice cream," and "helado."

Figure 5.1.   Home observation checklist.

Performance Assessment: IEP/IFSP Objectives Individual Observation Form

Child's name: _Shona_

Objective: _Manipulates two small objects at same time_

Criteria: _Places appropriate objects/pieces together and with precision_

Scoring: _Frequency counts_

Dates	Observer	Observations	Product/work samples
11/26/00	R.N.	Placed caps on markers	
11/28/00	M.L.	Strung five large beads	
12/5/00	M.L.	Built five-piece tower with Legos	Photograph of construction
12/12/00	R.N.	Strung eleven large beads	Photograph
12/20/00	R.N.	Strung eight large beads and five small beads	Necklace for display
12/21/00	M.L.	Placed key in cupboard padlock	

Figure 5.2. Performance assessment IEP/IFSP objectives data collection form for an individual child.

Performance Assessment: IEP/IFSP Objectives Data Collection Form

Date: _1/25/00_   Observer(s): _Rena Nguyen_

Activity/task: _Making masks from paper plates_

Child	IEP/IFSP objective	Observations
Shona	Fits object into defined space	Placed crayons back in box four out of five times
Kihyum	Uses adult-like sentences	Said: "I'm making a cat mask." "I want blue crayon."
Jon	Draws recognizable figures	Drew a flower on one "cheek" of mask and a bird on the other. Both recognizable.

Figure 5.3.   Performance assessment IEP/IFSP objectives data collection form for multiple children.

Performance Assessment: Observation Form

Date: _12/8/00_   Observer(s): _Marcia Lew_

Activity/task: _Playdough animals_

Child	Observations	Products/work samples
Jon	Formed rectangular shape with playdough. Said: "I'm trying to make something." "A horse house." "How do I do that?" "See I make a horse house."	Playdough = Two figures: barn horse
Anna	Rolled ball, then flattened it. Said: "Spider." "Spider get wet." "The spider dry off." "The spider eat."	Playdough shape

Figure 5.4. Performance assessment observation form for monitoring the progress of several children.

share some of her observations in her monthly parent newsletter to inform families about what their children were doing in school.

THEORETICAL FRAMEWORK

Performance assessment uses actual samples of children's work completed in the context of meaningful everyday home, school, and community environments. This type of assessment draws on ecological approaches that recognize the active role children play in constructing their own knowledge.

Social-Constructivist Approach

A **social-constructivist approach** emphasizes the social and cultural nature of mental activity (New, 1998). Children actively contribute to their own development and learn within a social context of culturally defined meanings and activities (Bruner, 1983; Rogoff, 1993). According to Malaguzzi, "What children learn does not follow as an automatic result from what is taught. Rather, it is in large part due to the children's doing as a consequence of their activities and our resources" (1998, p. 67). Performance assessment recognizes children's active role. It requires children to construct rather than select a response, and it focuses on tasks that have meaning within their daily life experiences.

As a qualitative methodology, performance assessment takes into account the role of the performer in selecting, interpreting, and evaluating work samples and behaviors (Ferguson, 1993). Children create their own work and participate in choosing a story to tell or a book to read. They provide their own explanations for science projects and identify strategies and solutions in math problems. Systematic documentation of work samples is a way for teachers to evaluate and analyze the quality and effectiveness of their teaching and share ideas with other professionals (Helm et al., 1998). Concrete and visible documents such as drawings, dictations, photographs, slides, and video recordings also serve as a "memory" for children, allowing them to "revisit" or reflect on and self-evaluate what they have said and done (Helm et al., 1998).

Ecological Approach

The Division of Early Childhood (DEC) Task Force on Recommended Practices encouraged that early intervention activities 1) be implemented in naturalistic or authentic contexts, 2) involve families, and 3) address cultural diversity (McLean & Odom, 1993). Children's behaviors are best observed when children are engaged in ongoing daily activities and routines. Often, children's behaviors in natural environments are complex and cannot be separated from relational, emotional, and contextual aspects. A holistic view is best rendered through methods such as anecdotal notes, videotaping, or children's actual products.

The ecological approach (Bronfenbrenner, 1979) stresses the interconnections among the diverse environments (e.g., home, school) in which a child participates. Home experiences have a strong influence on the child's performance at school. Children from literacy-rich homes may learn to read earlier than children who encounter little or no print materials at home. Also, children may take back to the home and community what they learn in school. A child from an immigrant family may help his or her parents learn to read and write in English. Documentation is an optimal means for connecting home and school. Teachers and parents can share and communicate information about a child's progress by exchanging written notes, diaries, photographs, and children's work (Helm et al., 1998). Written and photographic documentation—assembled in folders or books or displayed on panels mounted on classroom walls—can serve as an important means of exchange and discussion among teachers, children, and parents (Rinaldi, 1996). Parents can see their child's work directly and can share work from home with the teacher.

MODELS AND APPLICATIONS

A performance assessment approach offers practitioners many options for assessing performance and monitoring progress. Because tasks are usually familiar activities that are part of daily routines, assessment and data collection procedures are easy to implement. The major challenge lies in keeping subjective biases to a minimum when interpreting and evaluating the data. Practitioners are encouraged to draw from scoring criteria, developmental norms, and other quantitative instruments to cross-validate their evaluations.

A variety of performance assessment approaches and methods have been described in the literature. Bond and Dean (1997) used video, audio, photographic recordings, written observations, and archives of drawings to document 4-year-old children's learning during dance sessions, followed by verbal reflections and drawing. Maxim (1997) suggested having children observe, discuss, and document environments (e.g., playground, classroom, neighborhoods) with photographs and maps and to build models of buildings and streets with Legos and blocks. Morrow (1989) described a system for coding children's responses during storybook reading, using a Story Retelling Evaluation Guide Sheet to assign points for the inclusion of diverse elements of story structure. Sulzby (1985) provided levels of categories for evaluating emergent reading of favorite storybooks. For scoring drawings of a person and early writing, a useful source is the Drawing and Writing component of the Developing Skills Checklist (California Testing Bureau, 1990).

Guidry, van den Pol, Keeley, and Neilsen (1996) used videotapes to supplement traditional assessment measures in an inclusive preschool program. Videotapes were made of different activities and for various purposes. For example, videotapes of children's activities during daily classroom routines were recorded for sharing with families; videotapes of children during preplanned periods or activities in which skills targeted on IEPs were likely to occur were recorded for review by the child study team to evaluate progress over time.

Early childhood programs often use a **project approach** to performance assessment and documentation. A project is an in-depth study, conducted over an extended period of time, of particular activities undertaken by small groups of young children (Katz & Chard, 1989). Using checklists, anecdotal notes, and work samples, practitioners carefully and systematically document the skills and concepts that children learn while participating in the project. At the end of the project, the practitioner selects work samples for display. These items should tell the story of the project and reveal children's growth and development over the course of the project (Helm et al., 1998). Within the larger display, the teacher may want to create a minidisplay that provides evidence of an individual child's growth and development.

Helm and colleagues (1998) described a comprehensive authentic assessment approach in an early childhood program in which they used a documentation web to guide the gathering of evidence about children's learning. The web included five types of documentation: 1) **project narratives,** 2) observations of child development, 3) individual portfolios, 4) products (individual or group), and 5) child self-reflections. Project narratives focus on "telling the story" of a learning experience, such as the development of a project through the use of visual displays, stories for and by children, teacher journals, and narratives for parents in the form of books and letters.

Observations of child development focus on documenting children's progress on specific skills and include methods such as checklists and anecdotal notes. Work the child has done (e.g., drawings, writing samples, maps, videotapes of conversations and activities, photographs of block constructions) is collected systematically for individual portfolios. Other products include work that children may have created together in a group, such as a large poster or a book; individual three-dimensional work, such as sculptures and construction; videotapes of musical activities and movement; and recordings of group discussions and conversations during a field trip or other activity. **Self-reflections** are statements children make that reflect their own knowledge and feelings. They can be transcribed by the adult, audiotaped, videotaped, or written by the child.

Performance assessment can be easily linked to the classroom curriculum by designing assessment tasks that incorporate a student's IEP objectives and use a point-based holistic scoring system to evaluate student progress. Day and Skidmore (1996) provided an example of a six-point scoring rubric for evaluating writing samples. Scores are determined according to certain criteria. For example, a score of 6 is defined by the following criteria: well-developed responses, elaborate with specific details, strong organization and sequence, and fluency. The criteria for a score of 1 include very brief responses, few descriptive details, a lack of organizational sequence, and awkwardness.

Fuchs and Fuchs (1996) proposed a model that combines performance assessment with assessment methods that are more well established and have stronger technical qualities, such as curriculum-based measurement (CBM; Deno, 1985), which offers a set of standardized procedures for measuring student progress in basic school curriculum areas. Fuchs and Fuchs's approach requires the identification of a core set of critical skills (e.g., competencies for a group of children based on the yearly curriculum), designing an authentic problem-solving context within which children are required to integrate critical skills, and developing a scoring system that provides information on correct responses, as well as strategies. Children complete the tasks (which may differ, but the critical skills remain the same) at regular intervals throughout the school year. These same skills are also assessed on the CBM. Early childhood special educators can adapt these procedures and use technically sound CBAs such as AEPS (Bricker, 1993a) or the Battelle Developmental Inventory (BDI; Newborg, Stock, Wnek, Guidubaldi, & Svinicki, 1984) in combination with performance assessments. An example of this approach follows:

Lauren was in her last year of preschool, and her parents identified learning pre-academic skills (e.g., recognizing letters and numbers, being able to count, being able to print letters and simple words) as a priority to ensure a successful transition into kindergarten. Based on Lauren's assessment results, the following skills had been identified as IEP goals and objectives: identifies letters, produces phonetic sounds for letters, and identifies printed numerals 1–10. Using the criteria for mastery indicated on the assessment, her teacher, Mr. Morales, planned to monitor Lauren's progress on these skills by recording frequencies of correct and incorrect responses during biweekly probes and graphing them on a chart. Mr. Morales also wanted to monitor and assess types of strategies and errors and generalization of skills across environments and materials. For this he developed a set of authentic performance-based tasks to assess Lauren's ability to apply these skills in real-life, meaningful situations. For example, at circle time, the daily calendar and the morning message offered many opportunities for Lauren to practice identifying letters, sounds, words, and numbers. Taking anecdotal notes would enable Mr. Morales to record Lauren's responses, strategies, and mistakes, as well as her ability to provide explanations, correct her errors, and respond to instruction. Once per week, he would also monitor Lauren's progress in writing letters and her name in her drawing and writing journal.

Fuchs and Fuchs (1996) proposed scoring three aspects in performance assessments: 1) acquisition of the skill according to weekly IEP probes, 2) whether the skill is successfully applied in real-life situations, and 3) the child's strategies. Remember that correct strategies do not always lead to a correct response. For instance, a young child's IEP goal is to put on her coat independently. She places her arms in the sleeves correctly but struggles to close the coat and pull up the zipper because it is not her coat and, thus, is too small. Yet, strategies at different levels of sophistication may all yield a correct response. Two children correctly read the word *dog*. One child recognizes familiar visual features of the word; the other uses a more sophisticated strategy of sounding out each letter phonetically.

Figure 5.5 is an example of a data collection form that includes these three aspects. Children's performance can also be quantified by using scoring systems which assign points for different levels of performance mea-

Performance Assessment: Data Collection and Scoring Form

Child's name: _Lauren_

IEP/IFSP objectives: _Identifies letters_
Produces phonetic sound for letters
Identifies printed numerals 1–10

Date: _1/27/00–2/1/00_

Objectives/skills	Correct responses	Performance environment	Performance/generalization responses	Performance/generalization strategies	Scores/responses/strategies
Identifies letters	3/3	Morning message	L in "ladybug" B in "bird" and "ladybug"	Said: "That's in my name."	5
Produces phonetic sound for letters	1/2	Morning message	/b/ for d in "dog" /t/ for t in "tiger"	Said: "B, that's /b/ /b/ /b/." "T for tiger."	2
Identifies printed numerals 1–10	3/3	Calendar	Identified 1, 2, and 9	Identified 1 and 2 immediately. Counted 1–8 before identifying 9.	4

Scoring system:
0 = Incorrect response/incorrect strategy
1 = Incorrect response/viable strategy
2 = Correct response/incorrect strategy
3 = Correct response/viable strategy in a contrived environment
4 = Correct response/viable strategy in a few environments
5 = Correct response/viable strategy generalized across environments

Figure 5.5. Performance assessment IEP/IFSP data collection and scoring form for an individual child.

sured along each of the three dimensions (skill mastery, generalization, and strategies).

ADVANTAGES AND LIMITATIONS

Performance assessment is an ideal approach for assessing children's abilities and skills in real-life tasks and situations. The focus of the assessment is usually on general skills and strategies that the child applies across tasks, materials, and contexts. Tasks and materials can vary to accommodate cultural diversity and individual developmental levels. Qualitative, descriptive data collection methods and actual work samples allow for a comprehensive, authentic assessment of the child's abilities.

Advantages

The major advantage of conducting a performance assessment is that it focuses on a child's strengths, takes place in a meaningful context, allows for collaboration and communication between professionals and families, and involves nonintrusive data collection. These characteristics are discussed in detail next.

Focus on Strengths

Performance assessment focuses on what a child can do. It provides in-depth information on various aspects of performance, including types of strategies and errors, enabling the teacher to better understand reasons and motives for behaviors. This is especially useful for adjusting teaching to meet the individual needs of a child who may be experiencing difficulties.

Meaningful Context

Performance assessment provides information on complex behaviors and gives a broad picture of the child's abilities. Performance assessment fits well with activity-based approaches that do not lend themselves as well to task analysis and quantification. Samples of children's works (e.g., drawings, photographs of block constructions) are a direct and accurate reflection of what a child actually did. Qualitative descriptions of behaviors that are difficult to quantify (e.g., emotional affective aspects) provide valuable documentation of important dimensions that are often neglected in traditional assessments.

Collaboration and Communication

Because multiple individuals are involved in the collection of data, collaboration and communication among team members are necessary. The collection of data can be coordinated across environments. Language skills can be assessed in the classroom, at home, on the school bus, and on the playground by teachers, specialists, paraprofessionals, and family members. Discussing data during team meetings provides a more accurate and comprehensive picture of the child's functioning. Children may perform differently in different environments and with different people. Various professionals may bring various insights to understanding a particular behavior. Data can be shared easily among professionals and families. Using actual work samples and qualitative descriptions makes it easier for nonprofessionals to participate in the assessment process. Parents can send in drawings that children made at home, photographs and written observations of new behaviors, and lists of new words.

Nonintrusive Data Collection

Performance assessment relies on nonintrusive data collection methods because tasks are part of everyday school and life experience. Language and literacy skills are not necessarily a requirement for this type of assessment. Videotapes, photographs, and drawings, for example, may be especially useful when working with families who are not fluent in English.

Limitations

One particular limitation of performance assessment is the lack of standards for scoring. Other limitations include the high level of expertise, planning time, and resources required to conduct this type of assessment. The following sections further explore these issues.

Lack of Standards

Although flexibility is a major advantage of performance assessment, the lack of standardization and evaluation criteria is a concern. A lack of set criteria and standards for judging performance makes monitoring progress on children's IEP goals and objectives difficult (Fuchs & Fuchs, 1996). Typically, objectives on an IEP need to be both observable and measurable (Notari-Syverson & Shuster, 1995). Performance measures attempt to capture real-life situations involving rich complex tasks and the integration of multiple skills that are not easily quantifiable. Thus, it is recommended that performance assessments be used in combination with other methods that offer stronger psychometric assurances.

High Level of Expertise Required

Performance assessment requires major participation on the part of the practitioner. Practitioners must develop tasks, select documentation methods, and determine criteria for evaluating performance. Therefore, it is important that the practitioner be familiar with child development and assessment and curriculum practices. The practitioner must also be comfortable with the subjective and self-reflective nature of the process.

Required Planning Time and Resources

As noted previously, set scoring procedures do not exist for performance assessment. Therefore, practitioners may need to develop specific scoring criteria for each type of performance assessment. Anecdotal notes, children's work samples, and videotaping require time and resources for implementation and analysis. Financial resources also may be necessary for certain types of documentation (e.g., film, film development).

GUIDELINES FOR IMPLEMENTATION

It is best to begin slowly when using a performance-based approach. Focus on one area, one IEP goal, or one activity or environment. Identify developmental goals and appropriate documentation (e.g., transcriptions, work products). Helm and colleagues (1998), for example, suggested designing a documentation web to illustrate which types of documentation will be used for recording and assessing various types of behaviors.

The documentation must be adjusted to match the needs of the individual child and family. Different types of performance methods can be used (e.g., anecdotal notes, checklists, photographs). When recording anecdotal notes, the practitioner should describe specific events and report rather than evaluate or interpret. Information on both processes and outcomes should be collected.

The interpretation and analysis of data may require a considerable amount of time. Attention to detail is important. The practitioner must avoid preconceived ideas and jumping to conclusions. This point is shown in the following vignette:

Four-year-old Rosa rarely followed her teacher's directions. As a result, her teacher, Mr. Binek, suspected that Rosa had a behavior disorder. Yet, Rosa's mother was able to spend a few hours volunteering in the classroom one day, and Mr. Binek noticed that Rosa responded well to her mother's directions. These consisted mostly of simple, direct commands (e.g., "Pick it up!" "Share the play-dough!"). Mr. Binek realized he had been using more complex, indirect forms (e.g., "Could you please pick up the crayon?" "Would you mind sharing the play-dough?"), which perhaps Rosa had difficulty following due to a language comprehension disorder.

The practitioner must relate the observations to other information about the child, then generate hypotheses for further observations. Time must be set aside to meet with other members of the team. Because of the dangers of subjective biases, it is important to validate perceptions of the child's learning with other staff and the child's family. Before concluding that a child is not able to perform a task, it is important to make sure the child understands the directions and is familiar with the assessment situation and materials. The next vignette illustrates this concept:

Five-year-old Sami was having difficulty cutting shapes, so it originally appeared that he had a fine motor problem. Yet, the occupational therapist, Ms. Allen, remembered seeing Sami adeptly button up his coat—a skill that requires two-hand coordination similar to cutting with scissors. Therefore, it was possible that Sami had no experience using scissors. Ms. Allen revised her assessment plan to include observations of other skills involving two-hand coordination: using food utensils during snack time and dressing and undressing at toileting and before and after recess. She also decided to gather additional information from Sami's teacher and parents.

Performance assessment takes time. It is important to begin by collecting documents for a specific purpose (e.g., monitoring one IEP goal, observing a child's behavior in a particular activity) and to develop a plan that indicates the types of data to collect, by whom, during which activities, and in which environments. Dates and times for team meetings should also be determined in advance. Table 5.1 is a summary of guidelines for implementing performance assessment.

SUGGESTIONS FOR PRACTITIONERS IN INCLUSIVE ENVIRONMENTS

Early childhood and early intervention/early childhood special education staff can easily use performance assessments to document the work and progress of children functioning at diverse developmental levels. Many types of per-

Table 5.1.   Guidelines for implementing performance assessment

Start slowly.
    Focus on one area, one IEP goal, or one activity or environment.
    Identify developmental goals and appropriate documentation.

Adjust documentation to match the needs of the individual child and family.
    Use different types of performance methods:
        Anecdotal notes (Post-It notes, small note pads in pocket)
        Children's work and products
        Checklists
        Photographs
        Recordings
    When recording anecdotal notes, describe specific events and report rather than evaluate or interpret.
    Collect information on both processes and outcomes.

Be prepared for the interpretation and analysis of the data to take a considerable amount of time.
    Avoid preconceived ideas and "jumping to conclusions."
    Pay attention to details.
    Relate the observations to other information about the child.
    Generate hypotheses for further observations.

Set aside time to meet with team.
    Because of the dangers of subjective biases, it is important to validate perceptions of the child's learning with other staff and the child's family.

formance assessment are nonintrusive and use data that are easy to collect during everyday classroom activities, even by nonprofessional personnel.

Initial Assessment

Similar to naturalistic and focused assessment approaches, a CBA can be used to identify the child's strengths and areas of concern prior to conducting a performance assessment. The practitioner and the caregiver need to determine the types of documentation that are most appropriate for a particular child and family. A documentation web can be used to illustrate what type of documentation will be used to assess which behaviors.

Goal Development

Based on the results of the CBA and caregiver input, goals and objectives may be identified. The agreed-on types of documentation for monitoring progress toward target goals and objectives should be recorded on the IEP/IFSP data sheet. Evaluation criteria will also need to be jointly selected and developed.

Intervention

When using performance assessment, real-life tasks are most appropriate for practicing target skills and gathering documentation. Gross motor skills, for example, are best observed during outside play or at arrival and departure time while children are getting on and off the school bus. Documentation should be collected across environments by various members of the team. The materials used should be familiar and available to children in typical activities. For instance, small cereals and beans, rather than pellets, can be used to assess fine motor skills. Picture books, magazines, and posters can be used in place of flashcards to assess vocabulary.

Evaluation

Record progress on children's skills and their strategies for accomplishing tasks. Practitioners should attend to children's error patterns and the effectiveness of various types of supports for particular tasks and situations. The data should be reviewed on a regular basis, and modifications of the instructional program should be made if progress does not meet the team's expectations. Ideally, evaluation should take place at the beginning, middle, and end of the school year, as conducting assessment at least three times provides a more accurate picture compared with only pretesting and post-testing at the beginning and end of the school year.

Performance-based assessments are best used in combination with CBAs. CBAs provide direct information on a child's strengths and needs that can help the IEP team and family members identify specific areas and skills for the development of IEP goals. Performance-based assessments are

Table 5.2. Suggestions for practitioners using performance assessment in inclusive environments

Initial assessment

A curriculum-based assessment (CBA) can be used initially to identify the child's strengths and areas of concern.

Goal development

Identify goals and objectives based upon the results of the CBA and parent input.

Identify which types of documentation will be used for each goal and objective and criteria for evaluation.

Intervention

Determine real-life tasks that are most appropriate for practicing targeted skills and gathering documentation.

Evaluation

Evaluate progress on skills but also on strategies, errors, and the effectiveness of various types of supports for a particular child, task, and situation.

Review data on a regular basis during team meetings.

Modify instructional program if progress does not meet expectations.

Conduct comprehensive assessments at the beginning, middle, and end of the school year.

most appropriate for the intervention and evaluation phases, providing comprehensive and diverse types of documentation that represent the child's work and progress over time. Table 5.2 summarizes suggestions for practitioners using performance assessments in inclusive environments.

CONCLUSION

Performance assessment expands the traditional view of assessment by using children's actual work, completed in real-life tasks and natural environments, as the basis for documenting their skill levels and abilities. In performance assessment, behaviors are not to be broken down into smaller components; rather, multiple methods of collecting data are used—including anecdotal notes, work samples, and videotapes—that allow for documentation of holistic, complex behaviors.

Performance assessment is ideal for sharing information among team members and with families. Work samples and notes are a relatively straightforward means of communication. Photographs, drawings, work samples, and videotapes are particularly useful when working with families who have low literacy skills or who are not fluent in English.

Performance assessment focuses on optimizing conditions for children to demonstrate their skills and abilities. When selecting assessment tasks and materials, it is important to consider their cultural relevance, as well as the child's familiarity with them. Multiple tasks and observations across contexts and people are needed to keep the risk of subjectivity to a minimum. Practitioners can compensate for the lack of standardization by developing specific evaluation criteria or by combining performance assessment with more traditional psychometrically validated tools.

Review Questions

■ Discuss the rationale for using performance assessment methods.

■ How do underlying theoretical perspectives and assumptions influence performance assessment methods and procedures?

■ What are four salient characteristics of performance assessment?

■ Describe and provide examples of each of the five types of documentation used in comprehensive performance-based assessment.

Portfolio Assessment

6

After reading this chapter, you will be able to:

- Define portfolio assessment, and discuss the rationale for its use

- Give examples of models and methods that fit into a portfolio assessment framework

- Identify considerations and guidelines for implementing portfolio assessment

*M*s. Lee was pleased with the end-of-year meeting. All of the team members believed that they had been able to get a clear picture of 4-year-old Robbie's accomplishments during the school year. They had seen samples of Robbie's drawings and writings and photographs of his block constructions. Ms. Cowan, the speech-language pathologist, had shown some videotapes of her sessions with him. His parents had sent lists of books they had read at home during the school year, as well as lists of new words he had learned in both Spanish and English during their nightly storybook readings. During the meeting, Ms. Lee, Ms. Cowan, and Mr. Jensen, the occupational therapist, had shared their notes and lists of new words they had heard Robbie say. It was interesting to compare the similarities and differences and to see which words he was using in Spanish and which words he was using in English. Being able to share documents had helped team members better communicate, clarify some conflicting opinions, and understand that Robbie reacted differently with different people and in different environments. Throughout the school year, team members had placed copies of their documentation in a file that Ms. Lee had prepared specifically for Robbie. With Robbie and his parents, Ms. Lee now planned to select pieces that best represented Robbie's work and progress. These would be placed in a "pass-along portfolio" that would be given to Robbie's kindergarten teacher for the next school year. Although it had taken time and effort to coordinate the data collection process, everyone agreed that the result was an accurate and meaningful portrait of Robbie's abilities and accomplishments.

Ms. Lee also noticed how proud his parents were when they looked at the notebook that documented what Robbie had done during the year. Robbie also loved to look at his special book, especially the photographs. Ms. Lee remembered how Robbie had insisted on having a picture taken of his last Lego construction to place in his "special book."

During the initial IEP meeting at the beginning of the school year, Robbie's parents and the team had agreed that language was a concern. At 4 years old, Robbie spoke about the same amount of words, both in English and in Spanish, as his 2-year-old brother. He was also having difficulties with fine motor movements. He could stack only a few blocks and had trouble using scissors, holding a pencil, and turning the pages of a magazine or book. His drawings consisted mostly of scribbles. Standardized test results confirmed these concerns.

Because Robbie was learning two languages, it was important to monitor his progress in school and at home. His mother, Ms. Morales, was eager to be involved. The team decided that she would look at picture books at bedtime, an activity in which Robbie's younger brother could also participate. Talking about the pictures in the books would facilitate Robbie's language, while manipulating the book and turning pages would be good for practicing fine motor skills. Robbie's mother already had both Spanish and English books at home, and she could easily get more from the school and the public library. Ms. Lee also gave Ms. Morales a blank notebook for Robbie to use at home for drawing pictures. This activity, along with discussing the drawings with his mother, would allow Robbie to practice his fine motor and language skills.

Based on the CBA test results, Robbie's parents and the team identified specific goals and objectives for language and fine motor development with performance criteria. They also drafted a plan for how to assess and monitor progress on IEP objectives during routine daily activities in the classroom and at home. Figure 6.1 is an example of their document collection planning sheet.

Using an activity-based intervention approach (Bricker, 1998), staff would record and graph frequencies of behaviors, transcribe verbalizations, and collect drawings and other artwork that involves cutting and pasting and holding a brush or crayons. In the course of his occupational therapy work with Robbie, Mr. Jensen also volunteered to make sketches or take photographs of block constructions, and Ms. Cowan would videotape her speech-language pathology sessions with Robbie at least three times during the school year. Robbie's mother would keep a list of books that Robbie read and write down new words in Spanish and English that Robbie said during picture book readings and at other times as well. She would also make sure to set aside a time, at least weekly, for Robbie to draw in his notebook and talk about his drawings. Ms. Lee suggested that Ms. Morales also write down exactly what Robbie said about his drawings.

Classroom staff would collect frequency data and anecdotal notes on IEP objectives twice per week. Drawings, artwork, and photographs would be placed in Robbie's cubby, and once per month, Robbie would review the work with the staff and select representative samples for his portfolio. Robbie's mother liked the speech-language pathologist's forms for recording words that Robbie said during their daily storybook readings. As she accompanied Robbie to school in the morning, she could bring her documentation to school at the end of each week, along with other items such as drawings or photographs that she and Robbie decided should be in the portfolio. On a quarterly basis, the team and Robbie's family would review progress toward goals and summarize observations on a progress review form, as shown in Figure 6.2.

The purpose of the portfolio was to provide coherent and comprehensive documentation of his progress in the two areas targeted in Robbie's IEP: language and fine motor skills. Because these skills were likely to occur simultaneously during the same activity (e.g., talking while drawing or cutting), the team decided to organize the portfolio by type of documentation rather than by domain area or IEP goal. There would be a section for drawings and artwork, photographs of constructions, anecdotal notes and written transcriptions, IEP frequency data and charts, checklists, and standardized test results. Each document would be dated and contain brief information on the environment (e.g., home, classroom, playground) and other environmental factors (e.g., adults and children present). Figure 6.3 is an example of the team's portfolio description of content for monitoring Robbie's progress on early language and literacy development.

Performance criteria would be used to evaluate the IEP goals. Ms. Cowan would meet with the teaching staff informally at least once per month to discuss progress on the language goals, and Mr. Jensen would provide input on the fine motor goals once per month. Robbie's parents and the team agreed to meet formally in February and in June to review the portfolio and summarize data in a narrative form. Figure 6.4 shows the team's portfolio summary review form.

Portfolio Assessment: Document Collection Plan

Child's name: Robbie   Date: 1/5/00

Team members: Ms. Lee (teacher), Ms. Cowan (SLP), Mr. Jensen (OT), Ms. Kane (TA), Mr. and Ms. Morales (parents)

Behaviors	Documents	Who	Where	When/how often
Two-word utterances (agent–action, action–object, agent–object)	Anecdotal notes	Teacher, TA	Classroom	Snack and free play 3 times per week each
	Dictations	SLP	Classroom/therapy room	Picture book reading 1 time per week
	Videotapes	SLP	Therapy room	1 time every 3 months
	Frequency data	Teacher	Classroom	Small group 1 time per week
	Anecdotal notes— parent report	Parents	Home	Picture book reading 1 time per week
Drawing recognizable figures	Work samples (drawings, paintings, photographs)	Teacher, TA, OT	Classroom	Art activities 1 time per week
	Anecdotal notes	Parents	Home	1 time per month
	Anecdotal notes	Teacher, TA, OT	Classroom	1 time per month

Figure 6.1. Data collection planning sheet for an individual child. (Key: SLP = speech-language pathologist; OT = occupational therapist; TA = teaching assistant)

Portfolio Assessment: Progress Review Form

Child's name: _Robbie_

IEP goal: _Robbie will use two-word utterances_

Portfolio review date: _2/11/00_ Criteria: _By May 30, Robbie will use 10 different two-word utterances to express agent–action, action–object, and agent–object (in Spanish and/or English)._

Documentation	Evaluations
Anecdotal notes	Robbie is beginning to use two-word utterances (e.g., "Me toys," "Want juice"), mostly following adult or peer model. Two spontaneous utterances noted: "Me jump" (1/26); "Truck go" (2/3)
Dictations	Following completion of a six-piece dinosaur puzzle, dictated, "Little dinosaur, big dinosaur—walking. He eat" (2/5).
Frequency data	Gradual upward trend beginning week of 1/20
Parent notes	Uses Spanish at home—mother reported Robbie saying, "Mira gato" (1/15) and "Esto frog" (1/29)
Checklists	See initial AEPS assessment. (4/17)
Standardized tests	See initial assessment. (4/8)
Audiotapes/videotapes	SLP videotape of individual session (1/30)—reading of "The Snowy Day." Said: "Snow melt." "He footprints." "Walk snow." "Boy, coat."

Figure 6.2. Progress review form for an individual child.

Portfolio Assessment: Description of Content

Child's name: _Robbie_

Period/dates: _9/1/99–5/30/00_

Purpose: _Monitor progress on early language and literacy development_

Goals/criteria:

1. _Robbie will use 10 different two-word utterances to express agent–action, action–object, and agent–object._

2. _Robbie will draw five different recognizable figures._

Types of documentation:

1. _Anecdotal notes, dictations, frequency data/charts, parent notes, AEPS checklist, PLS initial assessment results, videotape of individual speech-language therapy session_

2. _Drawings, paintings, photographs, and anecdotal notes from school and home_

Figure 6.3.   Portfolio description of content for an individual child.

Portfolio Assessment: Summary Review

Child's name: Robbie   Age: 4:10   Date: 6/2/00   Reviewer(s): D.L., A.C., L.F.

Area/objectives: Language—Robbie will use 10 different two-word utterances to express agent–action, action–object, and agent–object.

Strengths/progress	Exemplary documents	Needs/recommendations
Robbie is eager to communicate. He initiates and responds appropriately to verbal interactions with adults and peers. In September 1999, he was using a variety of one-word utterances in English and Spanish.	Anecdotal notes (4/15; 5/1; 5/5)	Still needs help and support to continue to develop his expressive language skills. Benefits from exposure to adult and peer modeling, especially during picture book reading.
Currently, he is consistently using two-word utterances to express agent–action, action–object, and agent–object.	Graphs (4/15–5/30)	
He uses mostly English at school and Spanish at home.	Parent report (4/11; 4/30; 5/17)	
Occasionally, he switches codes. He appeared to learn new words the easiest by imitating adult or peer models.	Anecdotal notes (3/12; 3/30; 4/15)	
His comprehension is age-appropriate.	PLS (4/30)	

Figure 6.4. Portfolio summary review form for an individual child.

Assessment portfolios are one of the most promising and innovative approaches to assessment. Arter and Spandel (1991) defined **portfolio** as a *purposeful* collection of a child's work that can be used to *document* the child's efforts, progress, and achievements *over time*. Diverse types of behaviors and actual samples of work across different environments are collected to document and show what a child can do in a variety of situations and contexts. The portfolio is a powerful means to facilitate communication among different professionals and with parents, and it provides coherent documentation of a child's progress over time. Portfolios often demonstrate to parents child skills of which they were unaware and teach parents how to interpret their children's work (Meisels, 1993; Neuman & Roskos, 1993). Photographs and videotapes of children during school activities may show parents child behaviors that do not occur at home. A child may, for example, eat independently at school but expect to be fed by his mother at home. Children's work samples are also powerful communication and educational tools. Sharing samples of children's pretend writing, for instance, is an excellent opportunity to show parents that their child is not just scribbling.

Portfolios are open-ended and flexible (LaBoskey, 2000). The content of the portfolio depends on educational goals and purposes and can include a variety of children's work as well as teacher and parent observations. Examples of children's items include performance-based samples such as artwork, picture journals, dictations, audiotaped conversations and songs, photographs of science projects, playdough manipulations, or Lego constructions. Videotapes can also be used to supplement paper-based records (Guidry et al., 1996). Although the portfolio consists mostly of children's work, it can also contain parent reports and records of systematic observations by teachers, including graphs, charts, anecdotal observations, and checklists. Test results from CBAs and standardized assessments are also included in the portfolio.

No specific rules dictate a portfolio's appearance. Basically, a portfolio is simply a container for carrying documents (LaBoskey, 2000). One can use ring notebooks, file boxes, expandable file holders, laser disks, or computers files. A portfolio should be well organized, however, so that relevant materials can be located with minimal effort. Depending on the purpose of the assessment, the portfolio can be divided into different sections according to IEP goals, types of documents (e.g., photographs, drawings, anecdotal notes, test results), developmental or curriculum areas, sources of information (e.g., teachers, specialists, family), or contexts (e.g., classroom, home, community).

THEORETICAL FRAMEWORK

Portfolio assessment approaches share the basic tenets of ecological and social-constructivist views of child development. They emphasize the importance of assessments based on a comprehensive picture of a child's performance across environments, as well as the child's active involvement in the evaluation process.

Ecological Approach

Bronfenbrenner's (1979) theory of human ecology stresses that the inter-connections between environments (e.g., the connection between home and school) influence what actually takes place within an environment (e.g., a child's learning in school). Portfolio assessment is a means to provide a comprehensive view of the child's performance across a variety of situations and environments. It recognizes that a person's behavior is influenced by a broad variety of contextual factors and that the assessment process must use several methods to obtain information from diverse sources on the child's behaviors across multiple environments. Although it may also include information on performance in contrived situations (e.g., standardized tests), it is primarily a type of performance assessment that documents a child's functioning in authentic, meaningful tasks that are part of daily routines.

Social-Constructivist Approach

Children learn best when they are actively engaged in meaningful interactions with people and objects. Traditional assessment does not account for all of the creative things children do. Portfolio assessment recognizes children's active participation in the construction of their own knowledge and the effects of social context on learning. It is both child-originated and adult-guided. The adult structures and suggests but also involves the child in the selection and evaluation of content and performance. This process provides information not only on what the child is doing but also on the how and why. Portfolios provide documentation of children's learning processes and their ways of constructing knowledge, including their mistakes. Portfolios should also contain information on dynamic aspects of learning and learning potential, such as the effect of diverse teaching strategies on improving children's performance (e.g., drawing from a model versus from memory). Portfolios focus on what the child brings to the learning situation in addition to what the learning situation brings to the child (Meisels, 1993). Furthermore, by collecting children's work, adults communicate to children that what children do is important (Helm, Beneke, & Steinheimer, 1997).

MODELS AND APPLICATIONS

A portfolio is not just a collection of a child's work. It is an assessment tool to be used for a purpose; it requires clear process and evaluation criteria and the child's active involvement. The broad purpose of portfolio assessment is to document a child's progress using authentic products and descriptions of behavior in real-life contexts. Specific purposes are individualized to meet the child's and family's needs (e.g., monitoring the child's progress on IEP objectives, communicating with parents). Another important aspect of portfolio assessment is that the child participates in the selection and evaluation of the content (Cohen & Spenciner, 1994). This helps the child develop self-evaluation skills and other cognitive abilities, such as making decisions and providing explanations. The child's active involvement also strengthens the dynamic interactive nature of the portfolio assessment process and enables a more in-depth understanding of the child's performance. It may foster the child's interests, thereby bringing out the best of his or her abilities.

Criteria for Selecting and Evaluating Content

Portfolio assessment requires clear criteria for selecting and evaluating the content. The type of information collected should reflect the overall program curriculum and the child's individual goals and objectives (Nolet, 1992). If children have an IEP in place, the selection of items for the portfolio should be based on the IEP (Wesson & King, 1996).

Specific criteria for evaluating the child's performance should be determined by the professionals and parents and possibly the child as well. Criteria can be drawn from various sources and methods to evaluate a child's progress and can include teacher-made tests, criterion-referenced tests, and standardized tests. To counteract possible reliability and bias problems, it is important to use multiple and diverse methods, with various types of documentation of the child's work across different environments (Gelfer & Perkins, 1998).

The overall portfolio can be evaluated using different narrative or numerical methods (Cohen & Spenciner, 1994). An optimal approach is to review the contents with other professionals, the parents, and the child. Then summarize the child's strengths and needs and formulate recommendations in a written evaluative narrative. Another approach is to use rating scales with numerical scores that reflect the teacher's impression of the child's progress on specific goals and objectives or other areas. Figure 6.5 is an example of a portfolio progress rating scale.

A number of approaches are available for evaluating children's progress in specific areas. Hanline and Fox (1994) described scoring scales for observations of block constructions, art products, and play behaviors. With the block construction, for example, a 19-point scale is used to score the following behaviors: 1) no construction to linear construction, 2) bidimensional and tridimensional construction, and 3) symbolic representations of objects using blocks. The Drawing and Writing component of the Developing Skills Checklist (California Testing Bureau, 1990) is helpful for scoring drawings of people and early writing. Sulzby (1985) provided levels of categories for evaluating emergent reading of favorite storybooks. Teams can also develop their own scoring systems. A good resource for cognitive, social, motor, and self-care domains are the observation guidelines and worksheets in the revised edition of *Transdisciplinary Play-Based Assessment (TPBA): A Functional Approach to Working with Young Children* (Linder, 1993). Neuman and Roskos (1993) and Notari-Syverson and colleagues (1998) offered guidelines for early literacy and language.

The Work Sampling System (WSS; Meisels, Jablon, Marsden, Dichtenmiller, & Dorfman, 1994) provides a comprehensive evaluation and documentation approach in seven domains (including language and literacy, scientific thinking, and art and music) for children in preschool through fifth grade. The WSS includes developmental guidelines and checklists, portfolios, and summary reports. Data from multiple sources are collected three

Portfolio Assessment: Progress Rating Scale

Child's name: _Robbie_ Reviewers: _D.L., A.C., L.K._ Date: _6/5/00_

Date	Behavior/objective	Criteria	Evaluation and comments					
			0	1	2	3	4	5
	Two-word utterances	10 different utterances to express agent–action, action–object, agent–object						
2/1/00					Some two-word utterances, but mostly following peer/adult model.			
6/1/00								Consistently uses two-word utterances in school and at home (English and Spanish).

Scoring system:
0 = No change
1 = Some improvement
2 = Significant improvement but still needs help
3 = Significant improvement
4 = Meets criteria with help
5 = Meets criteria independently

Figure 6.5. Portfolio progress rating scale for an individual child.

times per year (fall, winter, and spring), and parents are involved in the assessment through conferences based on review of the portfolio, checklists, and summary reports. The checklists provide an individualized profile of children's progress based on teacher observation and include reference to well-recognized criteria and expectations. The portfolio section allows for documenting qualitative aspects of children's work. It consists of children's work samples and includes two types of work: 1) core items (e.g., record of language use, records of problem-solving skills) for all children and 2) individualized items (e.g., IEP goals). The summary report contains specific criteria for evaluating children's performance and progress in each domain based on data from the checklist and portfolio. The WSS has been successfully implemented in a variety of early childhood programs (e.g., Helm et al., 1998) and has strong to moderate internal and interexaminer reliability and predictive validity (Meisels, Liaw, Dorfman, & Nelson, 1995).

Portfolio systems of assessment are particularly meaningful for children with significant disabilities, for whom traditional assessments are inappropriate. Kentucky implemented a statewide inclusive assessment and accountability system that includes writing portfolios; on-demand, open-response performance tasks; and traditional, standardized achievement tests (Kearns, Kleinert, Clayton, Burdge, & Williams, 1998). Kearns, Kleinert, and Kennedy (1999) described an alternative portfolio approach that enables students with significant disabilities to participate in the assessment program. Specific standards are available for evaluating the portfolios along five dimensions:

1. Performance of targeted skills within the context of academic expectations

2. Appropriate supports that lead to independence

3. Generalization of skills to multiple environments

4. Social interactions with peers

5. Participation in the portfolio content selection and evaluation

Based on specific scoring criteria that are similar to those used for typical portfolio assessments, each dimension is rated using a single score of "novice," "apprentice," "proficient," or "distinguished."

Child Participation

Regularly scheduled portfolio review conferences are an important part of the portfolio assessment process (Gelfer & Perkins, 1998). These conferences should include both children and team members. When children review their work, they are able to remember, rediscover, and communicate their accomplishments (Rinaldi, 1996). They also learn important self-evaluation skills. Young children may require assistance understanding that they can participate in developing their portfolios and evaluating their work (Helm et al., 1998). Adults need to actively teach children the skills needed to document their own learning and assist them in selecting samples to place in their portfolios and evaluating their work. Young children can participate in this process in various ways (Neuman & Roskos, 1993).

They can choose favorite works to include in the portfolio. They can also say why they like or dislike a piece and what they may have learned from doing the work (Paratore, 1995). Adults can facilitate this process by asking the following questions:

- "Which drawing did you like best?"

- "Which book was the easiest (or the hardest) for you to read? Why?"

- "What did you learn about the most?"

- "What do you need help with?"

Children can also participate by completing self-evaluations that are either handwritten or dictated. See Figure 6.6 for an example of a child self-evaluation form.

ADVANTAGES AND LIMITATIONS

Portfolios are an integral part of educational practices. Gathering information and placing documentation in children's files should become a systematic activity for teachers and practitioners. The open-ended nature of the portfolio allows for different documentation formats—including work samples, photographs, and other visual media—that can be powerful communication tools for sharing information with families and colleagues.

Advantages

Notable advantages to using portfolio assessment include a link to classroom curriculum, continuity across environments and over time, flexibility and individualization, and child participation. These aspects are explored in the following sections.

Link to Classroom Curriculum

The portfolio reflects a child's work and performance during regular classroom routines. This enables the documentation of actual progress on curriculum goals and objectives. Products that are connected to curriculum work progress have the added bonus of being meaningful to the children and parents.

Continuity Across Environments and Over Time

Portfolios help teachers remember and share information with other colleagues and caregivers. Permanently visible products—such as drawings, paintings, and photographs—can serve as a communication tool among family members, school staff, and team members. Products can be added to a book or folder over a long period of time, and selected pieces can be placed into a pass-along portfolio (Jervis, 1996) that children can take from preschool to kindergarten to grade school. In addition, portfolio assessment may be more sensitive to changes over time and to small amounts of progress on functional tasks and activities.

Portfolio Assessment: Child Self-Evaluation

Child's name: _Tim_   Date: _4/26/00_

What I liked best and why:

> I liked when we played restaurant with Amy. She's my best friend. I was the cook. I was cooking pizza and new potatoes.

What I liked the least and why:

> Telling a story. That's a lot of words and sentences to tell someone.

What I learned:

> That's my picture of Abiyoyo. I learned a lot about Africa.

What was difficult and why:

> It was hard to draw the caterpillar and the butterfly. I got the colors mixed up. I colored the butterfly green.

What I want to learn to do better and how:

> I want to write my name. You can show me, then I can copy.

Figure 6.6. Self-evaluation form for an individual child.

Flexibility and Individualization

The selection of portfolio content and the criteria for evaluation are determined for each child and context. Multiple ways of documenting the child's work allows for a multimethod and multidimensional approach. In turn, this provides a comprehensive picture of the child's functioning, as well as a choice of ways to gather and communicate information that is culturally sensitive.

Child Participation

As noted previously, portfolio assessment encourages child participation. Children help select the materials that compose the portfolio. This promotes self-confidence and mastery by communicating to the child that his or her work is valuable. Involving the child in self-evaluation also promotes communication, problem-solving, and metacognitive skills.

Limitations

Extensive planning and coordination, reduced efficiency, storage issues, the lack of standardized evaluation criteria, and the need for an experienced and qualified team are all limitations of portfolio assessment. Each of these characteristics is discussed next.

Required Planning Time and Coordination

A portfolio assessment approach requires team members to plan ahead and coordinate documentation procedures and evaluation criteria. It involves regular meetings—some among the team members, others also including school staff and parents—to review documentation and monitor and evaluate progress.

Reduced Efficiency

Portfolio assessment is not as efficient as standardized assessment approaches. It requires team members to spend time recording observations, gathering documentation, and managing and organizing records. Additional time is required to properly evaluate children's work samples.

Storage Issues

Storage problems may arise when children's work samples are bulky, numerous, or fragile. In addition, if more than one child per class has a portfolio, a space dedicated to portfolio storage is required. The portfolios should be located in a specific area of the classroom, preferably one that is secure yet easily accessible to staff, children, and family members.

Evaluation Criteria

The nature of portfolio assessment does not allow for standardized evaluation criteria. Specific guidelines and expectations for evaluating children's work need to be developed on an individual basis by practitioners and caregivers. Clear procedures are important because they help team members avoid bias. Another way to increase reliability is to use multiple evaluation methods. Team members also must collect documentation systematically and engage in discussion with colleagues to monitor the portfolio assessment process (Helm et al., 1998).

Experienced and Qualified Team Required

When using a portfolio assessment approach, a strong background in child development is imperative. Understanding the benchmarks of child development is fundamental to evaluating children's work samples. Only those in the field are likely to have access to child development literature, which includes information on developmental ages and sequences of skills, and a background regarding existing normed and curriculum-based assessment tools.

GUIDELINES FOR IMPLEMENTATION

Portfolios should be started at the beginning of the school year. Caregivers and other team members must identify in advance the purpose of the portfolio, as well as expectations for the child's work. Children should be told the purpose of their portfolios. This can be done in simple terms: "This is your own special book (or box or file) where we can save some of your favorite schoolwork. Later, we can look at them and show them to your parents, friends, and other teachers and talk about all the new things you have learned." Or, "This will help us look at all the new words you learn at school."

The type of documentation for children's goals and the criteria for evaluating children's work should be discussed and agreed on by all team members, particularly for behaviors that are likely to occur across contexts and activities. The SLP, for example, may propose a common format for all team members to use when recording a child's communicative gestures and oral language. Then a plan must be developed for collecting documentation, including when and how data will be obtained and by whom. Practitioners should promptly date all work samples. Practitioners should also create a caption statement for each item included in the portfolio. Caption statements consist of short, written comments that describe the context in which the item was developed and the reasons that the practitioner or the student included the piece in the portfolio (Salend, 1995). Finally, it is important to identify the team members who will evaluate the portfolio and develop strategies to involve the child and family in work selection and evaluation. (Figures 6.7 and 6.8 contain examples of reporting forms for parents to use at home.) If necessary, teach children the skills that they will need to participate in this process.

Once these matters have been established, content, organization, and ownership issues must be addressed. The portfolio contents should be representative of children's work, growth, and accomplishments. (Practitioners may find it necessary to explain to caregivers and children the reasons for selecting particular samples.) Portfolios may then be organized by

- Content areas (e.g., art activities; language and literacy; motor, social, cognitive/academic skills)

Portfolio Assessment: My Child Learning to Talk

Child's name: _Simona_   Parent's name: _Rita_

My child learned to say a new word or sentence!

What: _Asked a lot of questions: "What does this say?"_

"Where did you buy that, Mommy?"

With whom: _Me_

Where: _Home_

When: _Looking at books, breakfast time_

My child said something funny!

What: _"Frosty wants some Chinese food."_

With whom: _Her brother_

Where: _Bedroom_

When: _Playing restaurant_

My child said something that surprised me!

What: _"Pay attention to me, Mommy."_

With whom: _Me_

Where: _Living room_

When: _While I was watching TV and wasn't listening to her_

My child said something that I thought was really smart!

What: _"The owl couldn't sleep because the birds were making noise."_

With whom: _Me_

Where: _Bedroom_

When: _Reading "Good Night Owl"_

Figure 6.7.   Caregiver form for recording a child's utterances when learning to talk.

Portfolio Assessment: Books We Read at Home

Child's name: _Eric_

Parent's name: _Mark_

Date	Name of book	Minutes spent reading	New words	Adult signature
9/00	"The Snowy Day"	10	snowman, snowballs	
9/00	"Chica Chica ABC"	5		
10/00	"The Very Hungry Caterpillar"	10	caterpillar, cocoon, butterfly	
10/00	"Nuts"	10	chestnut, parachute	
11/00	"Time to Get Out"	5	adventure, crocodile	
11/00	"Potluck"	15	corn on the cob	
11/00	"Where the Wild Things Are"	15	mischief, rumpus	
12/00	"Three Billy Goats Gruff"	10		

Figure 6.8. Form for storybook reading at home for an individual child.

- IEP goals
- Themes (e.g., family and friends, favorite books and stories, pets, nature discoveries)
- Chronological order of work

The team will also need to decide who gets to keep the portfolio (e.g., teacher, child, family) and where it will be stored. Establish clear, agreed-on guidelines to manage access to the portfolio and to ensure confidentiality.

Now the team is ready to determine criteria for monitoring children's progress. Formal and informal meetings will be necessary. Practitioners can schedule quarterly conferences with children, family, teachers, and other team members to review the portfolios. At these meetings, team member observations and documentation can be discussed to check for subjectivity and bias. Daily debriefings with other team members can help track the various types of documentation being gathered.

Salend (1998) suggested a series of criteria for evaluating the portfolio, which considers the following:

1. Quantity, quality, and diversity of items
2. Organization of the portfolio
3. Level of student involvement
4. Meaningfulness of caption statements
5. Quality of summary statements about growth and change

The portfolio assessment process should begin with careful planning. Caregivers and all members of the team should discuss the purpose for the portfolio as well as identify the types of documentation, the criteria for evaluation, and practical procedures for organizing and storing the portfolio. Table 6.1 is a summary of guidelines for implementing portfolio assessment.

SUGGESTIONS FOR PRACTITIONERS IN INCLUSIVE ENVIRONMENTS

Portfolio assessments are excellent tools for coordinating the efforts of all practitioners and family members involved in a child's educational program. Team members can contribute different types of documentation that are consistent with their discipline and philosophy.

Initial Assessment

Similar to models previously discussed in this book, CBA can facilitate the portfolio assessment process. These tools are useful to practitioners in determining a child's strengths and areas of concern, and they provide information on developmental sequences of behaviors that help identify the child's educational goals. CBAs often provide formal mechanisms for soliciting input from caregivers, as assessment items illustrate specific examples of behaviors that parents can expect from their child. Interviews with care-

Table 6.1.   Guidelines for implementing portfolio assessment

Start portfolios at the beginning of the year.

Caregivers and other team members should identify in advance the purpose for the portfolio, as well as expectations for children's work.

Children should be told the purpose of their portfolios.

Establish types of documentation for each goal and criteria for evaluating work.
  Develop plan for when and how data will be collected and by whom.
  Date all work promptly.
  Determine who will evaluate the portfolio.
  Identify ways to involve the child and the family in work selection and evaluation. If necessary, teach children the skills needed to participate in this process.

Portfolio contents should be representative of children's work, growth, and accomplishments.
  Explain to caregivers and children the reasons for selecting samples.

Decide how to organize the portfolio:
  Content areas
  IEP goals
  Themes
  Chronological order of work

Decide who owns the portfolio and where it will be stored.
  Establish clear, agreed-on guidelines to manage access to the portfolio and ensure confidentiality.

Determine criteria for monitoring children's progress.
  Practitioners can schedule quarterly conferences with children, family, teachers, and other team members to review the portfolio.
  At these meetings, discuss team member observations and documentation to check for subjectivity and bias.
  Daily debriefings with other team members can help track the various types of documentation being gathered.
  Criteria for evaluating the portfolio may include
    Quantity, quality, and diversity of items
    Organization of the portfolio
    Level of student involvement
    Meaningfulness of caption statements
    Quality of summary statements about growth and change

givers should also be conducted to get input on the types of documentation that fit with family preferences. Some families may prefer detailed descriptions of behaviors with anecdotes and examples; others may want a quick "snapshot" view with graphs and test scores. For instance, a family with low literacy skills may find visual documentation easier to understand.

Goal Development

Goals and objectives for children are based on the results of the CBA and caregiver preferences. IEP goals and objectives should reflect family priorities. Professionals may need to assist families in translating priorities into developmentally appropriate and observable goals and objectives. If a parent suggests a goal that seems too advanced for the child, the practitioner can break the skill into smaller steps. Goals and objectives also should be consistent with the family's cultural values and beliefs. Should these differ significantly from the practitioners' values and beliefs, open discussion with the family is necessary in order to reach a mutual understanding and agreement on goals (Kalyanpur & Harry, 1999). Criteria for judging whether the child has attained the goals and objectives must be agreed on by all team members and documented on the IEP/IFSP data form. Specialists can contribute information based on assessment tools and standards from their respective disciplines to be used as evaluation criteria.

Intervention

Intervention activities, like assessment activities, occur in the context of child-initiated, routine, and planned activities. Practitioners can use these activities as a vehicle for the systematic collection of documentation for portfolios. Authentic and real-life activities are most appropriate for practicing target skills and gathering documentation. Team members should identify daily home and classroom routines that present opportunities for practicing and observing target skills. Adults provide varying degrees of structure to these activities, from simple verbal encouragement and suggestions to more direct elicitation of targeted skills. As data are gathered, team members may place them in their own individual files but should then regularly transfer the documentation to a common file or portfolio.

Evaluation

Team members need to develop plans for how they will collect data on IEP objectives (e.g., determine schedule, types of data, criteria for mastery, portfolio format). The data collected should reflect children's progress on these objectives, as well as their strategies and errors and the effectiveness of various supports. Again, it is important to involve the child and the family in the selection of portfolio materials and the evaluation of the child's performance. The degree and type of involvement will vary according to individual child characteristics. Some children may simply choose favorite work samples to include in the portfolio, whereas other children may also provide interpretations and make judgments on the quality of their work.

When information is reviewed on a regular basis, team members can make more informed decisions on the instructional program (e.g., whether modifications are necessary). CBAs are administered at the beginning, middle, and end of each school year to monitor children's overall progress, and the results should go in the child's portfolio. Written summaries of the child's progress resulting from regular team meetings should also be included in the portfolio. At the end of the school year, team members, the child, and the family may select or make copies of documentation and work samples from the child's portfolio that are representative of the child's progress throughout the year. These are to be assembled in a notebook, saved on a computer disk, or recorded by any other appropriate medium and passed on to the child's next-grade teacher. Table 6.2 summarizes suggestions for practitioners using portfolio assessment in inclusive environments.

CONCLUSION

Portfolios are a type of performance-based assessment that provides a complex, comprehensive, and meaningful portrait of a child. Format and content are flexible and open ended and are chosen to best meet the individual child's specific educational needs. Assessment tasks, materials, data collection methods, and documentation formats can be easily accommodated to ensure cultural sensitivity.

Representative samples of a child's work are selected and gathered together into a notebook or other format. The portfolio usually includes different types of data, including visual documentation, making it a powerful and effective means of communication for sharing information about the child with family members and other colleagues.

The portfolio is more than a mere collection of documents. It must involve learner participation, evaluation criteria for performance, and procedures for systematic review of progress. It offers an optimal vehicle for coordinating team collaboration efforts and provides a structure for educational planning and regular review of progress.

Table 6.2.   Suggestions for practitioners using portfolio assessment in inclusive environments

Initial assessment

A curriculum-based assessment (CBA) can be used initially to identify the child's strengths and areas of concern.

Goal development

Identify goals and objectives based on the results of the CBA and caregiver preferences.

Authentic and real-life activities are most appropriate for practicing target skills and gathering information.

Intervention

Intervention activities occur in the context of child-initiated, routine, and planned activities.

Practitioners can use these activities as a vehicle for the systematic collection of documentation.

Adults provide varying degrees of structure to these activities.

Evaluation

Develop a data collection plan for gathering information on IEP objectives, determining:

Schedule

Types of data

Criteria for mastery

Portfolio format

Data collected should reflect children's progress on these objectives, as well as their strategies and errors and the effectiveness of various supports.

Review the portfolio on a regular basis during team meetings in order to make informed decisions on the instructional program.

Conduct comprehensive assessments at the beginning, middle, and end of each school year to monitor children's overall progress.

Review Questions

■ Explain the rationale for using portfolio assessment.

■ What types of materials might be included in a child's portfolio?

■ Describe the Work Sampling System (WSS) method of portfolio evaluation.

■ Discuss three reasons why it is important to include children when reviewing their portfolios.

Dynamic
Assessment

After reading this chapter, you will be able to:

■ Define dynamic assessment, and discuss the rationale
for its use

■ Give examples of models and methods that fit into a
dynamic assessment framework

■ Identify considerations and guidelines for implementing
dynamic assessment

*M*s. Jackson was concerned about Daraaraa, the new 4-year-old student in her class. He was very quiet, sat and observed other children without participating in activities, and only nodded or shook his head in response to her questions. He had just arrived from Ethiopia, where he had lived in harsh conditions for 2 years, and his first language was Oromo. Ms. Jackson wanted to be sure he would get the support and help he needed. She was uncertain whether he would eventually settle in, learn the classroom routines, make friends, and learn English. Ms. Jackson needed help determining whether Daraaraa was going through the typical process of learning a new language and assimilating to a new environment or whether he had an actual language disability and required individualized therapy with the speech-language pathologist.

Ms. Jackson decided to talk to the speech-language pathologist, Ms. Hesse. Ms. Hesse told Ms. Jackson that she had recently tested 3-year-old Suejin, who was learning to speak both Korean and English, using an expressive vocabulary test. Suejin's mother spoke English well enough to translate what Suejin said. To calculate Suejin's score, Ms. Hesse combined all of the items that Suejin identified correctly in both Korean and English. The results showed that Suejin's total vocabulary was well within the typical range for her age, but had Ms. Hesse counted only the English words, Suejin's score would have been well below the norm. Suejin's mother said she was not concerned about her daughter's language, and Ms. Hesse believed that Suejin was interacting appropriately with her peers, using English words and various communicative gestures. Both had observed that Suejin was mixing the two languages in her sentences. The teacher, for example, heard Suejin begin to count in Korean and then continue in English: "Hana, dul, three!" During the testing, Ms. Hesse heard Suejin say, "Boat itseo!" while pointing at a picture of a boat. Her mother translated as, "There boat." Ms. Hesse recognized this as an example of code-switching, a typical stage in bilingual development, and expected that Suejin would gradually learn to separate the two languages.

Roberto, a 5-year-old, was also bilingual and code-switching between English and Spanish. Roberto had not done well on English or Spanish versions of receptive vocabulary tests. With the help of Roberto's teacher, Ms. Rodriguez, who also spoke Spanish, Ms. Hesse had interviewed Roberto's mother using the Spanish version of a parent questionnaire. Roberto's mother was concerned about his language development. She remembered his older sister's mixing English and Spanish words in her sentences. She would say things such as, "My perro is marrón" [My dog is brown] or "I want dos tortillas" [I want two tortillas]. Although she mixed languages, her sentences were linguistically correct. Roberto's utterances were much harder to understand, and he seemed to be making errors in word order and grammar, saying things such as, "Roberto gato me mira" [Roberto cat I see] and "I want dos naranja" [I want two orange].

Ms. Rodriguez also had noticed during her initial assessment in class that Roberto had difficulty focusing his attention on tasks and understanding verbal directions. She decided to model the task for him and keep reminding him of the different components of the tasks. Roberto refused to try something if he did not feel he would be successful. If Ms. Rodriguez insisted and encouraged him, however, he would make some attempts, while continually checking with her for feedback. With his teacher's help and encouragement, Roberto actually was able to successfully perform new tasks.

After reviewing Suejin's and Roberto's experiences with Ms. Jackson, Ms. Hesse decided to test Daraaraa. He did not do well on tests of comprehension or expressive language, but the speech-language pathologist questioned whether the tests were culturally relevant. Ms. Hesse decided to schedule additional testing, and she asked Daraaraa's family to bring some toys, pictures, and books from home and Ms. Jackson to bring some objects from the classroom. During the second testing, Ms. Hesse requested that Daraaraa's father ask his son to label objects in Oromo and then tell her whether the response was correct. Then Ms. Hesse told Daraaraa the English word and asked him to repeat the word to her in English. Ms. Hesse wanted to see how easily Daraaraa could learn new words in English. She improvised a short comprehension task using four objects for which Daraaraa had just learned the English names. Daraaraa pointed correctly to the objects. Then Ms. Hesse tried the same process with a receptive vocabulary test. First, she labeled each picture in English and had Daraaraa repeat the words. Then she administered the test in the standardized way. Daraaraa did well but quickly got tired. Nonetheless, Ms. Hesse felt that Daraaraa would do well in school because he demonstrated motivation and the ability to learn the new words.

The practitioners working with Daraaraa, Suejin, and Roberto used a dynamic assessment approach. **Dynamic assessment** refers to various distinct approaches that are characterized by guided support or learning for the purpose of determining a child's potential for change (Palincsar, Brown, & Campione, 1994). Dynamic measures gauge performance prospectively, indicating not only what a child has learned but also what the child is capable of learning. These measures also indicate the types of assistance that will help the child do his or her best. What is being assessed is not the amount of knowledge and skill but the potential for the individual to change when guided to do so (Nelson, 1994).

As illustrated in the vignette, dynamic approaches can help determine whether a child's behavior is due to a cultural or linguistic difference, as in Daraaraa's case, or is a reflection of a developmental delay, as in Roberto's case. This is because the dynamic approach is based on the clinical method of assessment. The clinical method, as defined by Rey (1958) and Ginsberg and Opper (1979) refers to the child-focused, flexible method of questioning, as opposed to using predetermined standardized sets of procedures. The focus of the clinical method is not just on what a child is able to do but also on how a child approaches a task and what is needed for the child to learn. The focus is not on a right or wrong answer but on understanding children's thought processes and discovering children's intentions and reasons for behaviors and responses. For example, comparing Roberto's code-switching behavior to his older sister's—by analyzing communicative functions and whether switches preserve word meanings and grammatical constraints—is a useful procedure for differentiating typical language differences from language disorders (Gutierrez-Clellen, 1996).

Process and intervention are two key elements of dynamic assessment. The practitioner assumes an interactive role to examine how the child uses internal cognitive and emotional resources in response to social interactions, tasks, and materials. For instance, during a dynamic assessment, the practitioner promotes the child's use of cognitive resources and strategies (e.g., problem solving, evaluating and self-correcting, controlling behavior, delaying gratification) that will enable the child to self-regulate in knowledge acquisition and processing. The practitioner also examines the child's ability to learn and change when the proper **scaffolding** and **mediation** are provided. Information on what the child can do independently and what he or she can do with assistance has been identified by the National Association for the Education of Young Children as an important characteristic of appropriate assessments (Bredekamp & Rosegrant, 1995).

COGNITIVE AND METACOGNITIVE PROCESSES

Cognitive processes that emerge in preschool– and early elementary–age children include problem-solving strategies (e.g., defining problems and identifying solutions) and early logical reasoning skills (e.g., comparisons, predictions). **Metacognitive skills** refer to children's awareness of cognitive processes, including the ability to plan, monitor, and check the results of their actions (Fry, 1992). During the assessment, the examiner may look at the child's attention to the task, how a child explores and manipulates materials, the kinds of explanations given for responses, the ability to notice mistakes and correct them, and whether a child can seek out help.

The emphasis on observing general processes and strategies rather than mastery of specific tasks can be helpful in differentiating whether the child has a true delay or problem or only lacks familiarity with a task or situation. As noted previously, children who do not perform well on standardized tests do not necessarily have a disorder. They may perform poorly because of unfamiliarity with the specific test content or with the examiner (Peña, 1996). As the next example shows, Daraaraa's speech-language pathologist was not the only practitioner to considered this:

Mr. Donaldson, the school psychologist, began his assessment of Daraaraa by administering a nonverbal subtest of a standardized intelligence test. At first Daraaraa merely stared at the puzzle pieces. Then he arranged them to form a beautiful and colorful design, but without fitting the pieces together. Mr. Donaldson was impressed by Daraaraa's ability to focus on this task and how he arranged the pieces in a very systematic manner. He seemed to have a plan in his head. When Daraaraa finished, Mr. Donaldson praised him, then proceeded to show Daraaraa how different pieces of the puzzles fit together to form a picture. Daraaraa was very attentive. When presented with another puzzle, he was able to complete it. Mr. Donaldson noticed how quickly Daraaraa caught and corrected mistakes. Although it took well beyond the time limits of the test to complete the tasks, Daraaraa had manifested excellent cognitive and metacognitive abilities—particularly considering that this was probably the first time Daraaraa had seen a puzzle.

SELF-REGULATION AND SOCIOEMOTIONAL PROCESSES

Dynamic assessment is also concerned with the development of self-regulation and what adults need to do to best support children's competence (Fry, 1992). **Self-regulation** is the capacity to plan, guide, and monitor behavior and flexibly change according to different circumstances (Diaz, Neal, & Amaya-Williams, 1990). Very early in the context of interactions with their caregivers, infants begin to self-regulate. They learn to modulate their neurophysiological states and to use strategies such as thumb sucking to soothe themselves when tired or stressed (Kopp, 1982). Infants gradually move from being highly dependent on adults (a form of "other-regulation") to developing self-regulatory skills (Wertsch, McNamee, McLane, & Budwig, 1980).

The following example demonstrates how caregivers can observe and support infants' neurophysiological organization through their children's use of self-regulatory strategies, as well as how the strategies can be used to assess progress. This example is based on the Neurobehavioral Curriculum for Early Intervention (NCEI), an early intervention model developed by Hedlund (1998) to support infants' self-regulatory abilities and neurobehavioral organization:

Ms. Kingston was getting ready for the IFSP update meeting with Ms. Wong, the early interventionist who regularly visited the Kingston family at home. Ms. Kingston's daughter Karla was born at 27 weeks' gestation with a very low birth weight of 885 grams. Karla had spent almost 2 months in the neonatal intensive care unit and had been treated for various complications including hyperbilirubinemia, apnea, bradycardia of prematurity, and gastroesophageal reflux. Once Ms. Kingston took Karla home, it was very hard to establish a regular feeding pattern. Karla was formula-fed on demand. She also took medication, but because she had a tendency to throw up, her body often did not absorb it. The medication was also interfering with her sleep. Because of the reflux, Karla often gasped for air and her respiration was very irregular, often with strident sounds. If Ms. Kingston happened to move Karla a little more abruptly than usual, she even noticed some tremors and startling with her arms. All of this was upsetting to Ms. Kingston, and she worried about her daughter most of the time.

With the help of Ms. Wong during the first IFSP meeting, Ms. Kingston and her husband identified for Karla the goals of looking at and reaching for toys. Now, 6 months later, Karla still was not able to look at or reach for objects. Ms. Kingston remembered her initial attempts to help Karla reach her goals. She had tried to talk to Karla and show her some toys, but Karla would avert her gaze and turn her head away. If Ms. Kingston insisted, Karla would arch her back and squirm. Ms. Kingston had so badly wanted a smile from Karla, but all she received were frowns, tightly clenched eyes, and compressed lips—as if Karla was always on the edge of crying. Lately, however, there seemed to be an improvement. This is because Ms. Wong had been trained in the NCEI and drew on this approach to show Ms. Kingston a strategy for encouraging Karla's response. Karla was seated on Ms. Kingston's lap, facing her mother. As the two sat quietly, Ms. Wong had Ms. Kingston hold Karla's hands together at mid-line and let Karla's feet brace against her chest. She also suggested that Ms. Kingston give Karla something to suck on (e.g., her thumb, a pacifier). When Ms. Kingston did this, without talking, Karla glanced at her for a few short moments.

The day before the follow-up IFSP meeting had been exciting because feeding had gone so well—one burp and absolutely no spit-ups. Then, while Ms. Kingston was changing Karla's diaper, Karla independently brought her hands to mid-line, braced her feet against the towel roll, put her hands up to her mouth, placed her thumb in her mouth, and looked at her mother. For the first time, Ms. Kingston felt like Karla was truly interacting with her.

This example shows Karla's gradual progress from other-regulation to self-regulation. Even though she had not made progress looking at and reaching for toys, it was clear that Karla was improving her ability to sustain interaction and engagement with her mother, an important step in the direction of her IFSP goal. Most important, although she initially needed intense adult support, she now was able to use the strategy independently.

Self-regulatory abilities are manifested in the young child's ability to increasingly comply with their caregivers' requests and directives (Kopp, 1982). As children grow older, the adult's role is to promote higher cognitive skills, enabling children to learn and problem solve independently (Diaz et al., 1990). Adults help children regulate their behaviors by using more complex cognitive and language strategies: providing directions and suggestions, describing, demonstrating, explaining, giving feedback, and simplifying tasks. Assessing a child's level of self-regulation provides a useful framework for understanding and helping children with behavior problems (Kopp, 1982; Normandeau & Gray, 1998). Inappropriate or aggressive behaviors may result from difficulties in controlling impulses, delaying gratification, accepting limits, following directions, and lack of skills (e.g., communication, social). It is important to assess and teach the following social-cognition skills: an awareness of others' actions, thoughts, feelings, and perspectives; an awareness of the effect of one's action on others; the ability to share, take turns, and communicate functionally; and the ability to problem-solve, which includes expressing needs, listening to others, negotiating, and identifying a mutually agreed-on solution (Flavell, Miller, & Miller, 1993). This concept is shown in the next vignette:

Linda's teacher was concerned; during transitions, 5-year-old Linda ran in all directions, bumping into furniture and other children, who were starting to react negatively to her. The physical therapist came to observe Linda in class and noticed that Linda had difficulty stopping and her movements were quite uncoordinated. She seemed unaware of her body and her movements. The physical therapist gave Linda's teacher some suggestions to help Linda become aware of how she could "make her body stop and make her body go" and control her body while moving at different speeds (fast, slow) and in different directions (up, down, in, under). The teacher used various movements with music (e.g., walking, hopping, stopping) to help Linda. The whole class enjoyed participating, too, and soon Linda's transitions improved.

THEORETICAL FRAMEWORK

Dynamic assessment was conceptualized by Vygotsky (1962) and later operationalized by Feuerstein, Rand, and Hofmann (1979). It is based on the view that it is not sufficient to simply identify the content of instruction (i.e., goals and objectives) and expose the child to opportunities to practice this content. Rather, one must also identify how to best facilitate the child's mastery and competence by modifying aspects of the task (materials and/or demands) and providing appropriate guidance and support (Lidz, 1991).

There are six major theoretical assumptions underlying a dynamic assessment approach. First is Piaget's **constructivist perspective,** which views the child as having an active role in constructing knowledge. Second, Vygotsky's social-interactionist view emphasizes the adult's or more capable peer's role in guiding the child's development. Children, including those with disabilities, develop and learn primarily from engaging in social interactions during which adults and more knowledgeable peers provide support and guidance (Berk & Winsler, 1995). Third, Vygotsky's concept of ZPD represents the difference between what a child can achieve independently and what a child can achieve when provided with adult assistance. Fourth, scaffolding (Wood, Bruner, & Ross, 1976), or guided participation (Rogoff, 1993), is a type of interaction in which the adult guides and supports the child's learning by building on what the child can already do. Fifth, Feuerstein's theory of mediated learning experiences (MLEs) proposes that an adult or a more knowledgeable peer interposes himself or herself between a child and the world to make experiences more meaningful. The meanings children give to situations and tasks affect performance expectations and strategies, and meanings assigned to tasks and situations will reflect cultural values (Ogbu, 1987). Finally, self-regulation derives from the metaphor of the human being as an open, self-organized system that continuously reorganizes itself in response to environmental influences in a dynamic, nonlinear way (Cherkes-Julkowski, 1996; Thelen & Smith, 1994). The development of self-regulatory capacities originates in caregiver–child interactions and is facilitated by the social environment (Luria, 1982; Vygotsky, 1978).

MODELS AND APPLICATIONS

Dynamic assessment is conducted primarily to evaluate a child's ability to learn and generally follows a test-teach-retest model. The child's initial performance on a task serves as a baseline, followed by intervention consisting of graduated prompts (Campione & Brown, 1987; Olswang, Bain, & Johnson, 1992; Spector, 1992) or MLEs (Feuerstein et al., 1979; Lidz, 1991). The child is then retested on the same task. The comparison of performances before and after the intervention provides a measure of the change created by the assessment intervention process. Research has shown that dynamic measures tend to be more predictive than static measures of children's future performance for typically developing children (Spector, 1992) and children with disabilities (Vye, Burns, Delclos, & Bransford, 1987).

Both quantitative and qualitative approaches can be used in dynamic assessment. Quantitative approaches focus on quantifying the ZPD by calculating the difference between scores before and after the teaching phase or by quantifying amounts and intensities of prompts and supports required by the child to learn a task. For instance, a preschool-age child's score on an expressive vocabulary reassessment might increase by 5 points after being taught the names of items that the child had not labeled during the first assessment. The following example details scoring for evaluating a toddler's increasing independence in mastering a task:

Two-year-old Jenna was learning to eat independently with a spoon. Initially, her parents needed to hold the plate and physically guide Jenna to scoop up the food and bring it to her mouth. Seven weeks later, Jenna was feeding herself, and her parents only needed to steady the plate and provide verbal encouragements. The early interventionist who assessed Jenna rated her increase in independence numerically (i.e., 3 = performs task independently, 2 = performs task with minimal adult assistance, 1 = performs task with significant adult assistance). In other cases, the early interventionist has measured decreases in assistance levels by assigning numerical scores based on the intensity of prompts (i.e., 3 = high, 2 = moderate, 1 = low). This second option is well suited for children who are not yet ready to master developmental tasks and when the focus of intervention is on helping the child sustain ongoing interactions with people and objects.

Qualitative approaches focus on the processes a child uses to perform a task or the types of scaffolding the adult provides to enable the child to complete the task successfully. For example, a father observes how his 2-year-old daughter visually inspects two lids and chooses the correct one to fit on a jar, whereas the day before she proceeded by trial and error. He describes his observation on the recording form that the early interventionist gave him. A 5-year-old's mother calls her son's teacher to say that he wrote his first name independently on his drawing of the neighbor's cat. Usually, he would ask his mother to write his name for him to use as a model.

Dynamic Assessment and Scaffolding Models

Scaffolding is central to dynamic assessment because it refers to adult strategies that guide and support the child's learning by building on what the child already knows. Effective scaffolding is flexible and child responsive, drawing on a broad variety of techniques and varying considerably across cultures (Berk & Winsler, 1995). Applications of scaffolding range from low-structured approaches with minimal adult assistance (e.g., asking questions to help children discover their own solutions) to high-structured approaches with more direct and explicit modeling and instruction (e.g., eliciting questions, giving directions). Assistance can be verbal, visual, or physical, including words and symbols on cue cards, drawings, maps, arrangement of materials, and physical guidance of actions (Bodrova & Leong, 1996; Notari-Syverson et al., 1998; Tharp & Gallimore, 1988). Scaffolding approaches have been recommended and used successfully in a variety of classrooms and intervention programs (Gutierrez-Clellen & Quinn,

1993; Juel, 1996; Norris & Hoffman, 1990; Notari-Syverson et al., 1998; Olswang et al., 1992; Palincsar & Klenk, 1992; Tharp & Gallimore, 1988).

Dynamic assessment approaches have often been recommended for assessing children who do not speak English as their first language. Because of a lack of communicative proficiency in English, these children have been overrepresented as having learning disabilities (Gutierrez-Clellen, 1996). Because dynamic assessment bases learning ability on actual learning experiences within a socially meaningful context, it is especially suited for the assessment of language and literacy, areas strongly influenced by the social and cultural environment. Narratives, storytelling, and the use of contextualization rules vary greatly according to culture and experience (e.g., Heath, 1983; Labov, 1972). Gutierrez-Clellen and Quinn (1993) proposed a dynamic approach to assessing narratives of children from various cultures. Samples of spontaneous narratives are collected in varying narrative contexts. The adult then describes the contextualization rules of different narrative situations (e.g., storytelling with an unfamiliar audience, repeating a story from a book, informal conversation) and provides specific examples for the child, scaffolding through the use of verbal cues and modeling. If the child speaks little English, the adult must be able to speak in the child's language or work together with an interpreter. Progress over time is measured by changes in the number of prompts (e.g., asking for clarification, asking for more information) needed to elicit the targeted narrative behaviors.

Olswang and colleagues (1992) proposed a model of dynamic assessment in early language acquisition. They described a dynamic assessment protocol that is based on a series of verbal cues organized in a hierarchy from minimal prompting (e.g., a general statement calling the child's attention to the task) to maximum verbal prompting (e.g., shaping by having the child imitate utterances). The prompts include, from least to most supportive, the following:

1. General statements that help the child focus on the task ("Oh, look at this.")

2. Elicitation questions that invite the child to give a response ("What's happening?")

3. Sentence-completion tasks in which the child has to provide the last word of the adult's sentence ("José is riding his _____.")

4. Indirect models in which the adult invites the child to repeat a model in a naturalistic indirect manner ("José is riding his bike. What's José doing?")

5. Direct models in which the adult waits for the child to spontaneously imitate an utterance ("Dog run." [pause])

6. Direct models plus an elicitation question by which the adult asks the child directly to imitate an utterance ("Dog run. Tell me 'dog run.' ")

7. Shaping in which the adult breaks down an utterance into smaller components for the child to imitate ("Dog. Tell me, 'Dog.' " [pause] "Tell me, 'Run.' " [pause] "Tell me, 'Dog run.' ")

Losardo, Notari-Syverson, and Coleman (1997) described a dynamic assessment protocol that provides both quantitative and qualitative assessments of children's oral retelling of a story. Figure 7.1 is an example of a dynamic assessment worksheet for oral retelling of a story. Figure 7.2 is a qualitative dynamic assessment for use in the context of play and daily routine intervention environments. It is designed to provide practitioners with information on the nature and types of scaffolding they use.

Figure 7.3 is a scaffolding strategies checklist that illustrates a similar approach to evaluating the use and effectiveness of scaffolding strategies in the assessment of early literacy and language skills (Notari-Syverson et al., 1998). In addition to assessing the effects of various types of guidance, feedback, and teaching strategies, the scaffolding strategies checklist also considers the effects of various task accommodations and modifications, as well as children's preferences for particular modalities (e.g., manipulatives, pictures, concrete objects, verbal).

Mediated Learning Approaches

Mediated learning approaches focus not on specific prompts but on the mediation of broader processes to give meaning and organization to the child's world. Rather than teach test items or a task, the adult engages the child in MLEs by teaching cognitive-linguistic skills that will enable the child to master a task or solve a problem. In turn, this helps the child become a self-regulated, active learner.

MLE assessment models are based on the dynamic assessment that Feuerstein used with school-age children (Feuerstein et al., 1979). Lidz (1991) developed a version for children ages 3–5 years, the Preschool Learning Assessment Device. The assessment consists of a test-intervene-retest format anchored to the Triangles subtest of the Kaufman Assessment Battery for Children (K-ABC; Kaufman & Kaufman, 1983). It includes specific interventions involving drawing and block tasks, as well as general guidelines for CBA. The practitioner chooses specific areas of mediation, such as task modifications, language and concept demands, memory aids, or comparisons and generalizations to other situations. The assessment battery contains samples of assessment protocols, summary sheets, IEPs, lesson plans, and data collection sheets.

The adult's or mediator's role is to facilitate the child's learning by acting on the environment to make it meaningful and relevant for the child. MLEs are characterized by three essential components:

1. Intentionality and reciprocity: The mediator intentionally modifies the situation to motivate the child and elicit his or her active participation. To help focus the child's attention in a naming task, for example, the examiner could let a child actively manipulate an object before asking him or her to name it.

2. Meaning and purpose: The mediator provides reasons for activities and emphasizes the value and importance of tasks. These can be expressed through attitudes and generic statements (e.g., an excited facial expression accompanied by an utterance such as, "Oh, this

Dynamic Assessment: Oral Retelling of a Story

Date of observation: _April 20, 2000_

Name of book: _"The Bright Red Rose"_

Observer: _Anne Stapleton_

Child's name: _Maya_

The oral retelling of a story may be used to assess the following abilities: 1) comprehension of story structure, 2) short-term memory for events of a story, 3) ability to sequence the events in a story, 4) understanding of vocabulary from a story, 5) expressive use of vocabulary to describe events in a story, 6) ability to use prior knowledge to make sense of events in a story, and 7) ability to use their personal experiences to make predictions about a story. The nature and types of assistance that children need in order to be successful at retelling a story may be determined through use of the following guided learning procedures:

Procedure	Example	Quantitative analysis	Qualitative analysis
Ask the child to retell a simple story after you have read it.	"Tell me about the story."	Child describes events in story: yes _x_ no ___ number of events _5_	Verbatim response: "Once there was a seed. It planted itself in the garden. The boy tended the garden and the rose grew and grew. One day the boy picked the rose and gave it to his mother. This made the rose very happy."
Encourage the child to look at a picture in the book.	"Let's look at this picture. What does this make you think about?"	Child describes picture: yes _x_ no ___ number of events _2_	Verbatim response: "It makes me think about planting a flower garden full of roses. My mom loves roses."
Provide a partial model while looking at a picture in the book.	"It looks like the boy is getting ready to do something. What is the boy going to do?"	Child describes picture: yes _x_ no ___ number of events _2_	Verbatim response: "It looks like the boy is going to pull some weeds. Now the rose has more room to grow."
Provide a complete model while looking at a picture in the book.	"The boy is going to pick roses. What is the boy going to do?"	Child describes picture: yes _x_ no ___ number of events _1_	Verbatim response: "The boy is going to pick roses."

Figure 7.1.   Dynamic assessment for oral retelling of a story.

Dynamic Assessment: Use of Supportive Scaffolding

Practitioner: _Anne Stapleton_   Observer: _Dave Shah_

Practitioners use supportive scaffolding to assist children to mobilize their internal cognitive and emotional resources in response to social interactions, tasks, and materials. This form is designed to provide practitioners with feedback on their use of supportive scaffolding in educational environments.

Procedure:

1. Consult with another practitioner to choose which time of day to observe.

2. Provide a running record during the observational period, and include the following:
   a. A brief description of instructional activities
   b. Specific examples of supportive scaffolds used by the teacher

3. Meet with the practitioner to share your observational notes.

Summary:

Activity description	Observed use of supportive scaffolding
Recognizing printed words of foods eaten at snack	Provides clues = "It's something made from milk" (cheese); "It's a vegetable" (carrot)
Singing rhymes and songs	Has pictures of nursery rhymes on wall
Block construction	Holds base blocks steady so that the child can add more blocks
Picture book reading	Models two-word utterances and asks the child to imitate
Outdoor play—riding tricycle	Provides guidance by gently pushing the child from behind
Writing name—letter "D"	"Give it a big tummy" "Remember, you go down"
Calendar—day of week	"No, after Tuesday comes . . ."
Block construction	Shows block, taps it, says, "We need one more right there." Points.

Figure 7.2. Dynamic assessment for use of supportive scaffolding.

SCAFFOLDING STRATEGIES CHECKLIST

Child's name: _____

Date: _____ _____ _____

Activity: _____ _____ _____

Circle strategies used during activity:	Used	Did it help?	Used	Did it help?	Used	Did it help?
Open-ended questioning descriptions predictions and planning explanations relating to the child's experience	☐Y ☐N	☐Y ☐N	☐Y ☐N	☐Y ☐N	☐Y ☐N	☐Y ☐N

Providing feedback
encouragements   evaluations
thinking aloud   clarification requests
interpretation of meaning   acknowledgments
                                     and information
                                     talk
	☐Y ☐N	☐Y ☐N	☐Y ☐N	☐Y ☐N	☐Y ☐N	☐Y ☐N

Cognitive structuring rules and logical relationships sequencing contradictions	☐Y ☐N	☐Y ☐N	☐Y ☐N	☐Y ☐N	☐Y ☐N	☐Y ☐N
Holding in memory restating goals summaries and reminders	☐Y ☐N	☐Y ☐N	☐Y ☐N	☐Y ☐N	☐Y ☐N	☐Y ☐N
Task regulation matching interests rearranging elements and experience reducing alternatives making more concrete	☐Y ☐N	☐Y ☐N	☐Y ☐N	☐Y ☐N	☐Y ☐N	☐Y ☐N
Instructing modeling orienting direct questioning elicitations coparticipation	☐Y ☐N	☐Y ☐N	☐Y ☐N	☐Y ☐N	☐Y ☐N	☐Y ☐N

Figure 7.3.   Scaffolding Strategies Checklist. (From Notari-Syverson, A., O'Connor, R.E., & Vadasy, P.F. [1998]. *Ladders to literacy: A preschool activity book* [p. 282]. Baltimore: Paul H. Brookes Publishing Co; reprinted by permission.)

looks like fun") or more specific explanations (e.g., "Use your spoon so you don't get food on your hand").

3.   Transcendence: The mediator goes beyond the basic goals and immediate context of the interaction. During a color-identification task, for example, the examiner may ask the child to identify the colors of objects in the room in addition to those of the test materials. Also, the adult may help the child relate to similar objects and experiences in other environments (e.g., "Do you have one of these at home?" "This dog reminds me of your new puppy, Moka").

The MLE assessment approach has been used successfully to identify children who are at risk for language disorders. Peña, Quinn, and Iglesias (1992) worked with a Head Start program predominantly comprised of Puerto Rican and African American children who scored below average on a standardized expressive vocabulary test. The children were told that it was important to pay attention to "special names" (intentionality and reciprocity). During activities and games, adults emphasized that "special names help us tell things apart" (meaning). They also talked about what would happen if the teacher did not know the children's names (transcendence). The children were assisted in developing a plan for working out or solving the games and remembering to name items they saw. On the pretest, there was no difference in score between typically developing children and children with a possible language disorder. After the MLEs, however, the typically developing children scored higher on the posttest.

There are a number of early intervention programs based on the mediated learning approach (e.g., Haywood, Brooks, & Burns, 1986; Klein, 1996). The Mediated Learning Program (Osborn et al., 1991) is a preschool curriculum that has been proven effective in improving cognitive and language outcomes for preschool-age children with disabilities (Cole, Mills, & Dale, 1989, 1991; Notari-Syverson, Cole, Osborn, & Sherwood, 1996). This model draws on the following basic principles of mediated learning:

1. All children can learn.

2. The role of the teacher is critical to learning.

3. Children learn more when you address their interests (intentionality and reciprocity).

4. Children benefit from knowing the meaning and purpose of activities (meaning and purpose).

5. Children learn more from activities that are applicable to their world (transcendence).

The curriculum is organized into 20 units. Each unit is designed to teach specific cognitive functions such as labeling and categorizing, changing perspectives, communicating, using symbols and abstract thinking, planning ahead, thinking before acting, and defining problems. It contains recommendations for specific mediation strategies for the teacher to use (i.e., intentionality, meaning, and transcendence). Each unit teaches a set of daily principles involving specific cognitive functions. For example, the "Getting Along with People" unit covers the principles and cognitive functions of how families are different (comparison) and how to understand other people's feelings (decentering). The "Learning the Importance of Signs" unit includes the topics recognition of signs in the environment (clear perception/spatial orientation) and how signs help people navigate (using a system). Assessment focuses on children's mastery of cognitive functions as translated into the daily principles, in addition to the types of mediation used by the adult. Figure 7.4 illustrates a data collection format based on the this approach.

Dynamic Assessment: Data Collection Form Based on the Mediated Learning Program

Unit: _Spatial relationships_   Activity: _Outdoor play_   Date: _4/11/00_   Recorder: _Ana Rodriguez_

Child	Objectives/principles/functions	Child behaviors and responses	Mediation/scaffolding
Linda	Different people have different perspectives	Describes to Ashanti what she sees from top of slide: "I see the fire station!"	Spontaneous
	Decentering	"No, Ashanti is down there!"	Adult question: "Can Ashanti see it, too?"

Figure 7.4.   Data collection form based on the Mediated Learning Program for monitoring the progress of several children.

Mediated learning assessments have been developed to evaluate mother–child interactions. Klein and Alony (1993) used the Observation for Mediational Interaction (OMI) to evaluate mothers' mediational interaction with infants and young children up to 4 years of age. The OMI involves counting the frequency of occurrence of behaviors defined as factors of mediation (focusing, affecting, expanding, rewarding, regulating behaviors). Kahn (1992) described the Mediated Learning Experiences Record, an observation instrument to record parent–child MLEs for children from birth to 6 years of age during play interactions and to assess changes over time.

Early Self-Regulation and Neurobehavioral Facilitation

Adults play a fundamental role in helping children develop awareness and control of their behaviors. Caregivers use a variety of strategies to soothe a crying infant, to keep a toddler out of trouble, or to help a preschool-age child delay self-gratification. These strategies change from mainly physical and sensory during infancy to more psychological (e.g., words, smiles, looks) as the child develops more sophisticated cognitive, linguistic, and motor abilities. Children gradually learn to regulate and control their own behaviors, thereby relying less on adults.

Dynamic approaches to infant assessment focus on identifying strategies that an adult can use to facilitate the infant's attempts to self-regulate over the course of an interaction. One example is the Infant Behavioral Assessment (Hedlund & Tatarka, 1991). This model is based on Als's (1986) neurobehavioral approach, which provides a framework for observing the neurosocial behavioral levels of infants and the types and effectiveness of self-regulatory strategies the infant uses to promote subsystem balance, sustain attention, or maintain an interaction. The Infant Behavioral Assessment provides information on the maturation of an infant's neurophysiological organization and self-regulatory capabilities. It was developed for early interventionists who work with infants who are at high risk, are medically fragile, or have disabilities and their families. This tool focuses on the infant's attempts to master a task and how his or her performance can best be facilitated. It allows for three types of facilitation strategies:

1. Environmental: factors in the environment (e.g., noise level, light)

2. Motor: handling and positioning the infant

3. Cue-matched: the infant's specific self-regulatory behaviors (e.g., mouthing, sucking)

Hedlund (1998) also developed the Neurobehavioral Curriculum for Early Intervention and a dynamic approach to monitoring and evaluating progress on IFSP goals and objectives. This approach looks at developmental progress on objectives, as well as degree and quantity of supports required for each objective. Hedlund's IFSP quarterly progress report is contained in Figure 7.5. This example shows that the early interventionist rated the infant as having made moderate progress on the cognitive/gross motor goal (denoted by "COG/GM" on the figure) of reaching for an object. Progress was facilitated by low environmental facilitation (positioning the infant away from competing visual stimuli) and moderate motor neurobe-havioral facilitation (helping the infant maintain one hand in mid-line when offered an object).

ADVANTAGES AND LIMITATIONS

Dynamic assessment is most appropriate when the evaluation focuses on identifying processes and strategies to support a child's learning rather than on whether a child has mastered a skill. This approach is particularly use-ful when assessing children who are not yet ready to learn the developmen-tal and academic skills represented in traditional tests or children who have had insufficient exposure to the school's underlying cultural norms.

Advantages

The link between assessment and intervention, taking into account learn-ing potential, sensitivity to progress, and the capacity for adaptations and accommodations are advantages of dynamic assessment. Each of these char-acteristics is explored next.

Link Between Assessment and Intervention

A dynamic approach to assessment provides information on the child as a learner, not just on performance or mastery of skills. Dynamic assessment emphasizes a child's strengths. In turn, it is an integral part of intervention because it generates information about which teaching strategies and task characteristics work best for a particular child.

Information on Children's Learning Potential

Dynamic assessment is future oriented and provides information on chil-dren's potential for learning. Testing generally follows a test-teach-retest procedure. The main goal is to gauge the child's ability to respond to in-struction and to learn new behaviors. This is useful when assessing chil-dren who are unfamiliar with school or the dominant culture, such as chil-dren learning English as a second language.

Sensitive to Progress

Dynamic assessment provides information on children's use of strategies in a learning situation. Some very young infants or children with severe dis-abilities may show little progress on mastering traditional developmental tasks, but they may be using more sophisticated strategies in their at-tempts or may need less intensive support from adults. For these children, assessing changes in types of strategies and intensities of support over time may be the most appropriate indicator of progress.

Ability to Include Adaptations and Accommodations

Dynamic assessment is especially useful for assessing children with dis-abilities. These children may benefit from various types of testing accom-

IFSP Quarterly Progress Report

Child's Name: _Gil_ Date: _5/22/00_

Child's Case Manager: _Vandana_

Domain	Objective by Domain	Developmental Progress				Neurobehavioral Facilitation											
						Environment				Motor				Cue-matched			
		0	1	2	3	NA	L	M	H	NA	L	M	H	NA	L	M	H
COG/GM	1. _Reaches for object_			✓			1					1					
	2.																
	3.																
	4.																
	5.																
	6.																
	New Objectives:																
	1.																
	2.																
	3.																
	Comments:																
	Still needs occasional breaks from social interaction (reduce voice level and face-to-face gaze)																
	Likes brightly colored objects																

Figure 7.5. IFSP Quarterly Progress Report. Please indicate the *number* of neurobehavioral strategies that you are currently using for each level of support (i.e., low, moderate, high). (Key: Developmental progress: 0 = No change, 1 = Slight, 2 = Moderate, 3 = Objective achieved. Neurobehavioral facilitation: NA = Not applicable, L = Low, M = Moderate, H = High. COG = cognitive goal, GM = gross motor goal.) (From Hedlund, R. [1998]. *Supporting neurobehavioral organizational development in infants with disabilities: The neurobehavioral curriculum for early intervention* [p. 1 in Appendix A]. Unpublished manuscript, Washington Research Institute, Seattle; adapted by permission.)

modations, such as rewording items and directions, allowing more time to complete a response, or using a braille version of a test (Elliott, Kratochwill, & Schulte, 1998). Children's initial performance on a standardized test can then be compared with their performance on similar but modified tasks, providing important information on children's abilities and functioning in optimal conditions.

Limitations

Among the limitations of dynamic assessment are reduced efficiency, the requirement of a high level of experience and expertise, and practicality issues. These items are further discussed in the following sections.

Reduced Efficiency

Dynamic assessment takes more time to administer because of the interactive nature of the procedures. The adult must observe and listen to the child and propose varying types and levels of support. Tasks and demands must be presented so that the child reveals the strategies used to solve a problem or to find an answer. Recording involves qualitative descriptions of strategies in addition to checking a correct or an incorrect answer. The observational process may include working with children across various activities and environments in order to obtain a representative sample. Finally, using a test-teach-retest model involves three phases (two testings and one teaching) rather than a single test administration.

Required Experience and Expertise

The practitioner must draw on clinical experience and child development knowledge during the testing. The adult's interventions and interactions are continually adapted to the specific needs and characteristics of each child. This requires the practitioner to engage in an ongoing hypothesis-formulation and decision-making process.

Limited Practicality

As of the beginning of the 21st century, most dynamic assessment methods have been developed for research or diagnostic purposes and are not always appropriate in classroom environments (Bricker, 1993c). Methods designed for use by specialized professionals in one-to-one research or diagnostic testing situations often do not represent features in terms of tasks, materials, activities, recording formats, and test procedures that are optimal for use by practitioners in everyday classroom activities. The practitioner may adapt these procedures from research methodologies, following specialized training in the original instruments or working together with colleagues who are familiar with dynamic assessment approaches.

GUIDELINES FOR IMPLEMENTATION

The fundamental assumption of the dynamic approach to assessment and intervention is that development and learning occur in social and cultural contexts (Ben Hur, 1998). Thus, it is important to gather information about a child's sociocultural background. This requires involving children's families in order to learn about the rules that apply to children's cultures and their impact on the assessment and intervention process. If children are unfamiliar with the unspoken expectations of mainstream American schools (e.g., making eye contact with the teacher during conversation), the practitioner must actively instruct them about the norms. Figure 7.6 is a list of guidelines developed by Cole (1997) to evaluate a mediated learning activity.

In dynamic assessment, it is important to focus observations and teaching not just on correct responses but also on strategies and processes used by the child. How does the child approach the task? Is he or she able to focus his or her attention easily and stay engaged? Does the child notice mistakes and self-correct? How does he or she respond to feedback? Are there aspects of the task or strategies used by the child that seem to hinder his or her performance? The practitioner must also determine the child's potential for learning and responsivity to instruction by comparing what the child does independently and what the child is able to do with additional support and assistance. This corresponds to the child's ZPD. A test-intervene-retest format should be followed.

The practitioner must consider a variety of teaching strategies and task accommodations in order to identify which supports and modalities work best for the child. Teaching strategies include stating what is important and clearly explaining rules and expectations before each lesson. The following statements or questions may encourage the child's participation:

- "We are here to work together to find the best ways to teach you in school."

- "Can you get yourself ready to pay attention?"

- "Listen so you will know what to do."

- "This is interesting."

The practitioner should provide feedback and encouragement throughout the lesson and ask the child for explanations or clarification when necessary.

Task accommodations may include balancing tasks in order to keep the child's interest, shortening tasks or breaking them down into smaller components, and allowing the child to take breaks when necessary. Visual markers or modifying the classroom environment may be necessary to eliminate distractions. Changing or rearranging materials will also assist in maintaining a child's interest in an activity. As often as possible, practitioners should relate tasks to experiences and situations already familiar to the child (e.g., "Do you have these kinds of blocks at home? Do you build things?"). Figure 7.7 lists some suggestions recommended by Notari-Syverson (1997) for planning and evaluating scaffolding strategies.

Mediated Learning Activity Evaluation Form

Activity: _____ Date: _____

Were the primary goals appropriate?

Were materials appropriate?

Was the activity engaging and interesting for the children?

Was the activity meaningful to the children?

Did children learn skills other than the primary goals?

How well did I relate the activity to other times, places and tasks?

Which types of mediations worked the best?

What can be improved?

Figure 7.6. Mediated Learning Activity Evaluation Form. (From Cole, K. [1997]. *Mediated learning activity evaluation form.* Unpublished document, Washington Research Institute, Seattle; reprinted by permission.)

Scaffolding Checklist

Teacher: *Ruth Hesse* _____   Date: *4/11/00* _____

Children: *Nathan, Suejin, Chandra* _____   Activity: *Drawing pictures about visit to natural history museum* _____

Used open-ended questions (asked for descriptions, explanations, predictions)
Asked Nathan what he was planning on drawing

Provided encouragement and feedback
Showed interest in each child's drawing by asking questions about pictures;
pointed out that Nathan's car didn't have wheels by asking, "Is your car sitting on the street?"

Described what children were doing
Labeled English names of colors Suejin used

Asked children to explain why they did or said something
Took dictations from each child—asked them to say something about their picture

Provided clear instructions and additional clarifications, if needed
Checked with Suejin to make sure she understood the task

Repeated what children said
Repeated Suejin's Korean word for "tiger" and translated it into English

Explained rules and tasks step by step, if needed
Helped Chandra copy her name by pointing with finger to one letter at a time

Provided reminders
Had children talk about the visit to the museum; showed Chandra photos taken during visit

Made sure materials and tasks were interesting for children
Made available different coloring tools (crayons, pencils, pens, markers)

Changed materials or tasks to make them easier, if needed
Let Chandra write letters—she didn't want to draw a picture

Provided models for children to learn from
Wrote Chandra's name for her to copy

Asked children directly to do something, if needed
Asked Nathan to pass the blue marker to Suejin following her request

Worked together to help children complete a difficult task
Counted crayons up to six in English with Suejin

Figure 7.7.   Scaffolding Checklist. (From Notari-Syverson, A. [1997]. *Scaffolding checklist.* Unpublished document, Washington Research Institute, Seattle; adapted by permission.)

Based on models of child development that recognize the role of culture on learning, dynamic assessment requires taking into account a child's and family's sociocultural background when gathering and interpreting information. Testing procedures aim to highlight strategies and processes used by the child rather than the mastery of skills. The main goal is to determine the child's potential for learning by observing how the child learns when offered assistance and support by an adult. Table 7.1 is a summary of guidelines for implementing dynamic assessment.

SUGGESTIONS FOR PRACTITIONERS IN INCLUSIVE ENVIRONMENTS

Early childhood education and early childhood special education practitioners can use dynamic assessment to determine which teaching strategies will best help a child learn. For a child who has experienced learning environments that differ significantly from those of schools, it is particularly helpful to focus on how well he or she responds to instruction rather than on what school-related skills the child has learned so far. For a child with disabilities, focusing the assessment on strategies will provide valuable information on effective instructional approaches and accommodations.

Initial Assessment

A dynamic assessment summary report should contain a profile of a child's strengths and weaknesses and consider his or her skill mastery, use of strategies, and learning processes. It should also include information on the child's degree of responsivity to intervention, such as the intensity of intervention required to produce change, and recommendations of teaching strategies and interventions that promote or impede mastery. Figure 7.8 is an outline of an assessment based on a dynamic approach.

Goal Development

Goals and objectives based on the results of a dynamic assessment represent general processes rather than specific skills (Notari-Syverson & Shuster, 1995). On a child's IEP/IFSP, the team should identify suggested supports and necessary modifications for these objectives. Figure 7.9 is an example of an IEP/IFSP format that is representative of a dynamic approach.

Intervention

When planning intervention, the intentionality, meaning, and transcendence of activities must be taken into consideration. Practitioners need to ensure that the purpose of a task is clear to the child and actively engage and involve the child in the task. Activities should be meaningful to the child and draw on the child's prior experiences. Supports and teaching strategies will need to be identified for each child. Figures 7.10 and 7.11 are examples of activity plans. The first lends itself to planning for specific intervention for a single child within a group activity. The second is for plan-

Table 7.1.   Guidelines for implementing dynamic assessment

Gather information about the child's sociocultural background, and involve the child's family in order to learn about cultural rules.

  Use these rules accordingly in assessment and intervention.

  If children are unfamiliar with the unspoken expectations of mainstream American schools, the practitioner must actively instruct them about the norms.

Focus observations and teaching on strategies and processes used by the child.

  How does the child approach the task?

  Is he or she able to focus his or her attention easily and stay engaged?

  How does he or she respond to feedback?

  Are there aspects of the task that seem to hinder his or her performance?

  Does the child use strategies that seem to hinder his or her performance?

Determine the child's potential for learning and responsivity to instruction.

  Compare what the child does independently and what he or she is able to do with additional support and assistance.

  Follow a test-intervene-retest format.

Try a variety of teaching strategies and task accommodations to identify which supports and modalities work best for the child.

  The practitioner should provide feedback and encouragement throughout the lesson and ask the child for explanations or clarification when necessary.

  Task accommodations may include:

    Balancing tasks in order to keep the child's interest

    Shortening tasks or breaking them down into smaller components

    Allowing the child to take breaks when necessary

    Using visual markers or modifying the classroom environment, if necessary, to eliminate distractions.

    Changing or rearranging materials to maintain a child's interest in an activity.

    Relating tasks to experiences and situations already familiar to the child.

ning the teaching of three different skills for three children functioning at diverse developmental levels. The teacher decides which three children to observe during the activity and marks their names and IEP objectives at the top of each of the three columns. Below, the teacher also notes specific types of teaching strategies that he or she plans to use to facilitate each child's learning of the targeted objective.

Evaluation

When the team is ready to develop comprehensive evaluation plans, the format can vary but should include space notations on the child's progress on target objectives, the amount and intensity of support needed to be successful, and the effectiveness of the supports used. A comprehensive assessment should be completed at the beginning, middle, and end of each school year. Figure 7.12 shows an example of a data collection form. Table 7.2 summarizes suggestions for practitioners using dynamic assessment in inclusive environments.

Outline for Dynamic Assessment

Background information:

    Child

    Family

Family priorities and comments:

Assessment context/situation:

Child's disposition:

Skills observed:

    Cognitive

    Communication

    Socioemotional

    Fine motor

    Gross motor

    Self-help

Child's strategies:

    Attention and motivation

    Approach to materials

    Responses to feedback

    Reactions to challenges

    Self-evaluation and corrections

    Initiations

    Facilitative factors

    Impediments

Effectiveness of adult scaffolding/accommodations:

    What helped?

    What did not help?

Summary:

    Strengths and weaknesses (please describe skills and strategies):

Suggested scaffolding:

Figure 7.8.　Outline for an initial dynamic assessment.

Dynamic Assessment:
Individualized Education Program (IEP)/Individualized Family Service Plan (IFSP)

Child's name: _Aram_   Date of birth: _12/19/97_   Age: _3:1_

Parent(s)/caregiver(s): _Mara_

Resource coordinator/teacher: _Ruth Hesse_

Services: _Speech-language therapy_

Area: _Cognitive_

Goal: _Groups objects based on general categories (e.g., food, clothes, animals)_

Objectives	Strategies
Groups objects on the basis of function (e.g., things to eat with, things that go in water).	Ask questions to help planning: "What do you need to build your fire station?"
Example:	Ask questions to help evaluate: "Do you have everything you need?" "Is there anything missing?"
Before an activity (e.g., water play, construction, art, pretend play, games) choose from a group of objects all those appropriate for the activity.	Help the child list items: "Tell me all the things you need to draw a picture . . . "
	Point out inconsistencies: "Is the puppet a water toy?"
	Provide reminders: "Remember, you need toys that go in water."
	Provide suggestions: "I think you need plates and cups for your restaurant."

Figure 7.9. Individualized education program (IEP)/individualized family service plan (IFSP) containing dynamic assessment strategies.

Dynamic Assessment: Activity Plan

Child's name: _Linda_   Date: _1/31/00_

Description of activity and materials:

> Making lemonade
>
> Materials: lemons, juicers, honey, water

How to get the child/children involved:

> Tell children that they will make lemonade for their afternoon snack. Show them the materials and explain steps involved. Draw pictures of each step on large flipchart for them to refer back to during the activity.

How to make the activity meaningful:

> Have children talk about their favorite drinks—hot and cold.

How to expand the activity beyond the immediate situation:

> Talk about lemons (where they come from, climate needs, acidic taste) and honey (how bees make honey, sweet taste).

Child objectives	Teaching strategies
Linda will focus on the activity for at least 5 minutes.	• Provide verbal and nonverbal encouragements.
	• Provide verbal reminders of the tasks (squeeze lemon, pour juice) and the purpose (making lemonade for snack).
	• Direct Linda's attention to visual cues (pictures of the steps on a flipchart).
	• Encourage Linda to verbally describe what she is doing.

Figure 7.10. Activity plan for an individual child.

Dynamic Assessment: Activity Plan

Teacher: _Ms. Jackson_   Date: _2/24/00_

Description of activity: _Circle time: Storybook reading. Read "The Three Little Pigs" (Big Book). Talk about the pictures and read the text. Encourage the children to comment on the pictures and story._

How to get children involved: _Begin by focusing the children's attention on the title page. Explain the concepts of title, author, and illustrator. Talk about main characters. Ask children if they know the story. Tell them to listen carefully and put on "their listening ears."_

How to make the activity meaningful: _Tell children that we learn new things by reading books. In "The Three Little Pigs," we learn about good materials for building houses. Also, the children will learn to read words, recognize letters, and label pictures._

How to relate the activity to other places, times, and tasks: _Ask the children what their homes are made of. Also ask the children to name other building materials._

	Child and goal _Nathan: Read simple words_	**Child and goal** _Chandra: Recognize familiar letters_	**Child and goal** _Sara: Label pictures_
Strategies to reach goal	Question: "What words do you see on this page?" Provide structure: Encourage the child to sound out letters. ("What letters do you see in this word? If you say the sound for those letters, you can read the word.") Modify task: Sound out initial letters and let the child complete the word. ("First there's a /p/, then a /i/. Pi...") Instruct: Read the word for the child.	Question: "What letters do you see on this page?" Provide structure: Point out distinctive features of letters. ("You said this is a /b/. Look carefully at which side of the circle the stick is on.") Instruct: Show a visual model. ("Here's an 'm.' Can you find another 'm'?")	Question: "What do you see in this picture?" Modify task: Make the task more meaningful by selecting a picture of a main character (wolf, pig). Instruct: Label, and have the child imitate.

Figure 7.11. Activity plan for several children.

144

Dynamic Assessment: IEP/IFSP Data Collection Form

Child's name: _Miriam_

IEP/IFSP goal/objective: _Miriam will be able to sit independently to play for 5 or more minutes._

Recommended supports: _Offer hands to help her pull to sit. Talk about sitting "up, up, up!"_
Make play activity easy so she can work on trunk and head control.

Date and observer	Context/activity	Child behavior	Support
1/5/00 Rena	Home, on floor with blocks and rattle	Sat for 3 minutes on the floor, grasped rattle, brought it to mouth, then banged it on the floor. Played Peekaboo with her mother. Began to avert visual gaze and changed facial expression to show that she was done!	Offered support at her trunk. Changed activity to interactive game (Peekaboo) with no objects as she began to show signs of being tired (increase in body tension)

Figure 7.12. IEP/IFSP data collection form for an individual child.

145

Table 7.2.   Suggestions for practitioners using dynamic assessment in inclusive environments

Initial assessment

A dynamic assessment summary report should contain:

A profile of the child's strengths and weaknesses, considering the mastery of skills, the use of strategies, and learning processes

Information on the child's degree of responsivity to intervention

Goal development

Identify goals and objectives that represent general processes rather than specific skills.

Identify suggested supports and necessary modifications for these objectives.

Intervention

Address intentionality, meaning, and transcendence of the activity.

Make sure that the purpose of the task is clear to the child.

Make sure that the child is involved and engaged in the task.

Choose activities that are meaningful to the child and draw on the child's prior experiences.

Identify supports and teaching strategies for each child.

Evaluation

Develop comprehensive evaluation plans.

Include notations on the child's progress on target objectives, the amount and intensity of support needed to be successful, and the effectiveness of the supports used.

Conduct comprehensive assessments at the beginning, middle, and end of each year.

CONCLUSION

Dynamic assessment is a broad term that includes a variety of quantitative and qualitative approaches, ranging from assessment tools with specified administration procedures and materials to more clinical methodologies that focus on observing learning strategies and processes. There are two major approaches to dynamic assessment. One is to assess the child's ability to learn over a brief period of time using a test-teach-retest paradigm within a single assessment session. This approach is best used for diagnostic purposes. The other approach is better suited to educational environments and involves ongoing assessment at multiple points in time. Information is focused on changes in the child's use of strategies to accomplish a task, as well as in the amounts and types of support that the adult provides to help the child. The key feature common to all dynamic approaches is the emphasis on the child's ability and potential to learn.

Dynamic approaches reflect early 21st-century models of human learning that emphasize the importance of metacognitive processes and strategies. How children use and monitor their attention and listening skills—as well as their ability to plan, identify appropriate solutions to problems, and self-evaluate performance—are all crucial cognitive and self-regulation strategies about which educators and other practitioners need information to help children learn.

Finally, dynamic assessment directly addresses a key element of intervention and teaching: the interaction between the child and the adult. It provides information both on what an adult can do to best help a particular child learn and on how well the child responds to the adult's assistance and support. Progress is evaluated not only on the basis of the child's mastery of skills but also—and more important—on how the child is able to learn from experience and instruction.

Review Questions

■ Explain the rationale for using dynamic assessment.

■ The text states that "the emphasis on observing general processes and strategies rather than mastery of specific tasks can be helpful in differentiating whether the child has a true delay or problem or only lacks familiarity with a task or situation." Provide an example that illustrates this principle.

■ Describe and provide an example of each of the three types of facilitation strategies used to promote self-regulatory behavior.

■ How do underlying theoretical perspectives and assumptions influence dynamic assessment tools and procedures?

■ What are the three essential components of mediated learning experiences (MLEs)?

■ What is the role of the adult in a mediated learning approach?

Curriculum-Based Language Assessment

After reading this chapter, you will be able to:

- Define curriculum-based language assessment, and discuss the rationale for its use

- Give examples of models and methods that fit into a curriculum-based language assessment framework

- Identify considerations and guidelines for implementing curriculum-based language assessment

*N*atasha is a second-grade student. She is bilingual, although English is the primary language spoken at home and school. Her teacher, Mr. Martin, describes her as a carefree and talkative child. Recently, however, Mr. Martin referred her to the school speech-language pathologist for a complete evaluation. On the referral form, he noted that Natasha reads below grade level, puts forth very little effort to attend to tasks that are difficult for her, and has difficulty following oral and written directions. She does not appear to notice that all of the other children in the class raise their hands when they need assistance. Natasha just calls out her questions, even during silent reading time. She has been enrolled in a remedial reading program for the entire year, yet she still has difficulty with reading comprehension. Natasha has difficulty memorizing her spelling words, but when it comes to math, she has memorized basic addition and subtraction facts. Mr. Martin pointed out that Natasha shows inconsistency in her work. For example, on some days she will approach problems with enthusiasm, and on other days, she assumes the attitude of "I can't do this, so I'm not going to try." Her method for coping on these days is to look at other students' work to see what to do next. She does not appear to make friends easily.

Ms. Sutton, the speech-language pathologist, read Mr. Martin's referral information with interest because the remedial reading teacher, Mr. Carson, had a conversation with her about Natasha a week earlier. Ms. Sutton decided to call the school's evaluation team together to obtain more information on Natasha and her difficulties in the classroom. At their first meeting, Ms. Sutton introduced Natasha's parents, Mr. and Ms. Pogoloff, to the team members. She began the meeting by asking the Pogoloffs whether Natasha appeared to enjoy school. Ms. Pogoloff commented that Natasha had loved kindergarten and first grade but that she had noticed a marked difference in her enthusiasm for school this past year. Mr. Martin agreed that he too had noticed a difference in Natasha's attitude toward school since the beginning of the year.

The team explained the available assessment options to Mr. and Ms. Pogoloff. The psychologist could administer the Wechsler Intelligence Scale for Children–Revised (WISC-R; Wechsler, 1974) to determine whether there was a possible learning disability. Ms. Sutton recommended that a comprehensive speech-language evaluation be conducted that would include both formal and nonformal measures. The Pogoloffs agreed that it was important to complete the testing before the end of the school year to discover whether there were any underlying language difficulties that could be contributing to Natasha's reading comprehension difficulties.

The formal testing conducted by the psychologist and Ms. Sutton revealed that Natasha did qualify for special education services in the resource room program with a documented language-learning disability. Ms. Sutton, Mr. Martin, and the resource room teacher decided to work collaboratively to conduct a language-based curriculum analysis. Results from this analysis would be used to identify potential gaps between the language demands of the academic curriculum and Natasha's linguistic competence.

First, the team developed a simple checklist (see Figure 8.1) that they used to identify the contextually based areas in which Natasha was experiencing the most difficulty. Natasha's parents, Mr. Martin, Ms. Sutton, and Mr. Carson each completed the checklist. The Pogoloffs noted that although Natasha loved to read and look at pictures in books at home, she appeared to have difficulty answering questions about the story afterward. Also, they noticed that Natasha was having difficulty remembering to do her chores and repeatedly getting into arguments with the neighborhood children. Mr. Martin reiterated his concerns about Natasha's inability to ask for help appropriately in the classroom. He described how Natasha called out questions during silent reading time and looked at other children's worksheets without noticing their displeasure with her actions. Both Mr. Martin and Mr. Carson identified two additional areas of concern: following oral directions and reading comprehension. Ms. Sutton noted that Natasha appeared to experience difficulty following oral directions and comprehending words with multiple meanings in reading passages. After the team reviewed the entries on the form, three patterns emerged. The team agreed to focus their attention on 1) following oral directions, 2) reading comprehension, and 3) pragmatic language skills.

The next step required a review of the specific vocabulary and language requirements of the second-grade curriculum. Mr. Martin gave the team members copies of his scope and sequence chart, which outlined the curricular objectives of his second-grade class and the language requirements necessary across content areas. The team noticed that new vocabulary in the basal reading series and in the spelling textbook contained many words with multiple meanings and that the course objectives required an understanding of multistep directions.

Next, the team focused on Natasha's current linguistic abilities and the types of support that she would need to successfully meet the outlined curricular objectives. Ms. Sutton shared the results of her standardized language assessment battery with the other team members. The results indicated that Natasha had receptive and expressive language delays. She would need contextually based support in the three areas identified by the team.

Finally, the team brainstormed about the ways that the curricular materials could be modified to ensure Natasha's academic success. The Pogoloffs commented that Natasha seemed able to tell what happened in a story if they read it to her first and then asked her to read it back. After repeated readings, Mr. Pogoloff said that Natasha enjoyed asking him whether he remembered what happened in the story. Mr. Martin explained that he had tried writing the directions for class assignments on the blackboard and encouraged Natasha to copy these prior to beginning an assignment. Mr. Carson had listened to Natasha reading orally and recorded reading errors. His analysis showed that Natasha's errors were more syntactically acceptable than semantically acceptable. Ms. Sutton proposed videotaping dialogue exchanges between Natasha and her teachers during various class activities that required following multistep oral directions and reading comprehension. She would use the scoring procedure guidelines outlined by Blank, Rose, and Berlin (1978a).

Curriculum-Based Language Assessment: Area(s) of Concern Checklist

Child: _Natasha Pogoloff_   Date: _April 22, 2000_

Observer	Description of concern
Mr. and Ms. Pogoloff	Unable to answer simple questions after reading story
	Does not always follow through on directions
	Has difficulty maintaining friendships
Mr. Martin	Following multistep directions in class
	Responding to comprehension questions in basal reading series
	Following appropriate classroom social rules
Mr. Carson	Following directions related to reading assignment
	Answering comprehension questions for reading
Ms. Sutton	Following oral directions
	Comprehension of figurative language in narrative discourse and written reading passages

Summary of patterns noted:

1. Following oral directions
2. Reading comprehension
3. Pragmatic language skills

Figure 8.1. Area(s) of concern checklist for an individual child.

Traditional curriculum-based approaches only measure children's mastery of the official curriculum, taking no consideration of many other kinds of "hidden" curricula that children must learn in order to succeed in school (Nelson, 1994). These hidden curricula can include various unspoken expectations for children, such as knowledge and familiarity with mainstream culture, rules for communication and behavior in school, and rules for peer acceptance and interaction (Nelson, 1989). The assessment of language must be expanded beyond an analysis of the three basic dimensions of language—content, form, and use—to an analysis of the contextual and cultural influences that either facilitate or hinder language understanding and use in school.

Language use in the context of the school curriculum is the most significant factor in determining whether children succeed academically (Miller, 1984). Differences exist between language spoken at home and in school (Adler, 1981; Barrera, 1993; Cazden, 1988; Heath, 1982; Labov, 1972; Snow, 1983). For example, the predominant language style used in school is formal and emphasizes early orientation toward the written word; it neglects language areas that are strong in some cultures, such as oral language expression through drama, poetry, and song (Hale, 1992; Kochman, 1972). Verbal and nonverbal discrepancies often occur when teachers and children have different cultural backgrounds. For example, Barrera (1993) found that bilingual children responded differently when their non-English home language was used in the intervention environment. Also, teachers may expect eye contact and answers to direct questions, but some Asian and Native American individuals consider these interactions inappropriate in child–adult communication (Gilmore, 1984; Locust, 1988).

Assessing the language of children from various backgrounds requires consideration of the influences of contextual and cultural factors on language (Adler, 1981; Gutierrez-Clellen & Quinn, 1993; Labov, 1972; Miller, 1984). For example, the use of culturally appropriate pictures improved the language performance of African American children (Cazden, 1970). Children from lower-income families achieved the same level of performance as children from middle-class families when they received additional adult support in the form of probes and questions (Heider, Cazden, & Brown, 1968, cited in Cazden, 1970). Au and Mason (1981) found that native Hawaiian children understood written texts better when they were read in the "talk-story" conversational format typical of their culture compared with turn-taking reading groups.

The pragmatic aspects of language—in terms of style, genre, speech acts, and narratives across contexts—are extremely important when assessing children from diverse cultures. Language development is the primary medium for instruction and for learning (Bartoli & Botel, 1988; Westby, 1985). Children may score below norms on tests not because they have speech-language impairments but because of a sociocultural mismatch between their language experiences at home and the academic language used in school (Nelson, 1993). External text biases result from differences in the environment, child rearing, schooling, and sociocultural status. Language variations may be due to cultural and stylistic differences or from language development problems. Traditional tests focus on written language and ignore many oral language skills in which African Americans, for example, may demonstrate greater competence (Hale, 1992). Also, acculturation factors can cause stress, which can be confused with learning disabilities (Adler, 1981; Gavillàn-Torres, 1984). Children display language and communicative competence differently in school than in social situations, so information from family members is critical in making decisions about children's need for language intervention services (Nelson, 1993).

The Individuals with Disabilities Education Act (IDEA) Amendments of 1997 (PL 105-17) acknowledge the influences of the family's cultural and linguistic patterns and include regulations aimed at ensuring opportunities to succeed in the mainstream curriculum for all children. Section 614(b)(2) states that the local education agency shall

> [U]se a variety of assessment tools and strategies to gather relevant functional and developmental information, including information provided by the parent, that may assist in determining whether the child is a child with a disability and the content of the child's IEP, including information related to enabling the child to be involved in and progress in the general curriculum or, for preschool children, to participate in appropriate activities.

Children with limited proficiency in school language must be conscious of both the instructional content and the language used to convey it. This task is especially challenging for children who are bilingual and dealing with learning difficulties in general (Barrera, 1993). This chapter describes **curriculum-based language assessment** as the identification and analysis of potential gaps between a particular context's linguistic demands and a learner's linguistic competence.

THEORETICAL FRAMEWORK

A transactional perspective on learning (Sameroff & Chandler, 1975) views development as an interactive process in which infants and their caregiving environment mutually alter one another. The organism's ability to respond appropriately is contingent on the interactive nature of the organism—environment exchange (Sameroff & Chandler, 1975). Many scholars believe that formal linguistic systems emerge from these early reciprocal transactions between infants and their caregivers (Bricker & Schiefelbusch, 1981; Carlson & Bricker, 1982).

One aspect of curriculum-based language assessment involves determining the type of support that a child needs to ensure mastery of the linguistic demands of the curriculum. In order to accomplish this, dynamic assessment procedures based on Vygotsky's (1962) social-interactionist perspective can be used. One important task involves determining the child's ZPD, that is, what the child can achieve both independently and with the assistance of an adult or more capable peer. The child's responsivity to instruction can be determined through an analysis of dialogue exchanges. The adult mediates the exchange, by providing scaffolding or guided support, to build on what the child already knows. The level and type of scaffolding that an adult provides are contingent on the child's response, and the child's response to the adult's scaffolding provides the basis for the child's next response.

MODELS AND APPLICATIONS

Although much has been written about general curriculum-based models of assessment, practitioners need more information on applications of curriculum-based language assessment. Only a few models have been described in the literature. One early model of assessment, the Preschool Language Assessment Instrument (Blank, Rose, & Berlin, 1978b), underscores the importance of identifying the variables that hinder or facilitate adult–child interactions in preschool. This informal assessment tool identifies the language demands of a classroom and provides information on how children handle those demands. Results from this type of assessment enable practitioners to use children's responses to questions or demands to identify their current language-processing abilities. The model outlines four broad categories of demands that exist in the realm of discourse at the preschool level: 1) matching perception, 2) selective analysis of perception, 3) reordering perception, and 4) reasoning about perception.

Matching perception refers to language demands that require children to respond to or report on salient perceptual information inherent to a task. Questions are aimed at identifying whether they can differentiate between the types of information expected from different questions. The required language skills include matching, identifying objects by sound or touch, labeling and describing, imitating, and remembering previously seen objects and information.

Selective analysis of perception requires children to focus more particularly on the characteristics of objects or events that are common to preschool classrooms. Questions are aimed at identifying skills such as whether they can identify functions of objects, describe events, recall information, and categorize objects. For example, can the child respond to questions that are aimed at identifying similarities and differences?

Reordering perception differs from the first two groups of demands by requiring children to evaluate material and ideas that exclude salient perceptual information and involve materials and events that are not being perceived currently. For instance, children may be told part of a story and then asked to describe events subsequent to being shown a picture (e.g., "What might happen next?"). In addition, they may be asked to draw on metalinguistic abilities, that is, use language to talk about language (e.g., "Tell me how the words *bear* and *bare* are the same and how they are different"). They also must follow sequences in discourse and change the order of or reverse sequences (e.g., "Tell me what happened before the little girl went on the walk").

Reasoning about perception requires children to respond to complex verbal problems that involve drawing inferences (e.g., "How do you know that the little girl is afraid?"), making predictions (e.g., "What would happen if the little girl asked for help?"), and formulating solutions (e.g., "What could you do if you were afraid?"). Children responding to language demands at this level use language as a vehicle for reflecting on their own perceptions, a skill some researchers believe to be critical to effective teacher–child exchanges.

Norris and Hoffman (1993) provided a framework for an integrated model of language assessment that examines the dynamic interrelationships among contexts, learners, and language used within communicative contexts. In the situational context, language demands range from **contextualized** to **decontextualized.** The practitioner must differentiate between when a child's language relates to people, objects, or events in the immediate environment (i.e., it is contextualized) and when language refers to an imagined context (i.e., it is decontextualized).

In the discourse context, the practitioner must determine whether the function of the discourse is narrative or expository in nature. **Narrative discourse** occurs frequently in classroom and social environments and involves skills such as the ability to relate personal experiences and retell stories. **Expository discourse,** perhaps even more critical to academic success, involves utilizing the formal language found in textbooks and teachers' presentations.

When examining the **semantic context,** the practitioner must determine whether the ideas and meanings of words, phrases, or sentences draw on a child's prior knowledge and experiences (i.e., they are experiential) or go beyond a literal interpretation and are embedded in historical, cultural, and world views (i.e., they are erudite). Norris and Hoffman (1993) noted that sometimes ideas expressed within an oral or written passage can be understood at the experiential and erudite levels of meaning. Using this model, the practitioner can examine children's language simultaneously in the situational, discourse, and semantic contexts. The adult's presentation style can then be modified to match the linguistic abilities of the child when necessary.

Nelson (1994) used the term *curriculum-based language assessment* to refer to the process of determining whether children have the language skills and strategies for processing information within the context of the school curriculum. Prelock (1997) suggested a four-part language-based curriculum analysis that is most effective when implemented collaboratively by all relevant team members: caregivers, speech-language pathologists, classroom teachers, and related personnel.

The first step in this four-part language-based curriculum analysis is identifying the curricular objectives that must be attained by students in a particular environment. Nelson (1994) described this process as identifying the **zones of significance** for a particular child. These zones refer to contextually based language areas that two or more team members determine are critical to the mastery of curricular objectives. Team members use participant interviews, artifact analysis, onlooker observations, and participant observations to assist them in this process. To identify zones of significance, Prelock (1997) suggested ascertaining the following: 1) whether the child is confused by a particular content area, 2) whether the contextually based areas are prerequisites for later objectives, and 3) whether a competency-based curriculum (observable and measurable outcomes delineated at each grade level) is approved by the school district.

The second step is a review of the curriculum's specific vocabulary and language requirements. The team members must examine the typical ways in which students are allowed to demonstrate comprehension of vocabulary. They must conduct observations to determine the oral and written language demands of a particular environment. The team also must identify the prerequisite and new vocabulary used in the curriculum across content areas. In addition, the team needs to ascertain how children meet the requirements or expectations for comprehension of the curriculum.

The third step is identification of the child's current inner resources for meeting the demands of the curriculum and the areas in which the child may need support to ensure mastery of the curricular objectives (Nelson, 1994; Prelock, 1997). The speech-language pathologist, working in conjunction with the classroom teacher, is ideally suited to identify specific language deficit areas.

The fourth step is determining which strategies the child might use that would make processing more effective and efficient (Nelson, 1994). In addition, the team must decide what modifications, if any, will be made to the curriculum or the way it is being taught.

ADVANTAGES AND LIMITATIONS

Curriculum-based language assessment is ideally suited to assess young children from various linguistic and cultural backgrounds and children with disabilities. This approach can be used to pinpoint trouble spots in the curriculum and determine whether the difficulty is related to the learner's linguistic competence relative to the language of the curriculum. A serious limitation of traditional assessment measures is their poor predictability for learning potential or future performance. Curriculum-based language assessment provides an option for practitioners and caregivers who wish to identify strategies and techniques that can be used to modify the presentation of curricular information and thereby increase a child's potential for academic success.

Advantages

The link between assessment and intervention is an inherent advantage of curriculum-based language assessment. Another advantage of this assessment approach is that it encourages collaboration and communication among those working with the child. These concepts are further discussed next.

Link Between Assessment and Intervention

The most obvious advantage of curriculum-based language assessment is its direct relationship to the curricular content in which the child is experiencing difficulty. Team members can identify rather easily the areas that are causing most difficulty for the child. Then intervention efforts are geared toward enhancing the child's linguistic abilities, making curricular modifications, or both.

Collaboration and Communication

A curriculum-based language assessment approach encourages caregivers and practitioners to work collaboratively to analyze curricular requirements and a child's language abilities relative to these requirements. In this way, a more holistic view of the child—including his or her linguistic strengths and difficulties across contexts—can be obtained.

Limitations

Two disadvantages of the curriculum-based language approach are reduced efficiency and the high level of expertise required to conduct such assessment. Both ideas are explored in the following sections.

Reduced Efficiency

When using a curriculum-based language assessment approach, it is necessary to conduct a thorough analysis of the areas in the curriculum that are causing a child the most difficulty, and a review of the curricular objectives that must be attained. This process can be time consuming. In addition, times must be arranged to enable meetings between the child's caregivers and the practitioners who work with the child.

High Level of Expertise Required

One aspect of curriculum-based language assessment is the analysis of dialogue exchanges to determine what level of assistance is needed to ensure a child's linguistic success. Practitioners must be skilled in analyzing a child's responses to various oral and written language demands. They then need to provide the necessary scaffolding to assist the child in comprehending language demands.

GUIDELINES FOR IMPLEMENTATION

Curriculum-based language assessment must first identify areas within the curriculum that are most problematic for a child. This process ought to involve the child if he or she is old enough, the child's caregivers, and practitioners who work with the child. For a preschool-age child, this type of assessment might involve the child's caregiver and preschool teacher. For school-age children, the child's classroom teacher and other related-services personnel who work with the child, such as a speech-language pathologist, might be involved. Although numerous areas of difficulty may be identified, the team should prioritize two or three critical areas.

Once the areas of difficulty are identified, the team is ready to examine contextual language demands. The child's classroom teacher can identify the curricular objectives that must be attained and, working in collaboration with a speech-language pathologist, identify the language abilities necessary to comprehend the curriculum.

Next, the team must determine the child's current language abilities. This process utilizes formal and nonformal assessment tools. Formal measures may include standardized, norm-referenced tests. Nonformal measures may include descriptive measures, such as transcripts of dialogue exchanges. Audiotapes or videotapes may be used. The analysis of these exchanges should be conducted by the speech-language pathologist in collaboration with other team members. It should provide information on two separate but related aspects of the communicative exchange: 1) the quality of the child's response relative to the contextual or linguistic demand and 2) the child's responsivity to instruction.

To evaluate the quality of a child's response, the guidelines outlined by Blank and colleagues (1978a) are useful. Rather than a simple correct/incorrect categorization, they recommended the use of a scale with the following range of scores:

- 3 for a "fully adequate" response

- 2 for an "acceptable" response

- 1 for an "ambiguous" response

- 0 for an "inadequate" response

The focus of the evaluation is not on the structural complexity of the response but rather on the appropriateness of the response relative to the contextual demand. Figure 8.2 shows the further scoring procedures for assessment of a child's response.

The literature describes several scaffolding techniques (e.g., Bradshaw & Harn, 1999; Norris & Hoffman, 1990) that initiate the second level of analysis and can be used to determine the child's responsivity to instruction. These include, but are not limited to, the strategies that are described in Table 8.1.

Curriculum-based language assessment requires collecting information on an ongoing basis to monitor changes in curricular requirements and the developmental growth of the child's linguistic abilities. Table 8.2 provides guidelines for implementing curriculum-based language assessment.

SUGGESTIONS FOR PRACTITIONERS IN INCLUSIVE ENVIRONMENTS

Curriculum-based language assessment requires collaboration among caregivers, early childhood personnel, and early intervention/early childhood special education personnel. Potential gaps between the linguistic competence of a learner and the linguistic demands of various contexts can only be determined if the team works together to identify the "trouble spots."

Initial Assessment

During an initial assessment of a child, nonformal measures can be used to document the language demands of the oral-written curriculum. This is best accomplished by the child's teacher, working in collaboration with a speech-language pathologist. Both formal and nonformal measures can be used to determine the child's current level of linguistic competence. Audiotape or videotape analysis of verbal exchanges helps identify the types of scaffolding that assist a child in meeting the linguistic demands of the curriculum.

Goal Development

After a thorough review of interview or referral information, formal and nonformal test results, and nonformal assessment of curricular areas in

Assessment of Child's Response

Sample task: Child is shown a toy balance scale containing weights on each side. The adult holds up a small weight and asks, "What will happen to the scale if I put another one here?" (pointing to one side).

Coding of response	Score	Rules for coding	Example
Fully adequate	3	Answer fully meets the demands of the task.	(pointing) "That side will go down."
Acceptable			
Imprecise	2	Answer is valid but is vague or poorly formulated.	(pointing) "Down."
Oblique		Answer is not directed to the focus of the problem.	"There'll be another thing in the cup."
Extraneous		Answer includes extraneous or irrelevant information.	"It will go down 'cos it's white."
Ambiguous	1	It is not possible to determine if answer is adequate or inadequate	"It'll move."
Inadequate			
Invalid	0	Answer shows an understanding of the question, but the answer is incorrect.	"It will go up."
Association to material		Answer indicates no understanding of the question, but it is focused on the material.	"It's red."
Irrelevant		a. Answer shows no understanding of the question or material.	"I got one of those at home."
		b. Answer is an imitation of all or part of adult's words or actions.	"It will happen."
		c. Answer is denial of the problem stated.	"You won't put it on."
"I don't know"*		Child states that he or she cannot answer.	"I don't know what'll happen."
No response*		Child offers no verbal response.	(shrugs)

Figure 8.2. Assessment of child's response. *These two types of failures to respond are separated because clinically they seem to represent different behaviors. The verbalization *I don't know* is usually a sign that the child wishes to continue the exchange, whereas the nonverbal response is more indicative of a withdrawal from the dialogue. (*Source:* Blank, Rose, & Berlin [1978a].)

Table 8.1.   Scaffolding strategies used in curriculum-based language assessment

Strategy	Description	Example
Preparatory set	The adult provides information about the concept that needs to be understood.	Adult: What do you do before you go to sleep?
Gestures	The adult provides the child with nonlinguistic cues.	Child: Little Bear got ready for bed. Adult: He _____ (pretends to brush teeth).
Binary choices	The adult offers the child alternate utterances.	Adult: Do you think Little Bear wants to go to sleep or read a story?
Relational terms	The adult uses prompts that tell the child that more information is needed.	Child: Little Bear needs a light. Adult: So that he can _____.
Phonemic cues	The adult uses prompts that contain the initial sound or syllable in a word.	Child: He said something. Adult: Before bed, Little Bear said, "Good n _____ ."
Expansion/modeling	The adult expands on the child's utterance and models appropriate language.	Child: He said "night." Adult: Big Bear said "good night" to Little Bear.
Cloze procedures	The adult's pause indicates that the child is to fill in the information.	Adult: So Little Bear looked at shadow on his wall and felt very _____.
Wh- questions	The adult elicits specific information.	Child: Little Bear sat up in bed. Adult: What did Little Bear do next?
Comprehension questions	The adult asks questions to identify the child's level of comprehension.	Child: Little Bear could not sleep. Adult: Why couldn't he sleep?
Summarization question	The adult asks the child to summarize or restate information.	Adult: So tell me how Big Bear helped Little Bear get to sleep.

From Bradshaw, M., & Harn, W. (1999, April). *Application of adult scaffolding within naturalistic situations.* Paper presented at the North Carolina Speech, Hearing and Language Association, Asheville; adapted by permission.

Source: Norris & Hoffman (1990).

which the child is experiencing the most difficulty, the child's IEP/IFSP goals and objectives are selected. A checklist can be used to identify and cross-validate areas of concern voiced by all team members. It is recommended that the team identify two or three critical areas of the curriculum that are problematic for the child.

Intervention

Intervention efforts should be directed toward increasing the child's linguistic competence relative to contextual demands of the curriculum. The practitioner should provide the necessary scaffolding throughout dialogue exchanges to identify the level of support that the child needs to master the

Table 8.2. Guidelines for implementing curriculum-based language assessment

The team must identify areas within the curriculum that are most problematic for the child.
This ought to involve the child if he or she is old enough, the child's caregivers, and other relevant team members.
It is best that the team prioritize two or three critical areas.

The team must examine the contextual language demands.
The child's classroom teacher can ascertain the curricular objectives that must be attained and work in collaboration with a speech-language pathologist to identify the language abilities necessary to comprehend the curriculum.

The team must determine the child's current language abilities.
Practitioners and caregivers work together to determine the child's language abilities.
This process utilizes formal and nonformal assessment tools.

The team must plan for an analysis of dialogue exchanges between the child and the adults who work with the child.
The analysis of dialogue exchanges should be conducted by the speech-language pathologist in collaboration with other team members.
The analysis should accomplish two tasks:
Determining the quality of the child's response relative to the contextual or linguistic demands
Documenting the child's responsivity to instruction

The team must monitor changes in curricular requirements and the developmental growth of the child's linguistic abilities.

curricular objectives. Scaffolding strategies can be used to determine what the child is capable of learning with support and the types of assistance that will best help the child.

Evaluation

Audiotape or videotape analysis of verbal exchanges can be used to compare the quality of the child's responses to the linguistic demands of the curriculum before, during, and after intervention. It is best to monitor possible changes in curricular requirements and linguistic abilities of children every 3–4 months. Results can be quantified, summarized qualitatively, or both. Table 8.3 summarizes guidelines for practitioners using curriculum-based language assessment in inclusive environments.

CONCLUSION

Curriculum-based assessment has been used for a number of years in early childhood and early childhood special education environments. The local curriculum serves as a guide to determine a child's instructional needs (Nelson, 1994). Because of the direct congruence among testing, teaching, and progress evaluation, curriculum-based assessment provides a direct link between the child's entry or baseline level of mastery and the child's level of ability after instruction is provided. Curriculum-based language assessment

Table 8.3. Suggestions for practitioners using curriculum-based language assessment in inclusive environments

Initial assessment

Informal measures can be used to document the language demands of the oral-written curriculum.

Formal and informal measures can be used to determine the child's current level of linguistic competence.

Audiotape or videotape analysis of dialogue exchanges helps identify the types of scaffolding that assist a child in meeting the linguistic demands of the curriculum.

Goal development

The goals and objectives selected for the IEP/IFSP should be based on a thorough review of interview or referral information, formal and informal test results, and an informal assessment of curricular areas in which the child is experiencing the most difficulty.

Intervention

Intervention efforts should be directed toward increasing the child's linguistic competence relative to contextual demands of the curriculum.

The practitioner should provide the necessary scaffolding throughout dialogue exchanges to assist the child in mastery of curricular objectives.

Evaluation

Audiotape or videotape analysis of dialogue exchanges can be used to compare the quality of the child's responses to the linguistic demands of the curriculum before and after intervention.

Results can be quantified, summarized qualitatively, or both.

is distinguished from **curriculum-based measurement (CBM)** by a difference in the type of information it provides. According to Nelson (1994), CBM is used to determine whether the child mastered the content of the general curriculum, whereas curriculum-based language assessment addresses whether the child possesses the linguistic competence to process the language of the general curriculum. The results of curriculum-based language assessment can be used to help bridge the gap between the child's current language abilities and the language abilities that he or she needs to succeed in school.

Review Questions

■ Explain the rationale for using curriculum-based language assessment.

■ The text states, "Language use in the context of the school curriculum is the most significant factor in determining whether children succeed academically. Differences exist between language spoken at home and in school." Give two examples that illustrate this principle.

■ Briefly describe the four broad categories of demands that exist in the realm of discourse at the preschool level.

■ Identify the four steps involved in language-based curriculum analysis.

Transdisciplinary Framework

After reading this chapter, you will be able to:

- Summarize specific characteristics of alternative assessment approaches

- Provide the rationale for using a transdisciplinary framework to implement alternative assessment approaches

- Give examples of models and methods that incorporate a transdisciplinary framework

- Identify potential barriers to the implementation of a transdisciplinary framework

- Identify advantages and limitations of a transdisciplinary framework

- Provide guidelines for implementing a transdisciplinary framework

*E*veryone seemed very satisfied. This meeting had been the culmination of several planning sessions. Not only had everyone agreed on all assessment and educational outcomes, but also the hospital educational coordinator assented to providing the necessary support services to Richard Birdsong at home and in the classroom. He was paralyzed from the neck down and required around-the-clock medical attention for a chronic respiratory condition. Although 5-year-old Richard was diagnosed with severe cerebral palsy at birth, his intellect and humor were sharp.

Initially, Richard's parents were concerned that he would not be accepted in an off-reservation community because of his physical impairments and medical issues. Ms. Birdsong's niece, Ms. Atkins, was a prekindergarten teacher in an inclusive classroom housed in a university hospital environment. When Mr. Birdsong was offered a position at the hospital, Ms. Atkins encouraged the family to relocate so that Richard could receive quality medical care and educational services and still be close to family.

As a child growing up on the reservation, Ms. Atkins was overwhelmed by the severity of Richard's physical impairment. Richard had to lie on his back on a gurney, and the only controlled movement that he demonstrated was turning his head from side to side. He experienced respiratory failure five times in his first year of life, and no one had really expected him to live.

After Ms. Atkins received a degree in early childhood education at the university, she received a telephone call from her aunt. Richard was 3 years old, and his mother asked Ms. Atkins to speak with a Head Start worker who was encouraging the family to enroll Richard in a program for children with disabilities. Mr. and Ms. Birdsong, in consultation with tribal elders, had decided that traditional healing ceremonies designed to protect Richard from further illness should be conducted prior to exposing him to outside influences that might harm him. When Ms. Atkins spoke with the Head Start worker, she knew that the individual neither understood the necessity for the delay nor respected her aunt and uncle's decision.

Prior to Richard's enrollment in Ms. Atkins's classroom, Ms. Norton, the hospital educational coordinator, scheduled a preliminary planning meeting to determine who should be invited to serve on Richard's team. Mr. and Ms. Birdsong were apprehensive about this meeting because of their negative experience 2 years earlier with the Head Start worker. The first item on the agenda was to plan for a complete assessment of Richard's developmental abilities. Ms. Norton began the meeting by asking the Birdsongs to describe Richard's typical schedule and daily care needs at home. Mr. Birdsong bathed and dressed Richard, whereas Ms. Birdsong fed him and cared for his toileting needs. At 5 years old, Richard was light enough for his parents to lift and carry him, but they realized that as Richard grew, caring for him would become more difficult.

When asked to describe Richard's ability to communicate, Mr. and Ms. Birdsong explained that although Richard could not communicate using words, he understood all that was said to him and laughed at appropriate times. His parents recognized slight changes in his facial expressions, and Richard could answer a series of yes/no questions by nodding his head and grunting. Although they were confident that he understood everything that was said to him, they were very interested in knowing the extent of his cognitive and communication abilities.

The Birdsongs, Ms. Norton, and Ms. Atkins decided that an audiologist would test Richard's hearing, a psychologist would administer a cognitive assessment, and a speech-language pathologist would assess his communication abilities. Ms. Atkins suggested that a physical therapist conduct an evaluation of Richard's motor skills and that an occupational therapist assess his adaptive abilities. A respiratory specialist and rehabilitation engineer would be assigned to the team to collaborate with the speech-language pathologist in designing a comfortable positioning arrangement for Richard's testing. The hospital social worker would be available to help with funding arrangements. Satisfied that a thorough assessment would be possible, Richard's medical records were distributed to the team so that everyone could be prepared for the next planning meeting.

Although Ms. Atkins tried to prepare her aunt and uncle for the number of professionals who would be assembled for the second meeting, they were somewhat intimidated when they entered the room. Ms. Norton was eager to put the family at ease. She began by explaining that the team was interested in working collaboratively with them to provide Richard with the best possible educational services. With Ms. Atkins's help, the conversation that followed included a rich discussion of the role of extended family and tribal elders in all decision making; the family's cultural background, heritage, and values regarding educational outcomes and services; explanations of tribal practices and ceremonies for Richard's medical needs; and the family's language preferences and literacy practices in the home.

Ms. Norton explained the advantage of using both formal and nonformal assessment measures to gain a representative profile of Richard's developmental abilities. Each team member was asked to describe available formal and nonformal assessment options related to his or her field. After listening intently, Mr. and Ms. Birdsong concluded that a portfolio assessment approach would provide the most coherent and comprehensive picture of Richard's developmental abilities. Based on Ms. Norton's earlier conversation with the Birdsongs about Richard's ability to nod to yes/no questions and his keen receptive language abilities, she suggested that audiometric testing be conducted in the traditional way. The audiologist and the parents readily agreed. The psychologist and speech-language pathologist described a number of available alternative assessment approaches that could be used to assess Richard's cognitive and social-communication abilities. Mr. and Ms. Birdsong indicated a preference for both a formal receptive test of intellectual functioning and nonformal focused and dynamic assessment procedures to determine the extent of Richard's receptive vocabulary, as well as his ability to expand his understanding of vocabulary with mediation and support.

The respiratory specialist and the rehabilitation engineer explained that in order to effectively test Richard's expressive language abilities, his positioning would need to be considered. The team decided that specialized wheelchair adaptations would allow Richard to sit in a semireclined position. Ms. Norton said that she would secure the necessary paperwork for funding adaptive equipment, and the social worker and the Birdsongs agreed to complete the paperwork together. After Richard's cognitive and receptive abilities were assessed and the wheelchair modifications were made, the speech-language pathologist made two suggestions: that she and the respiratory specialist determine Richard's potential for spoken language and that, in the meantime, the team consider some type of AAC system. Mr. and Ms. Birdsong agreed to work with the team to teach them to read Richard's nonverbal cues, facial expressions, and grunts. Finally, the motor specialist explained that videotapes could be used to document Richard's response to a range of motion exercises.

All of the team members decided that assessment data should be collected in the classroom and at home. At the next meeting, Mr. and Ms. Birdsong and the other team members shared the assessment results and began the initial discussions about Richard's IEP. Mr. and Ms. Birdsong were much more comfortable in their team role than they were in the initial two meetings, as were the other team members. Differences of opinion were no longer followed by uncomfortable periods of silence; in fact, it appeared that hearing diverse points of view helped the team to see all sides of an issue. After the IEP was finalized, the team agreed to meet at 3-month intervals to review Richard's progress and plan for his future needs.

This chapter summarizes the characteristics of the alternative assessment approaches, designed to assist caregivers and practitioners in choosing the application(s) that best fit different situations, that are discussed throughout this book. Following the summary is the rationale for using a transdisciplinary framework to implement these assessment approaches. Two comprehensive, multidimensional programs that use a transdisciplinary framework are described, along with barriers to successful implementation of **transdisciplinary assessment** procedures. Finally, the advantages and limitations of using a transdisciplinary framework are identified and guidelines are provided for practitioners who wish to adopt this model.

SUMMARY OF ALTERNATIVE ASSESSMENT APPROACHES

The alternative assessment approaches discussed in this book are used to evaluate the comprehensive and ongoing development of young children from birth to 8 years of age. These approaches fall into three main categories (embedded, authentic, and mediated). Embedded models of assessment are those in which opportunities to observe children's behavior are embedded within a natural context. These include naturalistic assessment and focused assessment approaches. Authentic models, which include performance assessment and portfolio assessment approaches, are those in which a profile of the abilities of children are documented by observing real-life tasks. Mediated models involve the use of guided teaching to provide information on children's mastery of the language of instruction and their responsivity to instruction. These models include dynamic assessment and curriculum-based language assessment approaches.

Each of these alternative assessment approaches incorporates the following dimensions:

- The type of skills being assessed
- The assessment tools used
- The role of the adult in the assessment process
- The type of activities in which the assessment occurs
- The methods used to record data
- The types of data collected

The practitioner must carefully consider each of these dimensions in order to select an approach that is right for a particular child and family. Table 9.1 contains a detailed summary of the characteristics of each approach.

To choose an assessment procedure, the type of skill being measured should be considered. For example, as illustrated in Table 9.1, it is true that naturalistic assessment and focused/play assessments are similar because opportunities to assess children's developmental abilities are embedded in the natural context. Naturalistic assessment, however, is used when the practitioner wishes to assess discrete developmental behaviors that can be operationalized or measured, such as the number of two-word utterances that a child uses in a 30-minute observational period. Focused/play assessment is used when it is necessary to assess more complex or holistic behaviors, such as affective behaviors, that are difficult to quantify or to break down into smaller components. Although performance and portfolio assessments are used to measure the same types of skills, performance assessment is best used when the practitioner wishes to document the performance of all children in a classroom for display on Parents' Night. Portfolio assessment may be used to provide a comprehensive picture of a child with a severe disability in that same classroom for whom traditional assessment procedures failed to measure or document progress. Likewise, dynamic and curriculum-based language assessments can be used to measure the same type of skill, but dynamic assessment would be the better choice if the practitioner is more interested in determining a child's responsivity to instruction. When the practitioner is interested in probing a child's mastery of the language used for instruction, curriculum-based language assessment may be used.

Various formal and nonformal tools are used to assess children's behaviors. Informal tools include categorical, narrative, and descriptive measures. As shown in Table 9.1, naturalistic and performance assessments use all three types of tools. Naturalistic assessment involves the use of CBA checklists (categorical), interview information and anecdotal notes (narrative), and/or language samples (descriptive). The same types of categorical and narrative tools are used for focused assessment. Performance assessment typically involves use of CBA checklists (categorical), work samples and anecdotal notes (narrative), and audiotapes or videotapes (descriptive). The tools used for portfolio assessment are similar to those used in performance assessment, although formal, standardized assessment measures may be included. Similarly, norm-referenced (formal) assessments may be used to document a child's performance in dynamic and curriculum-based language assessments. Dynamic assessment also can include checklists

Table 9.1. A summary of characteristics of alternative assessment approaches

Model	Approach	Types of skills measured	Tools	Role of adult	Type of activity	Assessment methods	Types of data
Embedded	Naturalistic	Discrete	Categorical, narrative, descriptive	High to moderate structure	Child-initiated routine, planned	Observation, direct test	Qualitative, quantitative
	Focused	Discrete, complex, holistic	Categorical, narrative	High to moderate structure	Planned	Observation	Qualitative, quantitative
Authentic	Performance	Discrete, complex, holistic	Categorical, narrative, descriptive	Minimum structure	Child-initiated, routine	Observation, report	Qualitative, quantitative
	Portfolio	Discrete, complex, holistic	Formal, categorical, narrative, descriptive	Varying degrees of structure	Child-initiated, routine, planned	Formal, observation, direct test, report	Qualitative, quantitative
Mediated	Dynamic	Discrete, complex, holistic	Formal, categorical	High to moderate structure	Child-initiated, routine, planned	Observation, direct test	Qualitative, quantitative
	Curriculum-based language assessment	Discrete, complex, holistic	Formal, narrative	High to moderate structure	Child-initiated, routine, planned	Formal, observation, direct test, report	Qualitative, quantitative

(categorical) and work samples and anecdotal notes (descriptive). In curriculum-based language assessment, videotapes of dialogue exchanges (narrative) can supplement the use of formal assessment tools.

The adult's role in assessment methods varies, ranging from the adult providing highly structured to less structured tasks (Teale, 1988). In addition, assessment can include formal, observation, direct test, and report methods. Formal, standardized tests place the highest restriction on performance and ask for specific tasks with a narrow range of acceptable responses. Modifications or adaptations in how the assessment items are presented generally are not allowed. Criterion-referenced tools, such as CBAs, are structured and may involve some direct testing, but they mainly use observational methods. Observational methods are open and nonintrusive and provide descriptive accounts of a child's behavior. For example, focused/play assessment solely relies on observational methods, whereas all other assessment approaches utilize a variety of procedures.

As shown in Table 9.1, the practitioner may use both quantitative and qualitative data to analyze the results of alternative assessments. All of the approaches offer the flexibility to adapt assessment activities, materials, and adult–child interactions to suit particular cultural, linguistic, and developmental characteristics of children and families. Prior to conducting the assessment, it is important for practitioners to gather information from families and colleagues on culturally appropriate procedures and situations, especially if the culture of the child being tested is different from their own. It is also important to consider whether data collection methods will communicate information and results effectively to families. For example, work samples and visual documentation may be more appropriate for families with lower literacy abilities.

RATIONALE FOR A TRANSDISCIPLINARY FRAMEWORK

The choice of assessment procedures should be determined, in part, by the respective roles that teachers, specialists, and families play in gathering information and making decisions about curricula. Selection of appropriate assessment approaches for children and families is facilitated by the use of a transdisciplinary framework. Traditionally, early childhood and early childhood special education practitioners adopted one of two models of service delivery: 1) multidisciplinary or 2) interdisciplinary.

Using a multidisciplinary approach, practitioners carry out assessment activities for a child in isolation from other professionals. Typically, this approach involved one-way communication from the practitioners to the caregivers, usually only to report test results (Thomas, 1993), and each practitioner develops separate educational plans for the same child. Practitioners who adopt an interdisciplinary approach conduct assessment activities and develop educational plans without interaction with other team members but instead meet periodically with them to share information. One serious consequence of using either the multidisciplinary or the interdisciplinary approach is a lack of coordination and formal input from caregivers, teachers, and other professionals (Silliman & Wilkinson, 1991). The lack of collaboration between caregivers and practitioners often resulted in incomplete information, influencing judgments about children and leading to possible placement errors (Bartoli & Botel, 1988). Transdisciplinary approaches to assessment attempt to overcome the inadequacies of these two models. Families and practitioners work collaboratively and reach decisions by consensus. This model facilitates the use of more integrated assessment and intervention activities and procedures.

Planning for assessment should be guided by three main considerations. First, a transdisciplinary framework is needed to formulate a holistic and representative view of children's abilities and needs. It can be argued that no one person or discipline has sufficient knowledge about the full range of disabilities and intervention options (Bailey, 1996). Nonetheless, a transdisciplinary framework is more apt to ensure that caregivers and practitioners work collaboratively and reach all decisions by consensus.

Second, transdisciplinary assessment helps obtain a more accurate and comprehensive picture of children's developmental abilities across environments. Assessment procedures must take into account the contexts in which children are experiencing problems and, thus, draw on opportunities in those contexts when devising interventions (Nelson, 1994). Assessing and intervening across contexts calls for a comprehensive plan of assessment, including the use of multiple methods and sources, and involves the collaboration among disciplines and the family (Neisworth & Bagnato, 1988; Silliman & Wilkinson, 1991; Thomas, 1993).

Third, transdisciplinary procedures must be individualized to match the unique characteristics of children and families (Bagnato & Neisworth, 1991; Lahey, 1988). Practitioners are faced with increasing variability among children, particularly in the areas of language and literacy, due to rapidly changing demographic conditions and the inclusion of children with disabilities (Wilkinson & Silliman, 1993). Assessment plans need to be individualized to take into account the different ways that children may respond to the assessment procedures (Lahey, 1988). Assessment procedures should draw from both quantitative frameworks (e.g., formal tests), which are used by specialists to gain information about a child's developmental milestones, and qualitative methods to gain information about the perspectives of others, such as caregivers, peers, and the child (Nelson, 1994). Most comprehensive and individualized plans of assessment are a combination of procedures that range from formal, standardized tests to nonformal, naturalistic observations (Lahey, 1988; Silliman, Wilkinson, & Hoffman, 1993).

MODELS AND APPLICATIONS

Responding to the needs of children from various cultures also requires practitioners to look beyond children's individual characteristics and integrate sociocultural realities into early assessment and intervention practices (Barrera, 1993; Bernheimer, Gallimore, & Weisner, 1990). Few assessment models provide specific guidelines for using a transdisciplinary framework to systematically collect and integrate this type of information from outside the classroom. However, two comprehensive models have been developed to translate state-of-the-art transdisciplinary theory into practice and combine various alternative assessment approaches and procedures. These two models are described next.

System to Plan Early Childhood Services

The System to Plan Early Childhood Services (SPECS; Bagnato & Neisworth, 1990) is a framework for professionals and caregivers that synthesizes information obtained from multiple measures (e.g., tests, interviews, observations), sources (e.g., professionals from different disciplines, caregivers), and environments (e.g., home, school, community). SPECS uses a consensus rating system to help teams make joint decisions about children's and families' needs. SPECS has three interrelated components: 1) Developmental Specs (D-Specs), which evaluate a child's development in different areas; 2) Team Specs (T-Specs), which organize team members' and caregivers' judgments to reach a consensus regarding the child's needs; and 3) Program Specs (P-Specs), which translate the T-Specs evaluation data into specific recommendations for service delivery, therapy, and educational therapy planning. SPECS serves a variety of purposes, including assessment, service delivery planning, progress evaluation, team organization, service coordination, and program impact.

The major purpose of this multidimensional assessment model is to obtain the most valid and representative appraisal of a child's developmental abilities. For example, if multiple sources provide similar information about a child's cognitive abilities, communicative repertoire, and motor skills, then the team can identify an IFSP or IEP objective, such as use of an AAC system, with greater confidence.

Primary Language Record

The Primary Language Record (PLR; Barrs, Ellis, Hester, & Thomas, 1989) was originally developed in England. It has been used in New York State public schools (Falk, MacMurdy, & Darling-Hammond, 1994) and in California (where it was renamed the California Learning Record) (Thomas, 1993). This assessment framework is designed to evaluate and support children's comprehensive development, especially in the areas of language and literacy. The PLR provides multiple perspectives on children and their learning and appears particularly suited for children from various cultural backgrounds and children with learning disabilities (Falk et al., 1994). Information about children's culture, languages, experiences, and interests is obtained through focused interviews with the children and their families. The PLR provides specific procedural guidelines and a structure for practitioners to systematically record observations of children's behaviors. It also requires the collection of children's work samples. Rating scales are included to assess children's literacy development.

The major purpose of the PLR is to encourage practitioners to work collaboratively to identify learning experiences and teaching strategies that will help children develop language and literacy competency. Its innovative approach to IEP development focuses on recommendations for types of instructional supports rather than educational objectives and skills and criteria to be mastered. Outcomes (Falk et al., 1994) for a child who speaks a language other than English may include providing familiar texts and simple-pattern language books around themes of interest, making copies of these books in both languages for the child to use at home, and providing opportunities for involvement in school plays or presentations to foster oral language development.

BARRIERS TO IMPLEMENTATION

Although these innovative and multidimensional models have important and positive implications for assessment and intervention, developing and adopting practical transdisciplinary assessment procedures have been slow for a number of reasons. Utilizing a transdisciplinary framework requires radical changes in the preparation of early childhood and early childhood special education practitioners. In the 1990s, the Division for Early Childhood (DEC) and the National Association for the Education of Young Children (NAEYC) collaborated to produce a set of professional standards that incorporated the complementary perspectives of the two organizations. These standards have been adopted by several states to develop preservice personnel preparation competencies. This trend toward unification of the fields of early childhood and early childhood special education has resulted in blended interdisciplinary personnel preparation programs in which students from both fields obtain the skills required to work together to serve all young children and their families (Miller & Losardo, 1999).

Collecting information across authentic, real-life settings requires additional time and training, which is not always available to team members (Bricker, 1992). For example, a formal, standardized assessment administered by a single practitioner generally can be completed in 1–2 hours, whereas portfolio assessment may involve data collection by a variety of practitioners over the course of a school year. Alternative assessment tools have not been sufficiently field-tested, and too little is known about their technical qualities. For instance, some instruments (e.g., dynamic assessments) have been developed for research purposes and are not suited for use in daily intervention environments. Others, particularly those based on qualitative approaches, may conflict with traditional, quantitative conceptualizations of measurement (Darling-Hammond, 1989). Caregivers and team members must have adequate time to work collaboratively to develop and field test alternative assessment measures, to share their expertise, and to receive consultation from other team members (Sandall, 1997). In addition, conflicting time schedules and/or lack of administrative support for release time can often sabotage the most well-intentioned efforts.

Central to implementing a transdisciplinary framework is the process of role release, in which individual team members may carry out activities that would normally be assumed by a member of a different discipline. The practitioner must be knowledgeable about his or her own role and responsibilities, as well as those of other people from other disciplines represented on the team. In addition to involving caregivers, assessment teams can include early childhood educators, special educators, speech-language pathologists, occupational therapists, physical therapists, psychologists, and so-

Table 9.2.   Responsibilities of assessment team members

Team member	Responsibilities
Early childhood educator	Educational assessment and the child's overall educational programming
Special educator	In-depth assessment of the areas in which the child is experiencing difficulty
Speech-language pathologist	Assessment of the child's speech, language, and communicative abilities
Audiologist	Assessment of auditory acuity and processing skills
Occupational therapist	Assessment of child's sensory development and integration
Physical therapist	Assessment of neurological functioning and gross motor development
Psychologist	Assessment of cognitive, emotional, and behavioral development
Social worker	Assessment of the home environment and relevant family background information

cial workers. A brief description of the major responsibilities of assessment team members is presented in Table 9.2.

A major barrier to effective team functioning arises when team members do not share a common theoretical or philosophical orientation to the assessment process. For example, developing a unified assessment plan would be challenging if team members had opposing viewpoints on family involvement. Some team members might adhere to a diagnostic-prescriptive model or pathology-seeking model (Harbin & McNulty, 1990), in which the child and family are viewed as patients and the emphasis is on identification of the problem by the practitioner with little or no input from the family (Mowder, 1996). This diagnostic-prescriptive view of assessment would be incompatible with approaches adopted by other team members to treat family members as equal partners on a team with a role in guiding the assessment process (Mowder, 1996).

Other barriers to effective transdisciplinary team functioning involve lack of the following:

- A clear goal or purpose for the task at hand
- The necessary negotiation and communication skills to solve problems
- A creative conflict management plan
- Clear decision-making procedures
- A common language with which to discuss issues related to the decision-making process

See Table 9.3 for a summary of the barriers to implementing a transdisciplinary framework.

ADVANTAGES AND LIMITATIONS

Using a transdisciplinary framework involves communication and collaboration among disciplines and with the family. Assessment activities and pro-

Table 9.3.   Barriers to implementing a transdisciplinary framework

Preservice and in-service preparation of practitioners

Additional time and training that are not always available to team members

Conflicting time schedules of team members

Team members' lack of knowledge about their own roles and responsibilities, as well as the responsibilities of the other disciplines represented

Lack of the following:

Administrative support

A common theoretical or philosophical orientation to the assessment process among team members

A clear goal or purpose for the task at hand

The necessary negotiation and communication skills to solve problems

A creative conflict management plan

Clear decision-making procedures

A common language with which to discuss issues

cedures are individualized to match the unique characteristics of children and families, and caregivers are viewed as equal partners in the decision-making process. A more comprehensive and holistic picture of a child emerges when a team of practitioners select a combination of procedures that range from formal, standardized tests to nonformal, naturalistic observations. Although using a transdisciplinary framework has positive implications for assessment practices, adopting this model can be difficult.

Advantages

Major advantages of using a transdisciplinary framework for assessment include family empowerment, coherence of the assessment plan, holistic assessment of a child, and enhanced communication and collaboration. These characteristics are explored in the following sections.

Family Empowerment

Active family involvement is viewed as critical to effective team functioning. In a transdisciplinary framework, caregivers are considered competent in their ability to participate in all aspects of the assessment process. To empower families, the practitioner assumes the role of an effective helper (Dunst & Trivette, 1989). The practitioner provides the necessary support to families to enable them to make and carry out their own decisions. Ideally, the family members become more knowledgeable and self-sufficient and able to solve their own problems.

Coherence of the Assessment Plan

Assessment planning involves making a series of decisions. These decisions involve 1) the child behaviors to assess, 2) the assessment tools to use, 3) the roles and responsibilities of team members in the assessment process, 4) the context or location of the assessment, and 5) the assessment methods to use. It is safe to assume that if all team members initially determine the questions and agree on a plan of action that incorporates these variables, then the plan will be more readily facilitated.

Holistic Assessment of a Child

When an assessment is carried out by a team of individuals, it yields multiple perspectives on a child's behavioral repertoire. Multiple perspectives are especially important when working with children and families from cultures that are different from those of the professionals involved. For example, involving culture-language mediators (interpreters) or siblings in the assessment process may provide insight about the appropriateness of certain responses or behaviors. Also, children with disabilities are extremely diverse; this requires practitioners to possess a high degree of specialization (Bailey, 1996). Successful transdisciplinary assessment depends on each team member's assumption that no one professional possesses all of the knowledge needed to obtain a holistic view of a child's abilities.

Communication and Collaboration

The transdisciplinary framework requires ongoing communication and collaboration among team members. Sandall (1997) reminded practitioners that teams do not coalesce simply because they agree to or have been assigned to work together. After a team has worked together for a period of time and relationships have been established, this framework stimulates respect for diverse opinions and myriad styles of communication. In turn, this understanding helps develop attitudes for working with children and families from various cultures, whose values and interaction styles may differ significantly from the practitioner's. A team that consists of practitioners from different cultural and linguistic backgrounds is a great advantage.

Limitations

Some limitations—such as policy constraints, information exchange difficulties, and reduced efficiency—do accompany the use of a transdisciplinary framework. These items are discussed next.

Policy Constraints

Professional organizations and governmental guidelines regulate who can deliver direct services, even when practitioners on a transdisciplinary team have established the type of relationships that allow for collaboration and role release. For example, the American Psychological Association and the American Speech-Language and Hearing Association can limit the extent to which teams who work with young children and their families can implement a transdisciplinary framework (Bergen, 1994b; Mowder, 1996). Role release may not be feasible for a psychologist or a speech-language pathologist working with a child when services are billed for third-party payments (e.g., Medicaid). Ethical guidelines and insurance regulations require that only those services provided by a certified psychologist or speech-language pathologist can be compensated.

Information Exchange Difficulties

Ideally, practitioners agree to a degree of role release. Nonetheless, it still may be difficult to share sufficient information with team members from other disciplines to ensure understanding of an assessment or intervention procedure's finer points (Bergen, 1994b). Practitioners from different disciplines may miss important behavioral observations, and they may miscommunicate or misinterpret assessment data.

Reduced Efficiency

Scheduling time for planning an assessment, conducting the assessment, implementing the education or intervention plan, and evaluating outcomes can be difficult for practitioners, particularly when they are working individually with caregivers. In addition, the schedules of professionals who work for different agencies frequently conflict. It is essential that a coordinated interagency effort be part of the team's plan.

GUIDELINES FOR IMPLEMENTATION

An essential consideration in utilizing a transdisciplinary framework is to actively involve caregivers as equal members of the team. McLean and Crais (1996) proposed the three strategies for involving caregivers in all assessment activities. The first strategy is a period of preassessment planning to develop an individualized plan for each child and family. Formal and nonformal measures can be used to obtain relevant background information and statements of concern from the family. During this preassessment phase, decisions regarding the location or the context of the assessment must be made. For instance, some families may prefer that the assessment be conducted at home, whereas others may be uncomfortable with that idea.

The second strategy is including family members in the assessment process. The role caregivers have in the assessment will vary depending on their values, availability, comfort level, experience, education, and background (Bricker, 1998). Some formal assessment tools provide a mechanism for including families, such as filling out parent questionnaires (Bricker & Squires, 1999) or acting as an evaluator in an arena-type format (Linder, 1993).

The third strategy for ensuring collaborative participation by caregivers on teams is to solicit their opinions about the assessment process. Caregivers can be asked to validate the representativeness of the assessment results. For example, a child may show reluctance to speak or respond in a testing situation by using one- or two-word utterances but speak in complete sentences at home. The caregiver can be given an initial draft of the assessment summary to make the necessary additions or correct misinformation on the report.

Another goal when working on a transdisciplinary team is to anticipate and plan for the various stages of team development that are necessary for effective functioning. Sandall (1997) referred to these stages as *forming, storming, norming,* and *performing.* Forming is the time when team members must establish the rules, methods, and expectations for functioning. The storming stage derives its name from the realization that periods of conflict and discord are certain to arise when various individuals begin to share their ideas and search to identify their roles on the team. The third stage, norming, is the period in the team's development when a sense of cohesion develops and team spirit grows. Finally, during the performing stage, procedural issues have been resolved and the team is ready to work cooperatively for the benefit of children.

Transdisciplinary models require ongoing team-building and team-evaluation activities. Thus, another goal when using a transdisciplinary framework is to continually evaluate the degree to which the team is functioning effectively. Shea and Guzzo (1987) proposed three requirements for efficient team functioning: 1) task interdependence, 2) outcome interdependence, and 3) potency. Task interdependence is the degree to which team members are involved in pursuing a common goal. Outcome interdependence is the extent to which team members find the consequences of their efforts rewarding. Potency is the extent to which the team believes it has the necessary support and expertise to achieve its goals.

Task interdependence is achieved when the team can interact effectively to pursue a common goal, such as setting a scheduled meeting time to review and evaluate the progress of children and families. Noonan and McCormick (1993) suggested taking the time to establish personal relationships with other team members before trying to establish agreement on teaming goals. When team members can identify, agree on, and value the outcomes of their efforts, outcome interdependence is achieved. For example, if using a transdisciplinary framework is a desirable outcome for the team, then the implementation of this framework becomes intrinsically rewarding. Potency is established when team members are not only confident but also successful in achieving the agreed-on outcomes. These requirements for evaluating team functioning are addressed in Table 9.4, which also provides guidelines for implementing a transdisciplinary framework.

There are few published instruments that evaluate the efficiency of team functioning. The Team Profile (Olson, Murphy, & Olson, 1995), however, is designed to provide teams with feedback on role clarification, quality communication, goal setting and planning, and effective meetings. This tool is a self-assessment that consists of 30 items that are rated on a five-point Likert scale. It can be used by early childhood teams to identify trouble spots or areas of strength in team functioning, as well as to evaluate team members' perceptions of outcomes.

CONCLUSION

Adopting a transdisciplinary framework will enhance a team's ability to obtain a comprehensive and holistic view of young children's developmental abilities. The alternative assessment approaches described in this book are facilitated when carried out under a transdisciplinary framework, in which practitioners work collaboratively with family members to determine the

Table 9.4.   Guidelines for implementing a transdisciplinary framework

Actively involve caregivers as equal members of the team.

   Establish a period of preassessment planning to develop an individualized plan for each child and family. Formal and nonformal measures can be used to obtain relevant background information and statements of concern from the family.

   Include family members in the assessment process. Some formal assessment tools provide a mechanism for including families.

   Solicit caregivers' opinions about the assessment process and results.

Anticipate and plan for the various stages of team development that are necessary for effective functioning:

   Stage 1 (forming): Team members must establish the rules, methods, and expectations for functioning.

   Stage 2 (storming): Periods of conflict and discord are certain to arise when various individuals begin to share their ideas and try to identify their roles on the team.

   Stage 3 (norming): A sense of cohesion develops and a sense of team spirit grows.

   Stage 4 (performing): The procedural issues have been resolved and the team is ready to work cooperatively for the benefit of children.

Continually evaluate the degree to which the team is functioning effectively.

   Three requirements in judging the effectiveness of team functioning:

      Task interdependence

      Outcome interdependence

      Potency

contexts and conditions that are best for children's development and learning. All decision making regarding assessment tools, methods, environments, and procedures is consensual. As stated previously, alternative assessment procedures are especially useful when assessing children for whom traditional assessment approaches may not be adequate, such as children with disabilities or children with different cultural and linguistic backgrounds. Thus, there is a growing demand for early childhood and early childhood special education practitioners who are familiar with alternative assessment and evaluation procedures and who are prepared to work as a member of a transdisciplinary team to develop and implement such approaches across contexts in children's natural environments. Working together as a team develops general awareness of cultural differences in values and communication styles, which is an essential skill for establishing trusting and respectful relationships with families. Cultural and linguistic diversity within the team itself can strengthen the benefits of a transdisciplinary team.

Review Questions

■ What are three main considerations that should guide assessment planning?

■ Define a multidisciplinary approach to assessment and an interdisciplinary approach to assessment. What is one problem associated with both of these approaches?

■ Name one advantage each for using the System to Plan Early Childhood Services (SPECS) and the Primary Language Record (PLR).

■ Name three potential barriers to successful implementation of a transdisciplinary framework, and suggest one solution for overcoming each barrier.

Future
Directions

10

After reading this chapter, you will be able to:

■ Highlight this book's recurrent themes

■ Provide guidelines for assessing children from various cultural and linguistic backgrounds

■ Provide the authors' perspectives on the issues involved in the development and adoption of alternative assessment approaches

*T*he alternative assessment approaches discussed throughout this book are consistent with an integrated, holistic view of child development and essential to encouraging children's resiliency and self-regulatory mechanisms. Alternative assessment approaches place great importance on how context and culture influence learning; therefore, families are involved in all aspects of the assessment process. Equally important is the collaboration between practitioners and families in the use of multiple sources of information and methods for assessment. One purpose of this chapter is to review these major themes. In addition, guidelines are provided for using alternative assessment approaches with children who are from various cultural and linguistic backgrounds. Successful implementation of alternative assessment models and applications depends on resolving some of the significant issues that are inherent to the assessment process. These issues are discussed in this chapter as well.

MAJOR THEMES

The major themes addressed in this book are a holistic view of child development, the role of context and culture, caregiver involvement in the assessment process, using a transdisciplinary framework, and using a multidimensional approach. Each of these overarching themes is discussed in detail next.

Holistic View of Child Development

Child development is an organized, dynamic, and continuous process of growth and adaptation to environmental conditions. This concept prompted the development and adoption of assessment models described in this book. Practitioners who adhere to this belief collect information on the multitude of factors influencing a child's behavior before making decisions (Meltzer, 1994). For example, instead of assuming a language delay for a child who speaks English as a second language, the practitioner will assess several factors, including the caregivers' levels of acculturation; whether the child has had sufficient exposure to English; and the child's cognitive, social, and hearing abilities.

Alternative assessment models are based on the premise that a child is an "open system," highly resilient and motivated to achieve competence and balance through self-regulatory mechanisms. This premise assumes that the child plays an active role in constructing knowledge and influencing his or her social and physical environment. *Self-regulation* is defined in this book as the capacity to plan, guide, and monitor behavior from within and flexibly change according to different circumstances (Diaz et al., 1990). These assessment practices take into consideration the child's motivation by strongly emphasizing qualitative descriptions of complex behaviors, which have not been included in traditional quantitative assessment tools. The unstructured context of play, for instance, provides an ideal environment to observe a child's ability to organize emotions, sensations, and self-regulatory behaviors (Wieder, 1996). Other behaviors that supply information are derived from the child's attention span, engagement with others, exploration of objects, and persistence in activities (Segal & Webber, 1996).

These measures provide valuable information on the how and why of behaviors and are important to consider if children perform poorly in formal testing situations.

Role of Context and Culture

Most traditional assessments have been based on descriptions of middle-class, monocultural, and monolingual children and families. To respond to the needs of children who are developmentally, culturally, and/or linguistically diverse from the mainstream culture, practitioners need to look beyond the child's performance in a traditional classroom or clinical assessment environments and recognize the contexts of family and community. Alternative models of assessment have attempted to address problems that arise when children perform poorly on standardized tests, which often fail to account for cultural or contextual influences on variations in performance.

Practitioners will benefit from being familiar with children's cultural backgrounds and utilizing this information when selecting assessment tasks and materials. This recognition—that the child cannot be separated from the family, the community, and the values and institutions of the society in which the child is developing—led to the creation of the alternative models of assessment and methodologies described in this book.

Caregiver Involvement in the Assessment Process

One characteristic of assessment models available at the beginning of the 21st century is the acceptance of the varied roles that caregivers assume in the assessment process, ranging from informant to examiner to evaluator. The involvement of caregivers in the assessment process is critical to any type of educational decision making. Caregivers are the adults who are most familiar with the child, so their participation in all aspects of assessment is essential. Bricker (1998) suggested that caregivers' involvement may vary depending on their values, availability, comfort level, experience, education, and background. Nevertheless, all assessment should, in part, be based on interactions with caregivers in natural environments. Issues such as language barriers and different views regarding disability (Lynch & Hanson, 1998) are more equitably considered in this way.

Caregivers are best suited to provide practitioners with an understanding of children's background, developmental history, learning styles, and preferences. This information is particularly relevant for children whose backgrounds may differ from the practitioners' and who may score poorly on traditional, norm-referenced tests. The external biases of traditional tests may obscure variations in performance due to cultural and stylistic differences. The authenticity of information supplied by caregivers warrants respect.

Using a Transdisciplinary Framework

No one individual or discipline has all of the necessary information or expertise to gain a holistic perspective of a child's behavioral repertoire.

Therefore, an organizational framework whereby multiple perspectives can be shared and exchanged among the different observers creates a more complete and complex picture of the child's abilities. Transdisciplinary frameworks can also ensure that caregivers and practitioners work collaboratively for the benefit of the child.

As members of a transdisciplinary team, caregivers are viewed as full and equal participants in all aspects of the assessment process. A caregiver and a key professional often serve as organizers of the framework. Thus, the transdisciplinary framework facilitates opportunities for family members and practitioners to seek advice and expertise from each other. The transdisciplinary model of service delivery is the recommended approach when working with young children and their families.

Using a Multidimensional Approach

A *multidimensional approach* is defined as a comprehensive plan of assessment that uses numerous methods and sources of information across multiple contexts. It involves collaboration among various disciplines and with the child's family (Neisworth & Bagnato, 1988; Silliman & Wilkinson, 1991; Thomas, 1993). The alternative assessment approaches discussed in this book recommend tapping into multiple sources of information and applying multiple methods and procedures. Results can be cross-validated when various methods of assessment and sources of information are used to document children's developmental abilities.

Alternative assessment approaches are conducted across relevant contexts in collaboration with professionals in different disciplines and with the family (Neisworth & Bagnato, 1988; Silliman & Wilkinson, 1991; Thomas, 1993). Comprehensive and individualized plans of assessment include a combination of procedures ranging from formal, standardized tests to nonformal, naturalistic observations (Lahey, 1988; Silliman et al., 1993). A valid portrayal of a child's stages of development is made more possible with a multidimensional approach.

GUIDELINES FOR ASSESSING CHILDREN FROM DIVERSE CULTURAL AND LINGUISTIC BACKGROUNDS

American society is becoming increasingly multicultural, with dynamic blendings of identities and cultures (Luke & Kale, 1997). The result is that old values and traditions are transformed and mixed with new technologies and methods of multimedia expression. People are forming new types of relationships and creating new ways to communicate, often discarding the cultural norms of the past. As noted throughout this book, traditional assessment tools and procedures are riddled with cultural biases. The content of most standardized assessment tools reflects the formal language used in the dominant, mainstream culture. The responses of children with limited proficiency using the English language may reflect various levels of acculturation into the mainstream. Often children are penalized for differences in response style (e.g., avoiding direct responses to questions). In addition, standardized tests seldom take into account contextual influences on the measurement of developmental behaviors. Yet, research has shown that children do better on language and cognitive tasks when materials are culturally appropriate.

Reliability and validity of data on standardized instruments are questionable for evaluating the range of abilities or acquired knowledge of children from various cultural and linguistic backgrounds (Bergen & Mosley-Howard, 1994). Cultural differences that exist in values, beliefs, and attitudes are not measured with standardized tools. For example, commonly used achievement tests focus on written language and do not take into account rich oral language traditions of nondominant cultural groups. Adaptive tests, which focus on "self-sufficiency" skills, do not take into account differences in child-rearing styles (e.g., separation from mother) among various cultural groups (Bergen & Mosley-Howard, 1994).

Traditional assessment tools and procedures do not measure children's abilities across contexts, nor do they draw from observations and interactions of children and families involved in actual tasks. They also do not measure children's learning potential. Table 10.1 outlines how the alternative approaches to assessment described in this book attempt to address each of these concerns.

Table 10.1.   Summary of how alternative assessment models address the limitations of traditional assessment

Problem with traditional tests	Alternative assessment model	Applications	How alternative assessment models address the concern
Do not measure children's functional abilities across contexts	Embedded model	Naturalistic assessment	Occurs across contexts in typical and routine activities
			Uses planned interactions and activities with caregivers and other adults in natural contexts
		Focused assessment	Uses checklists and anecdotal notes
Do not measure how and why children learn in real-life tasks	Authentic model	Performance assessment	Provides opportunities to observe children demonstrating their knowledge and applying it in real-life tasks
			Uses documentation to provide possible explanation for the child's learning process
		Portfolio assessment	Uses open-ended documentation, multimedia methods, and work samples
Do not measure children's potential for learning	Mediated model	Dynamic assessment	Provides information on what the child is capable of understanding and learning with guided support
			Identifies the types of assistance a child needs to be successful
		Curriculum-based language assessment	Uses checklists and anecdotal notes

Alternative Assessment Approaches

Naturalistic and focused/play approaches, which are examples of embedded models of assessment, provide opportunities to observe children in typical and routine activities across natural environments. Interactions among caregivers, professionals, and others who interact with the child regularly form the base from which assessment activities occur. Usually observations are recorded with checklists or anecdotal notes. Information that is collected in the child's natural environment contributes most to an accurate picture of the child's functioning needs.

Authentic models of assessment, such as performance and portfolio approaches, involve observation and documentation of children engaged in actual tasks at home and in the community. The types of documentation used are open ended and can include visual media (e.g., photographs, videotapes, samples of children's work, drawing three-dimensional models). Performance documentation is obtained from culturally relevant and meaningful materials and contexts. Many behaviors, such as language, reflect influences of cultural contexts (e.g., home, school), which reinforce the importance of observing children in real-life activities and culturally relevant environments.

Mediated models of assessment, such as dynamic and curriculum-based language approaches, are used to determine children's learning potential. Curriculum-based language assessment provides valuable information on a child's knowledge of language for learning. The main focus of dynamic assessment is not so much on the child's initial mastery of skills on a test but whether the child is able to improve performance following instruction. It also identifies optimal conditions and strategies for learning. Mediated models offer promising alternatives to practitioners who wish to gain expertise in assessing children who lack experience with and knowledge of the dominant school culture and language. These models consider not only what a child is able to do but also how a child approaches a task and what type of support is needed for him or her to learn. Practitioners must focus on discovering a child's intentions and reasons for behaviors and responses, as well as how the child mobilizes internal cognitive and emotional resources in response to social interactions. A child's responsivity to instruction can be evaluated when the proper scaffolding and mediation are provided.

Assessment Process

All of the alternative approaches to assessment described in this book can be used to capture a more accurate picture of a child's developmental abilities than is possible with traditional measures. In the following sections, some general guidelines are provided for practitioners who wish to use these approaches when working with children and families from different cultural and linguistic backgrounds.

Before the Assessment

Before conducting an assessment, it is important to learn about the child's learning style, as well as his or her family, cultural, and linguistic background. Information can be sought in various ways: talking directly to the family with an interpreter if necessary, consulting with colleagues or members of the community who are familiar with the culture, reading about the culture and language, and visiting local businesses (e.g., ethnic grocery stores). The team members need to determine the family's level of acculturation to the U.S. culture (e.g., length of time the family has lived in the country, preservation of heritage culture and values, assimilation of new values and routines). The practitioner can determine the literacy practices in the home by observing the use of written materials, oral stories, television, films, and computers. Of course, they can always ask which languages the child and family can understand and speak.

During the Assessment

The team coordinator(s) can first explain the purpose and procedures for the assessment to family members, the child, and others who may be present (e.g., interpreters). During the assessment, the examiners' main concern is to provide the child with meaningful and culturally appropriate learning experiences (Gregory, 1997). This can be accomplished in the teaching phase by making modifications to test items or introducing additional tasks and materials in diverse forms with assistance from other adults. Whenever possible, culturally relevant materials and activities (e.g., pictures, books, toys) are used. Examiners need to be aware of cultural differences in communication styles that may influence the child's responsiveness to their prompts and teaching strategies.

Individuals from some cultures are comfortable with direct, verbal interactions, whereas others prefer more indirect, nonverbal styles. Consider having a family member or the interpreter assist in the teaching if the child does not respond well to the examiner. If the child has difficulty speaking English, observe whether he or she makes efforts to communicate nonverbally. Use visual nonverbal prompts and teaching strategies. If the child speaks more than one language or dialect, observe whether the child is aware of the differences between languages and can translate and explain words. Use simple words and sentences, and attempt to learn a few words or phrases in the child's and family's language.

After the Assessment

It is important to avoid making assumptions. The team needs to take time to discuss and reflect on the information gathered during the assessment. Family members should be asked for their interpretation of their child's behaviors during the testing and how it compares with the child's behavior at home and in other environments. Feedback about the cultural appropriateness of communication and teaching styles can be solicited from the family and/or the interpreter, if present. These guidelines are summarized in Table 10.2.

FUTURE DIRECTIONS FOR ALTERNATIVE ASSESSMENT

In spite of the promise of alternative models of assessment, significant challenges remain for researchers, practitioners, administrators, and caregivers

Table 10.2.   Guidelines for assessing children from different cultural and linguistic backgrounds

Before the assessment

Learn about the child's and family's cultural and linguistic background, as well as the child's learning style.

    Talk directly to the family with an interpreter if necessary.

    Consult with others who are familiar with the culture.

    Read and visit local businesses (e.g., ethnic grocery stores).

Ask the following questions:

    What is the family's level of acculturation to the U.S. culture?

    What are the literacy practices in the home?

    Which languages can the child and family understand and speak?

During the assessment

Explain the purpose of and procedures for the assessment to the child and family members and others who will participate in the process.

Provide the child with meaningful and culturally appropriate learning experiences.

    Use culturally relevant materials and activities.

    Be aware of cultural differences in communication styles that may influence the child's responsiveness to the examiner's prompts and teaching strategies.

    Consider having a family member or an interpreter assist in the teaching if the child does not respond well to the examiner.

    Use visual nonverbal prompts and teaching strategies if the child has difficulty speaking English.

    If the child speaks more than one language or dialect, observe whether the child is aware of the differences between languages and can translate and explain words.

    Use simple words and sentences. Try to learn a few words and sentences in the child's and family's language.

After the assessment

    Avoid making assumptions.

    Take time to reflect on the information gathered during the assessment.

    Ask caregivers for their opinions on the representativeness of the assessment results.

    Solicit feedback from the family and/or the interpreter, if present, on the cultural appropriateness of communication and teaching styles.

who wish to adopt and implement them. The IDEA Amendments of 1997 included provisions for states to develop alternative assessment tools and evaluation procedures (Ysseldyke & Olsen, 1999). However, practitioners need standards on how to interpret and use data collected through alternative assessment measures. The efficiency of the data collection efforts must also be addressed. When informed clinical judgment is used to analyze assessment outcomes, as recommended for many of the alternative models discussed in this book, practitioners must be aware of their own biases, limitations, and preconceived attitudes, especially toward caregivers who are different from themselves (Harry et al., 1999; Leung, 1996).

Giving up reliance on standardized measures leads to more work, such as determining ways to cross-validate assessment findings from formal and nonformal measures. For example, when working with children who have limited English proficiency, alternative procedures for assessment are essential in addition to standardized testing. Therefore, more information would need to be collected through parent interview, observational methods, and parent report.

School administrators face another challenge: employing qualified interpreters when assessors cannot communicate directly with children or caregivers who speak a different language (Leung, 1996). Lynch and Hanson (1998) suggested that interpreters be

- Proficient in the language of both the family and the practitioner

- Experienced and familiar with the dynamics of cross-cultural communication

- Sufficiently trained and knowledgeable in the professional field relevant to the interaction

- Respectful of cultural values, attitudes, and traditions of both parties involved in the transaction

Administrators, albeit willing, may not be able to find people who meet these qualifications.

In most cases, radical changes will be required by the institutions that prepare personnel to work with young children and families. Preparation at both the preservice and in-service levels is needed for practitioners to implement alternative models of assessment. At the preservice level, early childhood and early childhood special education programs should be interdisciplinary and prepare students for work on teams (Straka, Losardo, & Bricker, 1998). Cross-disciplinary coursework and practicum experiences are unquestionably desirable. These courses can provide information on the different learning styles of children, the integration of views on child development, and cultural factors that influence learning (Anstey & Bull, 1991). Professionals at the in-service level also face radical changes, not only because of new assessment techniques but because of the changing demographics of the individuals they serve. They will need opportunities to exchange information and experiences with other colleagues both within and across disciplines (Falk et al., 1994; Silliman & Wilkinson, 1991).

Assessment is expected to be fair, unbiased, and respectful of children's and families' cultural and linguistic differences. Although the development of innovative and alternative assessment models is exciting, evaluation of them is in its infancy stage. This book presents alternative models of assessment that offer practitioners options, but research is needed to determine their reliability and validity. The professionals involved must not lose sight of the overall goal of assessment, which is to ultimately improve educational outcomes for children. Progress toward that goal will require reckoning with the issues and problems associated with radical change.

Review Questions

How do alternative assessment approaches address some of the limitations of traditional assessment approaches?

What important aspects should be kept in mind when assessing children from different cultural and linguistic backgrounds?

Discuss three challenges facing practitioners who wish to adopt and implement alternative models of assessment.

References

Alder, S. (1981). *Poverty children and their language: Implications for teaching and treating.* New York: Grune & Stratton.

Als, H. (1986). A synactive model of neonatal behavioral organization: Framework for the assessment and support of neurobehavioral development of premature infants and their parents in the environment of the NICU newborn intensive care unit. In J.K. Sweeney (Ed.), *Physical and occupational therapy in pediatrics* (pp. 3–55). Binghamton, NY: The Haworth Press.

Anstey, M., & Bull, G. (1991). From teaching to learning: Translating monitoring into practice. In E. Daly (Ed.), *Monitoring children's language development: Holistic assessment in the classroom* (pp. 3–15). Westport, CT: Heinemann.

Aram, D.M., & Nation, J.E. (1980). Preschool language disorders and subsequent language and academic difficulties. *Journal of Communication Disorders, 13,* 159–170.

Arter, J.A., & Spandel, V. (1991). *Using portfolios of student work in instruction and assessment.* Portland, OR: Northwest Regional Education Laboratory.

Au, K.H., & Mason, J.M. (1981). Social organizational factors in learning to read: The balance of rights hypothesis. *Reading Research Quarterly, 17,* 115–152.

Bagnato, S.J., & Neisworth, J.T. (1990). *System to Plan Early Childhood Services (SPECS).* Circle Pines, MN: American Guidance Service.

Bagnato, S.J., & Neisworth, J.T. (1991). *Assessment for early intervention: Best practices for professionals.* New York: The Guilford Press.

Bagnato, S.J., & Neisworth, J.T. (1994). A national study of the social and treatment "invalidity" of intelligence testing for early intervention. *School Psychology Quarterly, 9,* 81–102.

Bagnato, S.J., Neisworth, J.T., & Munson, S.M. (1989). *Linking developmental assessment and early intervention: Curriculum-based prescriptions.* Gaithersburg, MD: Aspen Publishers.

Bagnato, S.J., Neisworth, J.T., & Munson, S.M. (1997). *LINKing assessment and early intervention: An authentic curriculum-based approach.* Baltimore: Paul H. Brookes Publishing Co.

Bailey, D. (1989). Assessment and its importance in early intervention. In D. Bailey & M. Wolery (Eds.), *Assessing infants and preschoolers with handicaps* (pp. 1–21). Columbus, OH: Charles E. Merrill.

Bailey, D.B. (1996). An overview of interdisciplinary training. In D. Bricker & A. Widerstrom (Eds.), *Preparing personnel to work with infants and young children and their families: A team approach* (pp. 3–21). Baltimore: Paul H. Brookes Publishing Co.

Bailey, D.B., & Wolery, M. (1992). *Teaching infants and preschoolers with disabilities* (2nd ed.). New York: Merrill.

Ball, E.W. (1993). Assessing phonemic awareness. *Language, Speech, and Hearing Services in the Schools, 24,* 130–139.

Ballard, K. (1991). Assessment for early intervention: Evaluating child development and learning in context. In D. Mitchell & R.I. Brown (Eds.), *Early intervention studies for children with special needs* (pp. 127–159). London: Chapman and Hill.

Barnett, D., Macmann, G., & Carey, K. (1992). Early intervention and the assessment of developmental skills: Challenges and directions. *Topics in Early Childhood Special Education, 12*(1), 21–43.

Barrera, I. (1993). Effective and appropriate instruction for all children: The challenge of cultural/linguistic diversity and young children with special needs. *Topics in Early Childhood Special Education, 13*(4), 461–487.

Barrera, I. (1996). Thoughts on the assessment of young children whose sociocultural background is unfamiliar to the assessor. In S.J. Meisels & E. Fenichel (Eds.), *New visions for the developmental assessment of infants and young children* (pp. 69–84). Washington, DC: ZERO TO THREE: National Center for Infants, Toddlers, and Families.

Barrs, M., Ellis, S., Hester, H., & Thomas, A. (1988). *The Primary Language Record.* Westport, CT: Heinemann.

Bartoli, J., & Botel, M. (1988). *Reading/learning disability: An ecological approach.* New York: Teachers College Press.

Bates, E., Benigni, L., Bretherton, I., Camaioni, L., & Volterra, V. (1979). *The emergence of symbols.* San Diego: Academic Press.

Bates, E., Camaioni, L., & Volterra, V. (1975). The acquisition of performatives prior to speech. *Merrill-Palmer Quarterly, 21*(3), 205–226.

Bates, E., Thal, D., & Marchman, V. (1991). From symbols to syntax. In N. Krasnegor, D. Rumbaugh, & R. Schiefelbusch (Eds.), *Language acquisition: Biological and behavioral determinants* (pp. 244–283). Mahwah, NJ: Lawrence Erlbaum Associates.

Ben Hur, M. (1998). Mediation of cognitive competencies for students in need. *Phi Delta Kappan, 9,* 661–666.

Bergen, D. (Ed.). (1994a). *Assessment methods for infants and toddlers: Transdisciplinary team approaches.* New York: Teachers College Press.

Bergen, D. (1994b). Speech pathology and audiology assessment perspectives. In D. Bergen (Ed.), *Assessment methods for infants and toddlers: Transdisciplinary team approaches* (pp. 140–156). New York: Teachers College Press.

Bergen, D., & Mosley-Howard, S. (1994). Assessment perspectives for culturally diverse young children. In D. Bergen (Ed.), *Assessment methods for infants and toddlers: Transdisciplinary team approaches* (pp. 190–206). New York: Teachers College Press.

Berk, L.E., & Winsler, A. (1995). *Scaffolding children's learning: Vygotsky and early childhood education.* Washington, DC: National Association for the Education of Young Children.

Berkeley, T.R., & Ludlow, B. (1992). Developmental domains: The mother of all interventions; or, the subterranean early development blues. *Topics in Early Childhood Special Education, 11,* 13–21.

Bernheimer, L., Gallimore, R., & Weisner, T. (1990). Ecocultural theory as a context for the individual family service plan. *Journal of Early Intervention, 14*(3), 219–233.

Blank, M., Rose, S.A., & Berlin, L.J. (1978a). *The language of learning: The preschool years.* New York: Grune & Stratton.

Blank, M., Rose, S.A., & Berlin, L.J. (1978b). *Preschool Language Assessment Instrument: The language of learning in practice.* New York: Grune & Stratton.

Bloom, L. (1970). *Language development: Form and function in emerging grammars.* Cambridge: The MIT Press.

Bodrova, E., & Leong, D.J. (1996). *Tools of the mind: The Vygotskian approach to early childhood education.* Upper Saddle River, NJ: Prentice Hall.

Bond, K., & Dean, J. (1997). Eagles, reptiles and beyond: A co-creative journey in dance. *Childhood Education, 73*(6), 366–371.

Bradshaw, M., & Harn, W. (1999, April). *Application of adult scaffolding within naturalistic situations.* Paper presented at the North Carolina Speech, Hearing and Language Association, Asheville.

Bredekamp, S., & Rosegrant, T. (Series & Vol. Eds.). (1995). *Reaching potentials: Vol. 2. Transforming early childhood curriculum and assessment.* Washington, DC: National Association for the Education of Young Children.

Bricker, D. (1989). *Early intervention for at-risk and handicapped infants.* Palo Alto, CA: VORT Corporation.

Bricker, D. (1992). The changing nature of communication and language intervention. In S.F. Warren & J. Reichle (Series & Vol. Eds.), *Communication and language intervention series: Vol. 1. Causes and effects in communication and language intervention* (pp. 361–375). Baltimore: Paul H. Brookes Publishing Co.

Bricker, D. (Series Ed.). (1993a). *Assessment, Evaluation, and Programming System (AEPS) for Infants and Children* (4 vols.). Baltimore: Paul H. Brookes Publishing Co.

Bricker, D. (Ed.). (1993b). *Assessment, Evaluation, and Programming System for Infants and Children: Vol. 1. AEPS measurement for birth to three years.* Baltimore: Paul H. Brookes Publishing Co.

Bricker, D. (1993c). Then, now, and the path between: A brief history of language intervention. In S.F. Warren & J. Reichle (Series Eds.) & A.P. Kaiser & D.B. Gray (Vol. Eds.), *Communication and language intervention series: Vol. 2. Enhancing children's communication: Research foundations for intervention* (pp. 11–31). Baltimore: Paul H. Brookes Publishing Co.

Bricker, D. (1998). *An activity-based approach to early intervention* (2nd ed.). Baltimore: Paul H. Brookes Publishing Co.

Bricker, D., & Littman, D. (1982). Intervention and evaluation: The inseparable mix. *Topics in Early Childhood Special Education, 1,* 23–33.

Bricker, D., & Losardo, A. (2000). Linking assessment and intervention for children with developmental disabilities. In T. Layton, L. Watson, & E. Crais (Eds.), *Handbook of early language impairments in children: Assessment and treatment* (pp. 111–136). Albany, NY: Delmar Publishers.

Bricker, D., & Pretti-Frontczak, K. (Eds.). (1996). *Assessment, Evaluation, and Programming System for Infants and Children: Vol. 3. AEPS measurement for three to six years.* Baltimore: Paul H. Brookes Publishing Co.

Bricker, D., & Schiefelbusch, R.L. (1981). Major themes: An epilogue. In R.L. Schiefelbusch & D. Bricker (Eds.), *Early language acquisition: Acquisition and intervention* (pp. 575–586). Baltimore: University Park Press.

Bricker, D., & Squires, J. (1999). *Ages & Stages Questionnaires (ASQ): A parent-completed child-monitoring system* (2nd ed.). Baltimore: Paul H. Brookes Publishing Co.

Bricker, D., & Waddell, M. (1996). *Assessment, Evaluation, and Programming System for Infants and Children: Vol 4. AEPS curriculum for three to six years.* Baltimore: Paul H. Brookes Publishing Co.

Bricker, W., & Bricker, D. (1974). An early language training strategy. In R. Schiefelbusch & L. Lloyd (Eds.), *Language perspectives: Acquisition, retardation, and intervention* (pp. 431–468). Baltimore: University Park Press.

Brigance, A.H. (1991). *Brigance Diagnostic Inventory of Early Development–Revised.* North Billerica, MA: Curriculum Associates.

Bronfenbrenner, U. (1979). *The ecology of human development.* Cambridge, MA: Harvard University Press.

Bronfenbrenner, U. (1993). The ecology of cognitive development: Research models and fugitive findings. In R.H. Wozniak & K.W. Fischer (Eds.), *Development in context: Acting and thinking in specific environments* (pp. 3–44). Mahwah, NJ: Lawrence Erlbaum Associates.

Brown, P., Collins, A., & Duguid, P. (1989). Situated cognition and the culture of learning. *Educational Researcher, 17*(1), 32–42.

Bruner, J. (1972). The nature and uses of immaturity. *American Psychologist, 27,* 687–708.

Bruner, J. (1975). The ontogenesis of speech acts. *Journal of Child Language, 2,* 1–19.

Bruner, J.S. (1983). Vygotsky's zone of proximal development: The hidden agenda. *New Directions for Child Development, 23,* 93–97.

Bufkin, L., & Bryde, S. (1996). Young children at their best: Linking play to assessment and intervention. *Teaching Exceptional Children, 29,* 50–53.

Calhoun, M.L., & Newson, E. (1984). Parents as experts: An assessment approach for hard-to-test children. *Diagnostique, 9*(4), 239–244.

California Testing Bureau. (1990). *Developing Skills Checklist.* New York: McGraw-Hill School Division.

Campione, J., & Brown, A. (1987). Linking dynamic assessment with school achievement. In C.S. Lidz (Ed.), *Dynamic assessment: An interactional approach to learning potential* (pp. 82–115). New York: The Guilford Press.

Carlson, L., & Bricker, D.D. (1982). Dyadic and contingent aspects of early communicative intervention. In D.D. Bricker (Ed.), *Intervention with at-risk and handicapped infants* (pp. 291–308). Baltimore: University Park Press.

Catts, H., & Kamhi, A. (1987). Relationship between language and reading disorders: Implications for the speech-language pathologist. *Topics in Language Disorders, 8,* 377–392.

Cazden, C. (1981). On evaluation. In C. Cazden (Ed.), *Language in early childhood education* (Rev. ed., pp. 153–156). Washington, DC: National Association for the Education of Young Children.

Cazden, C. (1984). Play with language and metalinguistic awareness: One dimension of language experience. *Urban Review, 1,* 23–39.

Cazden, C.B. (1970). The neglected situation in child language research and education. In F. Williams (Ed.), *Language and poverty: Perspectives on a theme* (pp. 81–101). Chicago: Markham.

Cazden, C.B. (1977). Concentrated versus contrived encounters: Suggestions for language assessment in early childhood. In A. Davies (Ed.), *Language and learning in early childhood* (pp. 40–59). London: Heinemann.

Cazden, C.B. (1988). *Classroom discourse: The language of teaching and learning.* Westport, CT: Heinemann.

Cherkes-Julkowski, M. (1996). The child as a self-organizing system: The case against instruction as we know it. *Learning Disabilities, 7,* 19–27.

Child Development Resources Training Center. (1992). *Transdisciplinary arena assessment process viewing guide.* Lightfoot, VA: Author.

Chomsky, N. (1957). *Syntactic structures.* The Hague, Netherlands: Mouton.

Cohen, L.G., & Spenciner, L.J. (1994). *Assessment of young children.* White Plains, NY: Longman.

Cole, K. (1997). *Mediated learning activity evaluation form.* Unpublished document, Washington Research Institute, Seattle.

Cole, K., Mills, P., & Dale, P. (1989). Comparison of effects of academic and cognitive curricula for young handicapped children one and two years post-program. *Topics in Early Childhood Special Education, 9,* 110–127.

Cole, K., Mills, P., & Dale, P. (1991). Individual differences in language delayed children's responses to direct and interactive preschool instruction. *Topics in Early Childhood Special Education, 11,* 99–124.

Cole, M., & Scribner, S. (1974). *Culture and thought.* New York: John Wiley & Sons.

Coleman, T., Losardo, A., & Notari-Syverson, A. (1999, November). *Cross-cultural assessment of children: The role of caregivers.* Paper presented at the American Speech-language-Hearing Association Annual Conference, San Francisco.

Crais, B. (1995). Expanding the repertoire of tools and techniques for assessing the communication skills of infants and toddlers. *American Journal of Speech-Language Pathology, 4*(3), 47–58.

Crais, E., & Wilson, L. (1996). The role of parents in child assessment: Self-evaluation by practicing professionals. *Infant-Toddler Intervention, 6*(2), 125–143.

Cripe, J., Slentz, K., & Bricker, D. (1993). *Assessment, Evaluation, and Programming System for Infants and Children: Vol 2. AEPS Curriculum for Birth to Three Years.* Baltimore: Paul H. Brookes Publishing Co.

Cummins, J. (1984). *Bilingualism and special education: Issues in assessment and pedagogy.* Austin, TX: PRO-ED.

Cunningham, C., Glenn, S., Wilkinson, P., & Sloper, P. (1985). Mental ability, symbolic play, and receptive and expressive language of young children with Down syndrome. *Journal of Child Psychology and Psychiatry, 26*(2), 255–265.

Darby, B.L. (1979). Infant cognition: Considerations for assessment tools. In B.L. Darby & M.J. May (Eds.), *Infant assessment: Issues and applications* (pp. 103–111). Seattle: WESTAR Publications.

Darling-Hammond, L. (1989). Curiouser and curiouser: Alice in testingland. *Rethinking Schools, 3*(2), 1–17.

Darling-Hammond, L., Ancess, J., & Falk, B. (1993). *Authentic assessment in action: Studies of schools and students at work.* New York: Teachers College Press.

Day, V.P., & Skidmore, M.L. (1996). Linking performance assessment and curricular goals. *TEACHING Exceptional Children, 29*(1), 59–64.

Delphit, L. (1995). I just want to be myself: Discovering what students bring to school "in their blood." In W. Ayers (Ed.), *To become a teacher* (pp. 34–47). New York: Teachers College Press.

Deno, S.L. (1985). Curriculum-based measurement: The emergent alternative. *Exceptional Children, 52*(30), 219–232.

Dewey, J. (1916). *Democracy and education: An introduction to the philosophy of education.* New York: Macmillan.

Diaz, R.M., Neal, C.J., & Amaya-Williams, M. (1990). Social origins of self-regulation. In L.C. Moll (Ed.), *Vygotsky and education* (pp. 127–154). New York: Cambridge University Press.

Dodge, D.T., & Colker, L. (1992). *Creative Curriculum for Early Childhood* (3rd ed.). Washington, DC: Teaching Strategies.

Donaldson, M. (1978). *Children's minds.* Glasgow, Scotland: Collins.

Dunst, C.J. (1980). *A clinical and educational manual for use with the Uzgiris and Hunt Scales of Infant Psychological Development.* Austin, TX: PRO-ED.

Dunst, C.J., & Trivette, C.M. (1989). An enablement and empowerment perspective of case management. *Topics in Early Childhood Special Education, 8*(4), 87–102.

Elliott, S.N., Kratochwill, T.R., & Schulte, A.G. (1998). The assessment accommodation checklist. *TEACHING Exceptional Children, 31,* 10–14.

Elman, J.L., Bates, E.A., Johnson, M.H., Karmiloff-Smith, A., Parisi, D., & Plunkett, K. (1996). *Rethinking innateness: A connectionist perspective on development.* Cambridge, MA: The MIT Press.

Evans, J.L. (1996). Plotting the complexities of language sample analysis: Linear and nonlinear dynamic models of assessment. In S.F. Warren & J. Reichle (Series Eds.) & K. Cole, P. Dale, & D. Thal (Vol. Eds.), *Communication and language intervention series: Vol. 6. Assessment of communication and language* (pp. 207–256). Baltimore: Paul H. Brookes Publishing Co.

Falk, B., MacMurdy, S., & Darling-Hammond, L. (1994, April). *Taking a different look: How the Primary Language Record supports teaching for diverse learners.* Paper presented at the Annual Meeting of the American Educational Research Association, New Orleans, LA.

Ferguson, D. (1993). Something a little out of the ordinary: Reflections on becoming an interpretivist researcher in special education. *Remedial and Special Education, 14*(4), 35–43.

Feuerstein, R., Rand, Y., & Hoffman, M. (1979). *The dynamic assessment of retarded performers.* Baltimore: University Park Press.

Fewell, R. (1986). *Play Assessment Scale (PAS)* (5th ed.). Unpublished manuscript, University of Washington, Seattle.

Fewell, R., Ogura, T., Notari-Syverson, A., & Wheeden, A. (1997). The relationship between play and communication skills in young children with Down syndrome. *Topics in Early Childhood Special Education, 17,* 103–118.

Fewell, R.R., & Kaminski, R. (1988). Play skills development and instruction for young children with handicaps. In S.L. Odom & M.B. Karnes (Eds.), *Early intervention for infants and children with handicaps: An empirical base* (pp. 145–158). Baltimore: Paul H. Brookes Publishing Co.

Fischer, K., & Silvern, L. (1985). Stages and individual differences in cognitive development. *Annual Review of Psychology, 36,* 613–648.

Flavell, J.H., Miller, P.H., & Miller, S.A. (1993). *Cognitive development.* Upper Saddle River, NJ: Prentice Hall.

Forman, G., & Fyfe, B. (1998). Negotiated learning through design, documentation and discourse. In C. Edwards, L. Gandini, & G. Forman (Eds.), *The hundred languages of children: The Reggio Emilia approach—advanced reflections* (2nd ed., pp. 239–260). Stamford, CT: Ablex Publishing Corporation.

Fry, P.S. (1992). *Fostering children's cognitive competence through mediated learning experiences: Frontiers and futures.* Springfield, IL: Charles C. Thomas.

Fuchs, L.S., & Fuchs, D. (1996). Combining performance assessment and curriculum-based measurement to strengthen instructional planning. *Learning Disabilities Research and Practice, 11*(3), 183–192.

Galda, L., & Pellegrini, A. (1985). *Play, language and stories.* Stamford, CT: Ablex Publishing Corporation.

Garvey, C. (1977). *Play.* Cambridge, MA: Harvard University Press.

Garwood, S.G. (1982). (Mis)use of developmental scales in program evaluation. *Topics in Early Childhood Special Education, 1*(4), 61–69.

Gavillàn-Torres, E. (1984). Issues of assessment of limited-English-proficient students and of truly disabled in the United States. In N. Miller (Ed.), *Bilingualism and language disability: Assessment and remediation* (pp. 131–153). New York: Croom Helm.

Gelfer, J.I., & Perkins, P.G. (1998). Portfolios: Focus on young children. *TEACHING Exceptional Children, 31*(2), 44–47.

Genishi, C., & Brainard, M.B. (1995). Assessment of bilingual children: A dilemma seeking solutions. In E. Garcia & B. McLaughlin (with B. Spodek & O. Saracho) (Eds.), *Meeting the challenge of linguistic and cultural diversity in early childhood education* (pp. 49–63). New York: Teachers College Press.

Gesell, A. (1940). *The first years of life.* New York: Harper & Row.

Gilmore, P. (1984). Research currents: Assessing sub-rosa skills in children's language. *Language Arts, 61,* 384–391.

Ginsberg, H., & Opper, S. (1979). *Piaget's theory of intellectual development* (2nd ed.). Upper Saddle River, NJ: Prentice Hall.

Gitlin-Weiner, K., Sandgrund, A., & Schaefer, C.E. (Eds.). (2000). *Play diagnosis and assessment* (2nd ed.). New York: John Wiley & Sons.

Greenspan, S., & Meisels, S.J. (1996). Toward a new vision for the developmental assessment of infants and young children. In S.J. Meisels & E. Fenichel (Eds.), *New visions for the developmental assessment of infants and young children* (pp. 11–26). Washington, DC: ZERO TO THREE: National Center for Infants, Toddlers and Families.

Gregory, E. (Ed.). (1997). *One child, many worlds: Early learning in multicultural communities.* New York: Teachers College Press.

Gregory, R. (1984). *Mind in science.* Harmondsworth, England: Peregrine Books.

Grisham-Brown, J. (2000). Transdisciplinary activity-based assessment for young children with multiple disabilities. *Young Exceptional Children, 3*(2), 3–10.

Guidry, J., van de Pol, R., Keeley, E., & Neilsen, S. (1996). Augmenting traditional assessment and information: The videoshare model. *Topics in Early Childhood Special Education, 16,* 51–65.

Gutierrez-Clellen, V.F. (1996). Language diversity: Implications for assessment. In S.F. Warren & J. Reichle (Series Eds.) & K.N. Cole, P.S. Dale, & D.J. Thal (Vol. Eds.), *Communication and language intervention series: Vol. 6. Assessment of communication and language* (pp. 29–56). Baltimore: Paul H. Brookes Publishing Co.

Gutierrez-Clellen, V.F., & Quinn, R. (1993). Assessing narratives of children from diverse cultural/linguistic groups. *Language-Speech-Hearing Services in Schools, 24,* 2–9.

Hale, J. (1992). Dignifying black children's lives. *Dimensions, 20*(3), 8–9, 40.

Hanline, M.F., & Fox, L. (1994). The use of assessment portfolios with young children with disabilities. *Assessment in Rehabilitation and Exceptionality, 1,* 40–57.

Harbin, G.L., & McNulty, B.A. (1990). Policy implementation: Perspectives on service coordination and interagency cooperation. In S.J. Meisels & J.P. Shonkoff (Eds.), *Handbook of early childhood interventions* (pp. 700–721). New York: Cambridge University Press.

Harry, B., Rueda, R., & Kalyanpur, M. (1999). Cultural reciprocity in sociocultural perspectives: Adapting the normalization principle for family collaboration. *Exceptional Children, 66*(1), 123–136.

Haywood, C., Brooks, P., & Burns, S. (1986). Stimulating cognitive development at developmental level: A tested, non-remedial preschool curriculum for preschoolers and older retarded children. *Special Services in the Schools, 3,* 127–147.

Heath, S.B. (1982). What no bedtime story means: Narrative skills at home and at school. *Language in Society, 11,* 49–78.

Heath, S.B. (1983). *Ways with words: Language, life and work in communities and classrooms.* New York: Cambridge University Press.

Heath, S.B. (1989). Oral and literate traditions among Black Americans living in poverty. *American Psychologist, 44,* 367–373.

Hedlund, R. (1998). *Supporting neurobehavioral organizational development in infants with disabilities: The neurobehavioral curriculum for early intervention.* Unpublished manuscript, Washington Research Institute, Seattle.

Hedlund, R., & Tatarka, M. (1991). *The infant behavioral assessment training manual.* Unpublished manuscript, Washington Research Institute, Seattle.

Helm, J., Beneke, S., & Steinheimer, K. (1997). Documenting children's learning. *Childhood Education, 73*(4), 200–205.

Helm, J., Beneke, S., & Steinheimer, K. (1998). *Windows on learning: Documenting young children's work.* New York: Teachers College Press.

Hodgkinson, H. (1992). *A demographic look at tomorrow.* Washington, DC: Institute for Educational Leadership.

Hohmann, M., Banet, B., & Weikart, D.P. (1979). *Young children in action.* Ypsilanti, MI: High Scope Educational Research Foundation.

Hutinger, P.L. (1988). Linking screening, identification, and assessment with curriculum. In J.B. Jordan, J.J. Gallagher, P.L. Hutinger, & M.B. Karnes (Eds.), *Early childhood special education: Birth to three* (p. 31). Reston, VA: Council for

Exceptional Children, Division for Early Childhood.

Individuals with Disabilities Education Act Amendments of 1997, PL 105–17, 20 U.S.C. §§ 1400 *et seq.*

Isenberg, J., & Jacob, E. (1983). Literacy and symbolic play: A review of the literature. *Childhood Education, 59,* 272–275.

Jervis, K. (1996). *Eyes on the child: Three portfolio stories.* New York: Teachers College Press.

Johnson, N.M. (1982). Assessment paradigms and atypical infants: An interventionist's perspective. In D. Bricker (Ed.), *Intervention with at-risk and handicapped infants: From research to application* (pp. 63–76). Baltimore: University Park Press.

Johnson-Martin, N.M., Attermeier, S.M., & Hacker, B. (1990). *The Carolina Curriculum for Preschoolers with Special Needs.* Baltimore: Paul H. Brookes Publishing Co.

Johnson-Martin, N.M., Jens, K.G., Attermeier, S.M., & Hacker, B.J. (1991). *The Carolina Curriculum for Infants and Toddlers with Special Needs* (2nd ed.). Baltimore: Paul H. Brookes Publishing Co.

Juel, C. (1996). What makes literacy tutoring effective? *Reading Research Quarterly, 31,* 268–289.

Kahn, R.J. (1992). Mediated learning experiences during parent/infant play interactions. *International Journal of Cognitive Education and Mediated Learning, 2*(2), 131–146.

Kaiser, A.P., Yoder, P.J., & Keetz, A. (1992). Evaluating milieu teaching. In S.F. Warren & J. Reichle (Series & Vol. Eds.), *Communication and language intervention series: Vol. 1. Causes and effects in communication and language intervention* (pp. 9–47). Baltimore: Paul H. Brookes Publishing Co.

Kalyanpur, M., & Harry, B. (1999). *Culture in special education: Building reciprocal family–professional relationships.* Baltimore: Paul H. Brookes Publishing Co.

Kamii, C., & DeVries, R. (1978). *Physical knowledge in preschool education: Implications of Piaget's theory.* Upper Saddle River, NJ: Prentice Hall.

Katz, L., & Chard, S. (1989). *Engaging children's minds: The project approach.* Stamford, CT: Ablex Publishing Corporation.

Kaufman, A.S., & Kaufman, N.L. (1983). *Kaufman Assessment Battery for Children (K-ABC).* Circle Pines, MN: American Guidance Service.

Kearns, J.F., Kleinert, H.L., Clayton, J., Burdge, M., & Williams, R. (1998). Principal supports for inclusive assessment: A Kentucky story. *TEACHING Exceptional Children, 31*(2), 16–23.

Kearns, J.F., Kleinert, H.L., & Kennedy, S. (1999). We need not exclude anyone. *Educational Leadership, 56,* 33–38.

Kennedy, M., Sheridan, M., Radlinski, S., & Beeghly, M. (1991). Play-language relationships in young children with developmental delays: Implications for assessment. *Journal of Speech and Hearing Research, 34,* 112–122.

Khattri, N., Kane, M.B., & Reeve, A.L. (1995). How performance assessments affect teaching and learning. *Educational Leadership, 53*(3), 80–83.

Klein, P. (1996). *Early intervention: Cross-cultural experiences with a mediational approach.* New York: Garland Publishing.

Klein, P., & Alony, S. (1993). Immediate and sustained effects of maternal mediating behaviors on young children. *Journal of Early Intervention, 17,* 177–193.

Kochman, T. (1972). Black American speech events and a language program for the classroom. In C.B. Cazden, V.P. John, & D. Hymes (Eds.), *Functions of language in the classroom* (pp. 135–151). New York: Teachers College Press.

Kohlberg, L., & Mayer, R. (1972). Development as the aim of education. *Harvard Educational Review, 42,* 449–496.

Kopp, C. (1982). Antecedents of self-regulation. *Developmental Psychology, 18,* 199–214.

LaBoskey, V.K. (2000). Portfolios here, portfolios there . . . Searching for the essence of 'educational portfolios.' *Phi Delta Kappan, 81*(8), 590–595.

Labov, W. (1972). *Language in the inner city: Studies in the Black English vernacular.* Philadelphia: University of Pennsylvania Press.

Lahey, M. (1988). *Language disorders and language development.* New York: Macmillan.

Lahey, M., Launer, P., & Shiff-Myers, N. (1983). Prediction of production: Elicited imitation and spontaneous speech productions of language-disordered children. *Applied Psycholinguistics, 4,* 319–343.

Lapp, D., Flood, J., Tinajero, J., Lundgren, L., & Nagel, G. (1996). Parents make a difference. *The Journal of Educational Issues of Language Minority Students, 16,* 263–280.

Largo, R.H., & Howard, J.A. (1979). Developmental progression in play behavior of children between 9 and 30 months: Spontaneous play and imitation. *Developmental Medicine and Child Neurology, 21,* 299–310.

Lazar, I., Darlington, R., Murray, H., Royce, J., & Snipper, A. (1982). Lasting effects of early intervention: A report from the Consortium for Longitudinal Studies. *Monographs of the Society for Research in Child Development, 47*(2–3, Serial No. 195).

Leung, B.P. (1996). Quality assessment practices in a diverse society. *TEACHING Exceptional Children, 28*(3), 42–45.

Lidz, C. (1991). *Practitioner's guide to dynamic assessment.* New York: The Guilford Press.

Lifter, K., & Bloom, L. (1989). Object knowledge and the emergence of language. *Infant Behavior and Development, 12,* 395–423.

Lifter, K., & Bloom, L. (1998). Intentionality and the role of play in the transition to language. In S.F. Warren & J. Reichle (Series Eds.) & A.M. Wetherby, S.F. Warren, & J. Reichle (Vol. Eds.), *Communication and language intervention series: Vol. 7. Transitions in prelinguistic communication* (pp. 161–195). Baltimore: Paul H. Brookes Publishing Co.

Lifter, K., Sulzer-Azaroff, B., Anderson, S., & Cowdery, G.E. (1993). Teaching play activities to preschool children with disabilities: The importance of developmental considerations. *Journal of Early Intervention, 17*(2), 139–159.

Linder, T.W. (1993). *Transdisciplinary Play-Based Assessment (TPBA): A functional approach to working with young children* (Rev. ed.). Baltimore: Paul H. Brookes Publishing Co.

Locust, C. (1988). Wounding the spirit: Discrimination and traditional American Indian belief systems. *Harvard Educational Review, 58*(3), 315–330.

Longhurst, T., & Grubb, S. (1974). A comparison of language samples collected in four situations. *Language-Speech-Hearing Services in Schools, 5,* 71–78.

Lopez-Reyna, N.A., & Bay, M. (1997). Enriching assessment: Using varied assessments for diverse learners. *TEACHING Exceptional Children, 29*(4), 33–37.

Losardo, A., Notari-Syverson, A., & Coleman, T. (1997, November). *Involving caregivers in the cross-cultural assessment of young children's language.* Paper presented at the International Early Childhood Conference on Children with Special Needs, Division for Early Childhood, Council for Exceptional Children, New Orleans, LA.

Lowe, M., & Costello, A.J. (1976). *The Symbolic Play Test.* Slough, England: NFER-Nelson.

Luke, A., & Kale, J. (1997). Learning through difference: Cultural practices in early childhood language socialisation. In E. Gregory (Ed.), *One child, many worlds. Early learning in multicultural communities* (pp. 11–29). New York: Teachers College Press.

Luria, A.R. (1982). *Language and cognition.* New York: John Wiley & Sons.

Lynch, E.W., & Hanson, M.J. (1998). *Developing cross-cultural competence: A guide for working with children and their families* (2nd ed.). Baltimore: Paul H. Brookes Publishing Co.

Malaguzzi, L. (1998). History, ideas, and basic philosophy. In C. Edwards, L. Gandini, & G. Forman (Eds.), *The hundred languages of children: The Reggio Emilia approach-advanced reflections* (2nd ed., pp. 41–89). Stamford, CT: Ablex Publishing Corporation.

Mallory, B. (1992). Is it always appropriate to be developmental? Convergent models for early intervention practice. *Topics in Early Childhood Special Education, 11*(4), 1–12.

Mareschal, D., French, R.M., & Quinn, P.C. (2000). A connectionist account of asymmetric category learning in early infancy. *Developmental Psychology, 36*(5), 635–645.

Marvin, C. (1989). Language and learning. In D.D. Smith (Ed.), *Teaching students with learning and behavior problems* (2nd ed., pp. 147–181). Upper Saddle River, NJ: Prentice Hall.

Maxim, G. (1997). Developmentally appropriate map skills instruction. *Childhood Education, 73*(4), 206–211.

McCune-Nicolich, L. (1980). *A manual for analyzing free play.* Piscataway, NJ: Rutgers University Press, Douglass College.

McCune-Nicolich, L., & Bruskin, C. (1982). Combinatorial competency in symbolic play and language. In D. Pepler & K. Rubin (Eds.), *The play of children: Current theory and research* (pp. 30–45). Basel, Switzerland: Karger.

McLean, M., & Crais, E. (1996). Procedural considerations in assessing infants and preschoolers with disabilities. In M. McLean, D.B. Bailey, & M. Wolery (Eds.), *Assessing infants and preschoolers with special needs* (2nd ed. pp. 46–65). Columbus, OH: Charles E. Merrill.

McLean, M., & Odom, S. (1993). Practices for young children with and without disabilities: A comparison of DEC and NAEYC identified practices. *Topics in Early Childhood Special Education, 13,* 274–292.

Meadows, S. (1993). *The child as thinker: The development and acquisition of cognition in childhood.* New York: Routledge.

Mehrens, W.A., & Clarizio, H.F. (1993). Curriculum-based measurement: Conceptual and psychometric considerations. *Psychology in the Schools, 30,* 241–254.

Meisels, S. (1993). Remaking classroom assessment with the Work Sampling System. *Young Children, 48*(5), 34–40.

Meisels, S.J. (1996). Charting the continuum of assessment and intervention. In S.J. Meisels & E. Fenichel (Eds.), *New visions for the developmental assessment of infants and young children* (pp. 27–52). Washington, DC: ZERO TO THREE: National Center for Infants, Toddlers, and Families.

Meisels, S.J., Jablon, J., Marsden, D.B., Dichtenmiller, M.L., & Dorfman, A. (1994). *The Work Sampling System.* Ann Arbor, MI: Rebus Planning Associates.

Meisels, S.J., Liaw, F., Dorfman, A., & Nelson, R.F. (1995). The Work Sampling System: Reliability and validity of a performance assessment for young children. *Early Childhood Research Quarterly, 10,* 277–296.

Meltzer, L.J. (1994). Assessment of learning disabilities: The challenge of evaluating cognitive strategies and processes underlying learning. In G.R. Lyon (Ed.), *Frames of reference for the assessment of learning disabilities: New views on measurement issues* (pp. 571–606). Baltimore: Paul H. Brookes Publishing Co.

Micklo, S. (1997). Math portfolios in the primary grades. *Childhood Education, 73*(4), 194–199.

Miller, L., & Robinson, C. (1996). Strategies for meaningful assessment of infants and toddlers with significant physical and sensory disabilities. In S. Meisels & E. Fenichel (Eds.), *New visions for the developmental assessment of infants and young children* (pp. 313–328). Washington, DC: ZERO TO THREE: National Center for Infants, Toddlers, and Families.

Miller, N. (1984). Some observations concerning formal tests in cross-cultural settings. In N. Miller (Ed.), *Bilingualism and language disability: Assessment and remediation* (pp. 107–114). New York: Croom Helm.

Miller, P., & Losardo, A. (1999). *Teacher preparation for inclusive early childhood settings: Quality of EC/ECSE blended pro-*

grams assessed. Manuscript submitted for publication.

Morrow, L. (1989). *Literacy development in the early years: Helping children read and write.* Upper Saddle River, NJ: Prentice Hall.

Mowder, B.A. (1996). Family dynamics. In A.H. Widerstrom, B.A. Mowder, & S.R. Sandall (Eds.), *Infant development and risk: An introduction* (2nd ed., pp. 125–153). Baltimore: Paul H. Brookes Publishing Co.

Myers, C., McBride, S., & Peterson, C. (1996). Transdisciplinary, play-based assessment in early childhood special education: An examination of social validity. *Topics in Early Childhood Special Education, 16,* 102–126.

Neisworth, J.T., & Bagnato, S.J. (1988). Assessment in early childhood special education: A typology of dependent measures. In S.L. Odom & M.B. Karnes (Eds.), *Early intervention for infants and children with handicaps: An empirical base* (pp. 23–49). Baltimore: Paul H. Brookes Publishing Co.

Nelson, N.W. (1989). Curriculum-based language assessment and intervention. *Language, Speech, and Hearing Services in Schools, 20,* 170–184.

Nelson, N.W. (1993). Language intervention in school settings. In D.K. Bernstein & E. Tiegerman (Eds.), *Language and communication disorders in children* (3rd ed., pp. 273–324). New York: Macmillan.

Nelson, N.W. (1994). Curriculum-based language assessment and intervention across the grades. In E. Wallach & K. Butler (Eds.), *Language learning disabilities in school-age children and adolescents* (pp. 104–131). New York: Macmillan.

Neuman, S., & Roskos, K. (1993). *Language and literacy learning in the early years: An integrated approach.* New York: Harcourt.

New, R. (1998). Theory and praxis in Reggio Emilia. In C. Edwards, L. Gandini, & G. Forman (Eds.), *The hundred languages of children: The Reggio Emilia approach—advanced reflections* (2nd ed., pp. 261–284). Stamford, CT: Ablex Publishing Corporation.

Newborg, J., Stock, J., Wnek, L., Guidubaldi, J., & Svinicki, J. (1984). *Battelle Developmental Inventory (BDI).* Allen, TX: DLM Teaching Resources.

Newson, E., & Newson, J. (Eds.). (1979). *Toys and play things in development and remediation.* New York: Penguin Books.

Nicolich, L. (1977). Beyond sensorimotor intelligence: Assessment of symbolic maturity through analysis of pretend play. *Merrill-Palmer Quarterly, 23,* 89–99.

Nolet, V. (1992). Classroom-based measurement and portfolio assessment. *Diagnostic, 18,* 5–26.

Noonan, M.J., & McCormick, L. (1993). *Early intervention in natural environments: Methods and procedures.* Pacific Grove, CA: Brooks/Cole Publishing.

Normandeau, S., & Gray, F. (1998). Preschool behavior and first-grade school achievement: The mediational role of cognitive self-control. *Journal of Educational Psychology, 90,* 111–121.

Norris, J.A., & Hoffman, P.R. (1990). Language intervention within naturalistic environments. *Language, Speech, and Hearing Services in Schools, 21,* 72–84.

Norris, J.A., & Hoffman, P.R. (1993). *Whole language intervention for school-age children.* San Diego: Singular Publishing Group.

Notari, A., Slentz, K., & Bricker, D. (1991). Assessment-curriculum systems for early childhood/special education. In D. Mitchell & R.I. Brown (Eds.), *Early intervention studies for children with special needs* (pp. 160–205). London: Chapman and Hill.

Notari-Syverson, A. (1997). *Scaffolding checklist.* Unpublished document, Washington Research Institute, Seattle.

Notari-Syverson, A., Cole, K., Osborn, J., & Sherwood, D. (1996). What is this? What did we just do? How did you do that? Teaching cognitive and social strategies to young children with disabilities in integrated settings. *TEACHING Exceptional Children, 28,* 12–16.

Notari-Syverson, A., O'Connor, R.E., & Vadasy, P.F. (1998). *Ladders to literacy: A preschool activity book.* Baltimore: Paul H. Brookes Publishing Co.

Notari-Syverson, A., & Shuster, S.L. (1995). Putting real-life skills into IEP/IFSPs for infants and young children. *TEACHING Exceptional Children, 27,* 29–32.

Odom, S., & Strain, P. (1984). Classroom-based social skills instruction for severely handicapped preschool children. *Topics in Early Childhood Special Education, 4*(3), 97–116.

Ogbu, J.U. (1987). Variability in minority school performance: A problem in search of an explanation. *Anthropology and Education Quarterly, 18,* 312–334.

Ogura, T. (1991). A longitudinal study of the relationship between early language and play development. *Journal of Child Language, 18,* 273–294.

Ogura, T., Notari, A., & Fewell, R. (1991). The relationship between play and language in young children with Down syndrome. *Japanese Journal of Developmental Psychology, 2*(1), 18–24.

Olson, J., Murphy, C.L., & Olson, P.D. (1995). *Team profile* [Survey]. Moscow: University of Idaho.

Olswang, L.B., Bain, B.A., & Johnson, G.A. (1992). Using dynamic assessment with children with language disorders. In S.F. Warren & J. Reichle (Series & Vol. Eds.), *Communication and language intervention series: Vol. 1. Causes and effects in communication and language intervention* (pp. 187–215). Baltimore: Paul H. Brookes Publishing Co.

Osborn, J., Sherwood, D., & Cole, K. (1991). *Mediated learning program.* Seattle: University of Washington Press.

Overton, W.F. (1994). Contexts of meaning. In W.F. Overton & D.S. Palermo (Eds.), *The nature and ontogenesis of meaning* (pp. 1–18). Mahwah, NJ: Lawrence Erlbaum Associates.

Palincsar, A., & Klenk, L. (1992). Fostering literacy learning in supportive contexts. *Journal of Learning Disabilities, 25*(4), 211–225.

Palincsar, A.S., Brown, A.L., & Campione, J.C. (1994). Models and practices of dynamic assessment. In E. Wallach & K. Butler (Eds.), *Language learning disabilities in school-age children and adolescents* (pp. 132–144). New York: Macmillan.

Paratore, J. (1995). Assessing literacy: Establishing common standards in portfolio assessment. *Topics in Language Disorders, 16,* 67–82.

Parks, S., Furuno, S., O'Reilly, K., Inatsuka, T., Hoska, C., & Zeisloft-Falbey, B. (1994). *Hawaii Early Learning Profile (HELP): Birth to 3* (6th ed.). Palo Alto, CA: VORT Corporation.

Parten, M. (1932). Social participation among preschool children. *Journal of Abnormal and Social Psychology, 27,* 243–269.

Peck, C.A. (1993). Ecological perspectives on the implementation of integrated early childhood programs. In C.A. Peck, S.L. Odom, & D.D. Bricker (Eds.), *Integrating young children with disabilities into community programs: Ecological perspectives on research and implementation* (pp. 3–15). Baltimore: Paul H. Brookes Publishing Co.

Pellegrini, A. (1983). Sociolinguistic contexts of the preschool. *Journal of Applied Developmental Psychology, 4*(4), 389–397.

Peña, E., Quinn, R., & Iglesias, A. (1992). The application of dynamic methods to language assessment: A non-biased procedure. *Journal of Special Education, 26*(3), 269–280.

Peña, E.D. (1996). Dynamic assessment: The model and its language applications. In S.F. Warren & J. Reichle (Series Eds.) & K.N. Cole, P.S. Dale, & D.J. Thal (Vol. Eds.), *Communication and language intervention series: Vol. 6. Assessment of communication and language* (pp. 281–307). Baltimore: Paul H. Brookes Publishing Co.

Piaget, J. (1962). *Play, dreams and imitation in childhood.* New York: Norton.

Piaget, J. (1973). Foreword. In M. Schwebel & J. Raph (Eds.), *Piaget in the classroom* (pp. ix–x). New York: Basic Books.

Popham, W.J. (1999). Why standardized tests don't measure educational quality. *Educational Leadership, 56*(6), 8–15.

Prelock, P. (1997). Language-based curriculum analysis: A collaborative assessment and intervention process. *Journal of Children's Communication Development, 19*(1), 35–42.

Prizant, B.M., & Rydell, P.J. (1993). Assessment and intervention considerations for unconventional verbal behavior. In S.F. Warren & J. Reichle (Series Eds.) & J. Reichle & D.P. Wacker (Vol. Eds.), *Communication and language intervention series: Vol. 3. Communicative alternatives to challenging behavior: Integrating functional assessment and intervention strategies* (pp. 263–297). Baltimore: Paul H. Brookes Publishing Co.

Prutting, C., Gallagher, T., & Mulac, A. (1975). The expressive portion of the NSST compared to a spontaneous language sample. *Journal of Speech and Hearing Disorders, 40,* 40–49.

Puckett, M.B., & Black, J.K. (1994). *Authentic assessment of the young child.* New York: Macmillan.

Rey, A. (1958). *L'examen clinique en psychologie* [Clinical testing in psychology]. Paris: Presses Universitaires de France.

Rice, M.L., & Wilcox, K.A. (Eds.). (1995). *Building a language-focused curriculum for the preschool classroom: Vol. 1. A foundation for lifelong communication.* Baltimore: Paul H. Brookes Publishing Co.

Rinaldi, C. (1996). Malaguzzi and the teachers. *Innovations in Early Education: The International Reggio Exchange, 3*(3), 1–3.

Rogers, S. (1988). Cognitive characteristics of handicapped children's play: A review.

Journal of the Division for Early Childhood, 12(2), 161–168.

Rogoff, B. (1993). Children's guided participation and participatory appropriation in sociocultural activity. In R. Wozniak & K. Fischer (Eds.), *Development in context: Acting and thinking in specific environments* (pp. 121–153). Mahwah, NJ: Lawrence Erlbaum Associates.

Rubin, K., Fein, G., & Vandenberg, B. (1983). Play. In P.H. Mussen (Series Ed.) & E.M. Hetherington (Vol. Ed.), *Handbook of child psychology: Vol. 4. Socialization, personality, and social development* (4th ed., pp. 693–774). New York: John Wiley & Sons.

Rule, S., Losardo, A., Dinnebeil, L., Kaiser, A., & Rowland, C. (1998). Translating research on naturalistic instruction into practice. *Journal of Early Intervention, 21*(4), 283–293.

Salend, S.J. (1998). Using portfolios to assess student performance. *TEACHING Exceptional Children, 31*(2), 36–43.

Sameroff, A.J., & Chandler, M.L. (1975). Reproductive risk and the continuum of caretaking causality. In F.D. Horowitz, M. Hetherington, S. Scarr-Salapatek, & G. Siegel (Eds.), *Review of child development research* (Vol. 4, pp. 187–244). Chicago: University of Chicago Press.

Sandall, S.R. (1997). The family service team. In A.H. Widerstrom, B.A. Mowder, & S.R. Sandall (Eds.), *Infant development and risk: An introduction* (2nd ed., pp. 155–172). Baltimore: Paul H. Brookes Publishing Co.

Schaefer, D.S., & Moersch, M.S. (Eds.). (1981). *Developmental Programming for Infants and Young Children—Early Intervention Developmental Programming and Profile* (Rev. ed.). Ann Arbor: The University of Michigan Press.

Schwartz, I., & Olswang, L. (1996). Evaluating child behavior change in natural settings: Exploring alternative strategies for data collection. *Topics in Early Childhood Special Education, 16*, 82–101.

Scott, F., & Bowman, B. (1997). Child development knowledge: A slippery base for practice. *Early Childhood Research Quarterly, 11*(2), 169–183.

Segal, M., & Webber, N. (1996). Nonstructured play observations: Guidelines, benefits and caveats. In S.J. Meisels & E. Fenichel (Eds.), *New visions for the developmental assessment of infants and young children* (pp. 207–230). Washington, DC: ZERO TO THREE: National Center for Infants, Toddlers, and Families.

Shea, G.P., & Guzzo, R.A. (1987). Group effectiveness: What really matters. *Sloan Management, 3*, 25–31.

Sheehan, R. (1982). Infant assessment: A review and identification of emergent trends. In D. Bricker (Ed.), *Intervention with at-risk and handicapped infants: From research to application* (pp. 47–76). Baltimore: University Park Press.

Sheridan, M.K., Foley, G.M., & Radlinski, S.H. (1995). *Using the supportive play model*. New York: Teachers College Press.

Shore, C. (1986). Combinatorial play, conceptual development, and early multiword speech. *Developmental Psychology, 20*, 872–880.

Shore, R. (1997). *Rethinking the brain: New insights into early development*. New York: Families and Work Institute.

Silliman, E.R., & Wilkinson, L.C. (1991). *Communicating for learning: Classroom observation and collaboration*. Gaithersburg, MD: Aspen Publishers.

Silliman, E.R., Wilkinson, L.C., & Hoffman, L.P. (1993). Documenting authentic progress in language and literacy learning: Collaborative assessment in classrooms. *Topics in Language Disorders, 11*(3), 58–71.

Skinner, B.F. (1957). *Verbal behavior*. New York: Appleton-Century-Crofts.

Snow, C. (1983). Literacy and language: Relationships during the preschool years. *Harvard Educational Review, 53*, 165–189.

Snow, C., Burns, S., & Griffin, P. (1998). *Preventing reading difficulties in young children*. Washington, DC: National Academy Press.

Spector, J. (1992). Predicting progress in beginning reading: Dynamic assessment of phonemic awareness. *Journal of Educational Psychology, 84*(3), 353–363.

Stillman, R. (1974). *Callier-Azusa Scale: Assessment of Deaf-Blind Children*. Reston, VA: Council for Exceptional Children.

Straka, E., Losardo, A., & Bricker, D. (1998). Early intervention preservice preparation: Program evaluation and reflections. *Infant-Toddler Intervention: The Transdisciplinary Journal, 8*(4), 345–363.

Sulzby, E. (1985). Children's emergent reading of favorite storybooks: A developmental study. *Reading Research Quarterly, 20*(4), 458–481.

Teale, W.H. (1988). Developmentally appropriate assessment of reading and writing in the early childhood classroom. *The Elementary School Journal, 89*, 173–183.

Tharp, R. (1989). Psychocultural variables and constants: Effects on teaching and learning. *American Psychologist, 44*, 349–359.

Tharp, R.G., & Gallimore, R. (1988). *Rousing minds to life: Teaching, learning, and schooling in social context.* New York: Cambridge University Press.

Thelen, E., & Smith, L. (1994). *A dynamic systems approach to the development of cognition and action.* Cambridge, MA: The MIT Press.

Thomas, S. (1993). Rethinking assessment: Teachers and students helping each other through the "sharp curves of life." *Learning Disability Quarterly, 16*(4), 257–279.

Thorp, E. (1997). Increasing opportunities for partnership with culturally and linguistically diverse families. *Intervention in School and Clinic, 32,* 261–269.

U.S. General Accounting Office. (1994). *Infants and toddlers: Dramatic increases in numbers living in poverty.* Washington, DC: Author.

VORT Corporation. (1995). *Hawaii Early Learning Profile (HELP) for Preschoolers.* Palo Alto, CA: Author.

Vye, N.J., Burns, S., Delclos, V.R., & Bransford, J.D. (1987). A comprehensive approach to assessing intellectually handicapped children. In C.S. Lidz (Ed.), *Dynamic assessment: An interactional approach to evaluating learning potential* (pp. 327–359). New York: The Guilford Press.

Vygotsky, L.S. (1962). *Thought and language* (E. Hanfmann & G. Vakar, Eds. & Trans.). Cambridge, MA: The MIT Press. (Original work published 1934)

Vygotsky, L.S. (1967). Play and its role in the mental development of the child. *Soviet Psychology, 12,* 62–76.

Vygotsky, L.S. (1978). *Mind in society: The development of higher psychological processes.* Cambridge, MA: Harvard University Press.

Warren, S.F. (1993). Early communication and language intervention: Challenges for the 1990s and beyond. In S.F. Warren & J. Reichle (Series Eds.) & A.P. Kaiser & D. Gray (Vol. Eds.), *Communication and language intervention series: Vol. 2. Enhancing children's communication: Research foundations for intervention* (pp. 375–395). Baltimore: Paul H. Brookes Publishing Co.

Warren, S.F., & Reichle, J. (1992). The emerging field of communication and language intervention. In S.F. Warren & J. Reichle (Series & Vol. Eds.), *Communication and language intervention series: Vol. 1. Causes and effects in communication and language intervention* (pp. 1–8). Baltimore: Paul H. Brookes Publishing Co.

Watson, L.R., Layton, T.L., Pierce, P., & Abraham, L. (1994). Enhancing emerging literacy in a language preschool. *Language-Speech-Hearing Services in Schools, 25,* 136–145.

Watson, M.W., & Fischer, K.W. (1980). Development of social roles in elicited and spontaneous behavior in the preschool years. *Developmental Psychology, 16,* 483–494.

Wechsler, D. (1974). *Wechsler Intelligence Scale for Children–Revised (WISC-R).* San Antonio, TX: Psychological Corporation.

Wertsch, J.V. (1985). *Culture, communication and cognition: Vygotskian perspectives.* New York: Cambridge University Press.

Wertsch, J.V., McNamee, G.D., McLane, J.B., & Budwig, N.A. (1980). The adult-child dyad as a problem-solving system. *Child Development, 51,* 1215–1221.

Wesson, C.L., & King, R.P. (1996). Portfolio assessment and special education students. *TEACHING Exceptional Children, 28*(2), 44–48.

Westby, C.E. (1980). Assessment of cognitive and language abilities through play. *Language, Speech and Hearing Services in Schools, 11,* 154–168.

Westby, C.E. (1985). Learning to talk—talking to learn: Oral-literate language differences. In C. Simon (Ed.), *Communication skills and classroom success* (pp. 81–218). Boston: Little, Brown and Company.

Westby, C.E., & Costlow, L. (1991). Implementing a whole language program in a special education class. *Topics in Language Disorders, 11*(3), 69–84.

Wetherby, A.M., & Prizant, B.M. (1992). Profiling young children's communicative competence. In S.F. Warren & J. Reichle (Series & Vol. Eds.), *Communication and language intervention series: Vol. 1. Causes and effects in communication and language intervention* (pp. 217–253). Baltimore: Paul H. Brookes Publishing Co.

Wetherby, A.M., & Prizant, B.M. (1993). *Communication and Symbolic Behavior Scales (CSBS).* Chicago: Applied Symbolix.

Wieder, S. (1996). Climbing the "symbolic ladder": Assessing young children's symbolic and representational capacities through observation of free play interaction. In S. Meisels & E. Fenichel (Eds.), *New visions for the developmental assessment of infants and young children* (pp. 267–288). Washington, DC: ZERO TO THREE: National Center for Infants, Toddlers, and Families.

Wiggins, G. (1989, April). Teaching to the (authentic) test. *Educational Leadership,* 41–46.

Wilkinson, L.C., & Silliman, E. (1993). Assessing students' progress in language and literacy: A classroom approach. In L. Morrow, L. Wilkinson, & J. Smith (Eds.), *Integrated language arts: Controversy to consensus* (pp. 241–269). Needham Heights, MA: Allyn & Bacon.

Winnicott, D.W. (1971). *Playing and reality.* New York: Routledge.

Wolery, M. (1996). Monitoring child progress. In M.E. McClean, D.B. Bailey, & M. Wolery (Eds.), *Assessing infants and preschoolers with special needs* (2nd ed., pp. 519–560). Upper Saddle River, NJ: Prentice Hall.

Wolery, M., & Dyk, L. (1984). Arena assessment: Description and preliminary social validity data. *Journal of The Association for the Severely Handicapped, 3,* 231–235.

Wood, D., Bruner, J.S., & Ross, G. (1976). The role of tutoring in problem-solving. *Journal of Child Psychology and Psychiatry, 17,* 89–100.

Yoder, P., & Davies, B. (1990). Do parental questions and topic continuations elicit replies from developmentally delayed children? A sequence analysis. *Journal of Speech and Hearing Research, 23,* 513–573.

Yoder, P.J., Davies, B., & Bishop, K. (1992). Getting children with developmental disabilities to talk to adults. In S.F. Warren & J. Reichle (Series & Vol. Eds.), *Communication and language intervention series: Vol. 1. Causes and effects in communication and language intervention* (pp. 255–275). Baltimore: Paul H. Brookes Publishing Co.

Ysseldyke, J., & Olsen, K. (1999). Putting alternate assessment into practice: What to measure and possible sources of data. *Exceptional Children, 65*(2), 175–185.

Glossary

Activity-based intervention A child-directed, transactional approach that embeds children's individual goals and objectives in routine, planned, or child-initiated activities and uses logically occurring antecedents and consequences to develop functional and generative skills.

Arena assessment A type of transdisciplinary assessment in which one person interacts with the child while other team members observe, record observations, and score on identical or different tests. Observers are typically seated in a circle around the child.

Assessment The process of observing, gathering, and/or recording information for the purpose of making evaluative decisions.

Authentic assessment A type of performance assessment in which a profile of the child's abilities are documented through completion of real-life tasks. Authentic models are based on the assumption that behavior must be observed in real-life contexts.

Behavioral perspective A theory of human development that stresses the role of experience in shaping behavior. Learning is believed to occur as a result of external reinforcement of associations between environmental stimuli and behavioral responses. Skinner was the major advocate of behaviorism.

Categorical tools Assessment tools that have predetermined categories into which all events and behaviors are coded during the observation. This type of observation can be quantified and summarized by a numerical representation. Typical examples of categorical tools are rating scales and checklists.

Child-initiated activities Activities that a child selects.

Concentrated encounters Assessment situations that represent real-life events and familiar interaction experiences but are condensed and focused by teacher direction to yield more information in less time.

Connectionist model A neurobiological model of information processing. The connectionist model draws an analogy to the central nervous system in which neurons activate and inhibit each other in complex networks. In turn, information processing involves large numbers of units stimulating or inhibiting each other through networks of connections.

Constructivist perspective A theory of knowledge that views the child as an active learner who organizes new information and relates it to his or her prior learning. Piaget's theory of child development represents this approach.

Contextualized language A type of language that relates to people, objects, or events in the immediate environment.

Criterion-referenced assessments Tests that measure mastery of specific objectives defined by predetermined standards of criteria. Items are usually sequentially arranged within developmental domains or subject areas. Numerical scores represent the proportion of the specific domain or subject area that the child has mastered.

Curriculum-based assessment (CBA) A form of criterion-referenced measurement in which assessment and curricular content are coordinated to address the same skills and abilities. It is used as a direct means for identifying a child's entry point within an educational program and for refining and readjusting instruction.

Curriculum-based language assessment An assessment aimed at identifying and analyzing potential gaps between a particular context's linguistic demands and a learner's linguistic competence. It also involves determining the type of support that a child needs to ensure mastery of the linguistic demands of the curriculum.

Curriculum-based measurement (CBM) A set of standardized procedures used to measure student progress in basic school curriculum areas.

Decontextualized language A type of language that refers to an imagined context or to objects and events that are detached from the immediate context.

Descriptive tools   Verbatim accounts of actual language use (e.g., language transcripts) that provide a detailed record of behaviors and a description of various contexts.

Diagnostic assessment   An assessment conducted to determine whether a problem exists, to identify the nature of the problem, and to ascertain whether the child is eligible for services.

Documentation   Any activity that provides a performance record with sufficient detail to help others understand the behavior recorded. Documentation goes beyond merely displaying or assessing performance; it also provides an explanation of the child's learning processes. It is typically used to assess the development of a group of children working together on a project and focuses on the social dynamics of learning.

Dynamic assessment   An assessment approach that determines the child's potential for learning and responsivity to instruction by comparing what the child does independently and what the child is able to do with additional support and assistance. This corresponds to the child's zone of proximal development (ZPD).

Ecobehavioral interviews   A type of interview used in naturalistic assessment. Caregivers and others who interact with the child on a regular basis are interviewed to obtain detailed information on the child's behavioral repertoire, including the child's abilities and areas in which the child may be experiencing difficulties.

Ecological approach   A model of human behavior that views the development of the child within the broader family and societal context. It stresses the interconnections among the diverse environments (e.g., home, school) in which a child participates.

Embedded approaches   Assessment approaches in which opportunities to observe the child's behavior are embedded within the natural context. This approach focuses on providing the child with multiple opportunities to perform skills across domains of development with different people, using different materials, in multiple environments.

Evaluation   An assessment conducted to determine progress over time by comparing a child's skills before and after intervention.

Event sampling   A method for collecting data that involves measuring specific behaviors by counting the number of times they occur or recording how long each lasts.

Expository discourse   A type of discourse, critical to academic success, that utilizes the formal language found in textbooks and teachers' presentations.

Focused assessment   Refers to observations using adult-structured interactions to elicit specific behaviors that usually occur within the context of familiar activities and situations. The assessor concentrates multiple behaviors across different areas into a single situation and uses specific strategies to elicit targeted skills.

Formal assessment   Tests that yield information on a preset content and have specified guidelines for administration. Information is usually collected on a one-time basis and compared with normative data. Standardized tests belong to this category.

Information processing model   A theory of human development that uses the computer as a metaphor for explaining thought processes. Similar to computers, humans transform information to solve cognitive problems. Development is viewed in terms of changes in memory-storage capacities and use of different types of cognitive strategies.

Interactionist perspective   A theory that views development as the result of an interaction between the organism and environment. Dewey and Piaget were advocates of the interactionist perspective.

Judgment-based assessment   A systematic method for rating behaviors based on professional judgment and expertise rather than on explicit criteria. It focuses on assessing broad dimensions of behavior, including tolerance for frustration, task persistence, attention, engagement, and motivation.

Linked systems approach   A program evaluation approach that directly connects assessment, intervention and evaluation. A linked system can be divided into four phases: 1) initial assessment, 2) goal development, 3) intervention, and 4) evaluation. Each phase is linked to the next, and all four components are reciprocally related.

Matching perception   Refers to language demands that require the child to respond to or report on salient perceptual information inherent to a task. The language skills required include matching, identifying objects by sound or touch, labeling and describing, imitating, and remembering previously seen objects and information.

Mediated assessment approach   Assessment approach in which guided teaching is used to provide information on the child's responsivity to instruction and his or her mastery of the language of instruction.

Mediated learning approach   An educational approach based on Feuerstein's theory of mediated learning experiences (MLEs). Rather than teach test items or a task, the adult engages the child in MLEs by teaching cognitive-linguistic skills that will enable the child to master a task or solve a problem and become a self-regulated, active learner.

Mediation   A form of adult–child interaction in which the adult or a more knowledgeable peer interposes him- or herself between a child and the world to make experiences more meaningful.

Metacognitive skills   The ability to reflect on and control one's cognitive processes.

Narrative discourse   A type of discourse that involves skills such as the ability to relate personal experiences and retell stories. It occurs frequently in the classroom and social environments.

Narrative tools   Systematic and detailed written descriptions of behaviors. Narrative tools include journals, running records, anecdotal notes of observations of critical incidents, and ethnographic notes recorded during observations.

Nativist perspective   A theory of human development that emphasizes the intrinsic potential for optimal development to occur, given a healthy environment. Development is viewed as genetically determined and occurring primarily through maturation.

Naturalistic assessment   An assessment approach based on naturalistic instruction. Multiple opportunities for the child to perform skills across domains of development occur or can be embedded in the context of child-initiated, routine, and planned activities. Caregivers and others who interact with the child on a regular basis are responsible for observing the child and recording assessment information. The adult observes the child in play or directly tests the child to obtain information on functional skills that will enhance the child's independence and social interactions across environments.

Naturalistic instruction   A group of strategies for teaching functional language skills during routine events and everyday activities in a variety of environments. This type of instruction is characterized by adult–child interactions in which the adult typically follows the child's lead or capitalizes on a child's interest.

Nonformal assessment   Structured and systematic observations of behaviors within meaningful, context-bound activities (e.g., children's block constructions, drawing, writing, dramatic play, conversations about books, participation in class discussions).

Nonstandardized elicitations   An assessment approach in which the adult takes an active role within naturalistic situations by suggesting certain tasks and probes in order to elicit particular responses from the child.

Nonstructured play observations   A type of observation in which play is most often used as a context for assessing behaviors across multiple domains of development. The child is observed in spontaneous play with a caregiver or another adult without restrictions on environment, toys, or timing.

Norm-referenced assessment   Tests that provide information on how a child is developing in relation to a larger group of children of the same chronological age. Items are chosen based on statistical criteria, such as the percentage of children who master a particular skill at a certain age or whether the item correlates well with the total test.

Performance assessment A broad term that refers to methods in which children are given the opportunity to demonstrate their knowledge and apply it (e.g., telling a story, building a model of a playground area, climbing a ladder, drawing a picture of a pet, creating a shopping list before a grocery store visit). The tasks can be developed specifically for the assessment, or they can occur as part of daily routines. When tasks are completed in a real-life context (e.g., writing a letter to a friend or the newspaper, reading a list of products to buy at the store, swimming at the local pool), then it is referred to as authentic assessment.

Planned activities Events designed for the child that ordinarily do not happen without adult intervention, such as making recipes, conducting science experiments, or visiting museums.

Portfolio A purposeful collection of a child's work that can be used to document the child's efforts, progress, and achievements over time. Portfolios are open ended and flexible. The content of the portfolio depends on educational goals and purposes and can include a variety of the child's work as well as teacher and parent observations.

Portfolio assessment Use of a portfolio to assess a child's progress over time. An important aspect of portfolio assessment is that the child participates in the selection and evaluation of the content.

Program assessment An assessment conducted to determine a child's current skill level or baseline skills before intervention.

Project approach An in-depth study, conducted over an extended period of time, of particular activities undertaken by small groups of children. Teachers carefully and systematically document the skills and concepts that children learn while participating in the project and select work samples for display at the end of the project.

Project narratives A type of documentation that "tells the story" of a learning experience, such as the development of a project through the use of visual displays, stories for and by children, teacher journals, and narratives for parents in the form of books and letters.

Qualitative perspective An approach in which assessment is viewed as the documentation of more complex and holistic behaviors as they occur in natural environments. Methods such as observations, interviews, and questionnaires provide information on qualitative aspects of behaviors.

Quantitative perspective An approach in which assessment is viewed primarily as an objective measurement process that results in a numerical representation of children's behaviors and abilities. The process begins with the identification of well-defined target behaviors, which are usually tested in prespecified and standardized conditions.

Reasoning about perception Refers to language demands that require the child to respond to complex verbal problems that involve drawing inferences, making predictions, and assuming another person's perspective.

Reductionist models Theories and methodologies that try to explain the properties of complex wholes (e.g., human beings, societies) by reducing or breaking them down into the units of which they are composed.

Reliability Refers to the consistency or stability of test performance over time and across observers. If a child is tested twice, within a short time period, the test should yield similar scores. Also, two testers independently testing a same child should obtain similar test results.

Reordering perception Refers to language demands that require the child to evaluate materials and ideas that exclude salient perceptual information and that involve materials and events that are not currently being perceived.

Routine activities Events that occur on a predictable or regular basis, such as mealtime, diapering, and dressing.

Scaffolding A dynamic process during adult–child interactions in which the adult provides appropriate levels of support to help the child accomplish more difficult tasks than he or she could normally accomplish independently.

Screening   An assessment conducted to determine whether the child needs further assessment in one or more areas of development.

Selective analysis of perception   Refers to language demands that require the child to focus more particularly on the characteristics of objects or events that are common to preschool classrooms. Questions are aimed at identifying skills such as whether the child can identify the functions of objects, describe events, recall information, and categorize objects.

Self-reflection   An essential component of portfolio assessment that refers to the statements children make that reflect their own knowledge and feelings about their work.

Self-regulation   Refers to the capacity to plan, guide, and monitor behavior from within and flexibly change according to different circumstances. Very early in the context of interaction with their caregivers, infants begin to self-regulate. They learn to modulate their neurophysiological states and gradually move from a state that is highly dependent on adults (other regulation) to the development of self-regulatory skills.

Semantic context   Refers to the meanings of words, phrases, or sentences. Can be experiential (i.e., draw on a child's prior knowledge and experiences) or erudite (i.e., the ideas and meanings expressed go beyond a literal interpretation and are embedded in historical, cultural, and world views).

Social-constructivist approach   A model of child development, based on Vygotsky's theory, that emphasizes the role of social interactions with adults in the child's learning process. The child actively contributes to his or her own development and learns within a social context of culturally defined meanings and activities.

Structured play observations   Structured assessments that are specifically designed to assess play behaviors. They usually consist of checklists or rating scales and involve predefined procedural protocols specifying the environment, toys used, and strategies for eliciting behaviors. Some may also use normed scales or developmental levels to rate a child's behaviors.

Systems theory   A theory designed to study unified whole and self-organizing systems. Systems theory is based upon the idea that the whole is different from the sum of the individual parts. It stresses the interdependent and interactional nature of the relationships that exist among all components of a system. The family, for example, is viewed as consisting of subsystems (parents, siblings, grandparents) in which events affecting any one member will have an impact on all family members.

Theory   An organized set of ideas that serves as a framework for interpreting facts and findings and a guide for scientific research

Transactional perspective   A perspective on learning that views development as a interactive process in which infants and their caregiving environment mutually alter one another.

Transdisciplinary assessment   A team approach to assessment in which families and practitioners from different disciplines work collaboratively and reach decisions by consensus. The adoption of this model facilitates the use of more integrated assessment and intervention activities and procedures.

Validity   Refers to the extent to which a test measures what it is supposed to measure. If a test is said to assess pragmatic language, for example, it is important that items represent an adequately comprehensive range of skills that are specifically pragmatic, such as turn taking and topic elicitation.

Zone of proximal development (ZPD)   A concept formulated by Vygotsky to represent the difference between what a child can achieve independently and what a child can achieve when provided with adult assistance.

Zones of significance   Refers to contextually based language areas that two or more team members identify as curricular objectives that must be attained by students in a particular setting. It is the first step in a language-based curriculum analysis.

Data Collection Sheets

Naturalistic Assessment: Assessment Schedule for an Individual Child

Child's name: _____

Child's routine	Area of assessment	Assessor	Where	How

Alternative Approaches to Assessing Young Children by Angela Losardo and Angela Notari-Syverson
© 2001 Paul H. Brookes Publishing Co., Baltimore

Naturalistic Assessment: Activity Schedule for Assessment in a Center-Based Program

Classroom routine	Area of assessment	Who	How

Alternative Approaches to Assessing Young Children by Angela Losardo and Angela Notari-Syverson
© 2001 Paul H. Brookes Publishing Co., Baltimore

Focused Assessment: Data Collection Form

Activity: _____   Date: _____   Observer(s): _____

Child:	Child:	Child:	Child:
Objective:	Objective:	Objective:	Objective:
Note:	Note:	Note:	Note:

Alternative Approaches to Assessing Young Children by Angela Losardo and Angela Notari-Syverson
© 2001 Paul H. Brookes Publishing Co., Baltimore

Focused Assessment: Individualized Observation Form

Child's name: _____ Activity: _____ Date: _____ Observer(s): _____

Objectives/focus	Child behavior	Where	With whom	Qualitative aspects

Performance Assessment: Things My Child Can Do at Home

Child's name: _____ Observer(s): _____

Observation period/dates: _____

Alternative Approaches to Assessing Young Children by Angela Losardo and Angela Notari-Syverson
© 2001 Paul H. Brookes Publishing Co., Baltimore

Performance Assessment: IEP/IFSP Objectives Individual Observation Form

Child's name: ———

Objective: ——

Criteria: ———

Scoring: ———

Dates	Observer	Observations	Product/work samples

Alternative Approaches to Assessing Young Children by Angela Losardo and Angela Notari-Syverson
© 2001 Paul H. Brookes Publishing Co., Baltimore

Performance Assessment: IEP/IFSP Objectives Data Collection Form

Date: _____ Observer(s): _____

Activity/task: _____

Child	IEP/IFSP objective	Observations

Alternative Approaches to Assessing Young Children by Angela Losardo and Angela Notari-Syverson
© 2001 Paul H. Brookes Publishing Co., Baltimore

Performance Assessment: Observation Form

Date: _____

Observer(s): _____

Activity/task: _____

Child	Observations	Products/work samples

Performance Assessment: Data Collection and Scoring Form

Child's name: _____ Date: _____

IEP/IFSP objectives: _____

Objectives/skills	Correct responses	Performance environment	Performance/generalization responses	Performance/generalization strategies	Scores/ responses/ strategies

Scoring system:
0 = Incorrect response/incorrect strategy
1 = Incorrect response/viable strategy
2 = Correct response/incorrect strategy
3 = Correct response/viable strategy in a contrived environment
4 = Correct response/viable strategy in a few environments
5 = Correct response/viable strategy generalized across environments

Alternative Approaches to Assessing Young Children by Angela Losardo and Angela Notari-Syverson
© 2001 Paul H. Brookes Publishing Co., Baltimore

Portfolio Assessment: Document Collection Plan

Child's name: _____ Date: _____

Team members: _____

Behaviors	Documents	Who	Where	When/how often

Alternative Approaches to Assessing Young Children by Angela Losardo and Angela Notari-Syverson
© 2001 Paul H. Brookes Publishing Co., Baltimore

Portfolio Assessment: Progress Review Form

Child's name: _____ IEP goal: _____

Portfolio review date: _____ Criteria: _____

Documentation	Evaluations

Alternative Approaches to Assessing Young Children by Angela Losardo and Angela Notari-Syverson
© 2001 Paul H. Brookes Publishing Co., Baltimore

Portfolio Assessment: Description of Content

Child's name: _____

Period/dates: _____

Purpose:

Goals/criteria:

Types of documentation:

Portfolio Assessment: Summary Review

Child's name: _____ Age: _____ Date: _____ Reviewer(s): _____

Area/objectives: _____

Strengths/progress	Exemplary documents	Needs/recommendations

Alternative Approaches to Assessing Young Children by Angela Losardo and Angela Notari-Syverson
© 2001 Paul H. Brookes Publishing Co., Baltimore

Portfolio Assessment: Progress Rating Scale

Child's name: _____ Reviewers: _____ Date: _____

Date	Behavior/objective	Criteria	Evaluation and comments					
			0	1	2	3	4	5

Scoring system:
0 = No change
1 = Some improvement
2 = Significant improvement but still needs help
3 = Significant improvement
4 = Meets criteria with help
5 = Meets criteria independently

Alternative Approaches to Assessing Young Children by Angela Losardo and Angela Notari-Syverson
© 2001 Paul H. Brookes Publishing Co., Baltimore

Portfolio Assessment: Child Self-Evaluation

Child's name: _____ Date: _____

What I liked best and why:

What I liked the least and why:

What I learned:

What was difficult and why:

What I want to learn to do better and how:

Portfolio Assessment: My Child Learning to Talk

Child's name: _____ Parent's name: _____

My child learned to say a new word or sentence!

What:

With whom:

Where:

When:

My child said something funny!

What:

With whom:

Where:

When:

My child said something that surprised me!

What:

With whom:

Where:

When:

My child said something that I thought was really smart!

What:

With whom:

Where:

When:

Alternative Approaches to Assessing Young Children by Angela Losardo and Angela Notari-Syverson
© 2001 Paul H. Brookes Publishing Co., Baltimore

Portfolio Assessment: Books We Read at Home

Child's name: _____ Parent's name: _____

Date	Name of book	Minutes spent reading	New words	Adult signature

Alternative Approaches to Assessing Young Children by Angela Losardo and Angela Notari-Syverson
© 2001 Paul H. Brookes Publishing Co., Baltimore

Dynamic Assessment: Oral Retelling of a Story

Date of observation: _____ Name of book: _____

Observer: _____ Child's name: _____

The oral retelling of a story may be used to assess the following abilities: 1) comprehension of story structure, 2) short-term memory for events of a story, 3) ability to sequence the events in a story, 4) understanding of vocabulary from a story, 5) expressive use of vocabulary to describe events in a story, 6) ability to use prior knowledge to make sense of events in a story, and 7) ability to use their personal experiences to make predictions about a story. The nature and types of assistance that children need in order to be successful at retelling a story may be determined through use of the following guided learning procedures:

Procedure	Example	Quantitative analysis	Qualitative analysis
Ask the child to retell a simple story after you have read it.	"Tell me about the story."	Child describes events in story: yes ____ no ____ number of events ____	Verbatim response:
Encourage the child to look at a picture in the book.	"Let's look at this picture. What does this make you think about?"	Child describes picture: yes ____ no ____ number of events ____	Verbatim response:
Provide a partial model while looking at a picture in the book.	"It looks like the boy is getting ready to do something. What is the boy going to do?"	Child describes picture: yes ____ no ____ number of events ____	Verbatim response:
Provide a complete model while looking at a picture in the book.	"The boy is going to pick roses. What is the boy going to do?"	Child describes picture: yes ____ no ____ number of events ____	Verbatim response:

Alternative Approaches to Assessing Young Children by Angela Losardo and Angela Notari-Syverson
© 2001 Paul H. Brookes Publishing Co., Baltimore

Dynamic Assessment: Use of Supportive Scaffolding

Practitioner:_____ Observer:_____

Practitioners use supportive scaffolding to assist children to mobilize their internal cognitive and emotional resources in response to social interactions, tasks, and materials. This form is designed to provide practitioners with feedback on their use of supportive scaffolding in educational environments.

Procedure:

1. Consult with another practitioner to choose which time of day to observe.

2. Provide a running record during the observational period, and include the following:

   a. A brief description of instructional activities

   b. Specific examples of supportive scaffolds used by the teacher

3. Meet with the practitioner to share your observational notes.

Summary:

Activity description	Observed use of supportive scaffolding

Alternative Approaches to Assessing Young Children by Angela Losardo and Angela Notari-Syverson
© 2001 Paul H. Brookes Publishing Co., Baltimore

Dynamic Assessment: Data Collection Form Based on the Mediated Learning Program

Unit: _____ Activity: _____ Date: _____ Recorder: _____

Child	Objectives/principles/functions	Child behaviors and responses	Mediation/scaffolding

Alternative Approaches to Assessing Young Children by Angela Losardo and Angela Notari-Syverson
© 2001 Paul H. Brookes Publishing Co., Baltimore

Dynamic Assessment:
Individualized Education Program (IEP)/Individualized Family Service Plan (IFSP)

Child's name: _____ Date of birth: _____ Age: _____

Parent(s)/caregiver(s): _____

Resource coordinator/teacher: _____

Services: _____

Area: _____

Goal: _____
_____
_____

Objectives	Strategies

Dynamic Assessment: Activity Plan

Child's name: _____ Date: _____

Description of activity and materials:

How to get the child/children involved:

How to make the activity meaningful:

How to expand the activity beyond the immediate situation:

Objectives	Strategies

Alternative Approaches to Assessing Young Children by Angela Losardo and Angela Notari-Syverson
© 2001 Paul H. Brookes Publishing Co., Baltimore

Dynamic Assessment: Activity Plan

Teacher: _____ Date: _____

Description of activity: _____

How to get children involved: _____

How to make the activity meaningful: _____

How to relate the activity to other places, times, and tasks: _____

	Child and goal	Child and goal	Child and goal
Strategies to reach goal			

Alternative Approaches to Assessing Young Children by Angela Losardo and Angela Notari-Syverson
© 2001 Paul H. Brookes Publishing Co., Baltimore

Dynamic Assessment: IEP/IFSP Data Collection Form

Child's name: _____

IEP/IFSP goal/objective: _____

Recommended supports: _____

Date and observer	Context/activity	Child behavior	Support

Alternative Approaches to Assessing Young Children by Angela Losardo and Angela Notari-Syverson
© 2001 Paul H. Brookes Publishing Co., Baltimore

Curriculum-Based Language Assessment: Area(s) of Concern Checklist

Child's name: _____   Date: _____

Observer	Description of concern
Summary of patterns noted:	

Alternative Approaches to Assessing Young Children by Angela Losardo and Angela Notari-Syverson
© 2001 Paul H. Brookes Publishing Co., Baltimore

Index

Page references followed by *t* or *f* indicate tables or figures, respectively.